SO-BDV-703

Let astrology guide you to wholeness:

Gloria Star, the editor of this collection, has been a professional astrologer for over twenty years. She has written for Llewellyn's *Sun Sign Book* since 1990 and authored the astrology book *Optimum Child.*

Jan Spiller has been a full-time practicing astrologer since 1977. Her nationally syndicated columns in *Dell Horoscope* and *Globe Midnight Horoscope* reach an audience of thousands.

Demetra George is an astrologer and mythologist who has been a counselor, teacher and writer since 1972. Her pioneering research synthesizes mythology and archetypal psychology with feminine-centered astrology.

M. Kelley Hunter has been studying astrology since 1967 and holds a master's degree in depth pyschology and creative communication from Norwich University.

Carol Garlick is a professional astrologer, teacher and lecturer. She is the former staff astrologer for Matrix Software, where she worked with others to develop the Microsoft Network's New Age Forum.

Barbara Schermer has practiced astrology since 1974. She is a pioneer in the field of experiential astrology who was nominated by her peers in 1993 and 1995 for the prestigious Regulus Award for her contributions to the astrological community.

Madalyn Hillis-Dineen has practiced and taught the Uranian system of astrology since 1980 and works for Astrolabe, Inc., a leading astrological software firm.

Ronnie Gale Dreyer is a consultant, lecturer and teacher who writes a monthly column for *American Astrology* magazine and who has written three books, two of them focusing on Indian or Vedic astrology.

Kim Rogers-Gallagher writes a monthly column for *Dell Horoscope* and is a teacher and lecturer who particularly enjoys political astrology.

Roxana Muise is a second generation astrologer and metaphysician. She lectures and has written two books and numerous articles on astrology.

To Write to the Authors

If you wish to contact the authors or would like more information about this book, please write to the authors in care of Llewellyn Worldwide, and we will forward your request. Both the authors and publisher appreciate hearing from you and learning of your enjoyment of this book and how it has helped you. Llewellyn Worldwide cannot guarantee that every letter written to the authors can be answered, but all will be forwarded. Please write to:

Llewellyn's New Worlds of Mind and Spirit
P.O. Box 64383-K850–5, St. Paul, MN 55164-0383, U.S.A.

Please enclose a self-addressed, stamped envelope for reply, or $1.00 to cover costs. If outside the U.S.A., enclose international postal reply coupon.

Llewellyn's New World Astrology Series—Book 16

Roles and Relationships

Astrology for Women

Edited by Gloria Star

1997
Llewellyn Publications
St. Paul, Minnesota 55164-0383 U.S.A.

FIRST EDITION
First Printing, 1997

Cover design by Anne Marie Garrison
Cover images by Digital Stock
Interior design and format by Peregrine Graphics Services
Project Management and in-house edit by Connie Hill

Library of Congress Cataloging-in-Publication Data
Astrology for women : roles & relationships / edited by Gloria Star.—
    1st ed.
        p.   cm.
    Includes bibliographical references.
    ISBN 1-56718-860-5 (trade paper)
    1. Astrology. 2. Women—Miscellanea. I. Star, Gloria, 1948–
BF1729.W64A88   1997
133.5'082—dc21   97-2183
                                                                    CIP

Llewellyn Publications
A Division of Llewellyn Worldwide, Ltd.
St. Paul, Minnesota 55164-0383, U.S.A.

Contents

Introduction

n today's world, a woman's role is not defined so much by society's expectations as by the woman herself. Many changes have arisen over the course of this century in regard to how a woman conceives, determines, and shapes her destiny. In the process, western society, as a whole, has also transformed. Yet despite the far-reaching alterations women have experienced collectively, individual women are still faced with the challenge of becoming themselves. This book is a first look, from the viewpoint of female astrologers, at some of the tasks each woman must embrace or overcome.

Rather than concentrating on just one aspect of a woman's expression, we attempt here to look at the *whole person.* Astrologers think in terms of wholes. The western astrological chart is itself drawn upon a circular wheel, which illustrates the concept of the whole. Astrology also creates a focus of integration and synthesis—no one factor stands alone. As women, we are naturally aware of cycles, thanks to our body rhythms, and of the continual process of change. Yet in the midst of all those changes resides the inner continuum: the constancy of the soul of the Self.

It is that soulful process of becoming whole which drives us, and it is that process which each of these writers is exploring through a particular dimension. Not only were we interested in sharing some astrological insights, but, more importantly, we wanted to share the concepts that we have developed and experienced through our work as women who are also astrologers.

In "The Total Woman," Jan Spiller introduces the concepts of integration of the feminine and masculine elements of the self through exploring the Moon, Venus, the Sun, and Mars. These archetypal qualities are easy to find in ourselves, but are not always easy to develop. From this beginning point, which also challenges a woman to integrate and achieve a sense of personal balance, a feeling of inner harmony forms an excellent basis for self-expression.

Demetra George weaves the fabric of the deep inner feminine by exploring "Women's Evolving Needs: The Moon and the Blood Mysteries." Here, the idea of the cyclic moon, continually moving through its phases and stages, sets the stage of a deeper mystery. Not only does Demetra offer us the experience of the cycles, but she also draws in the complete cycle of life, from menarche, through menstruation, to pregnancy and into menopause.

"The Mother-Daughter Bond" by M. Kelley Hunter tells a story dear to each of us: the story of mothers and daughters and their life long connections. Kelley shares the myth of Demeter and Persephone, the archetypal mother and daughter who must lose one another in order to find themselves, and then to be able to come back together. Each woman faces this challenge with her own mother, and, if she has daughters, from the other side of the picture.

Carol Garlick writes "Daughters and Fathers: The Father's Role in the Development of a Whole Woman." In telling the story of a family of four daughters, Carol paints an intimate portrait of the dichotomy of tremendous consistency and variability in the perception and experience of father. Through this tale, we can see the father's impact on a woman's sense of self.

"Psyche's Task: A Path of Initiation for Women," by Barbara Schermer opens the door to discovering the inner self and the experience of love and beauty. With the help of Megan Wells, who tells the story of Psyche and Eros, Barbara takes us on an arduous and inspiring journey through the many twists and turns of love, passion, recollection and self-discovery.

We each have relationships, and in "Creating Healthy Relationships," I offer some ideas which allow you to discover yourself while creating a relationship which provides growth, support and wholeness for both partners. Although the concepts presented are based upon astrological factors, I have attempted to share a view of astrology from your perception of yourself: tempting you to recognize yourself in your chart! If you are to have a healthy relationship, the most intimate connection you create is with yourself.

Madalyn Hillis-Dineen has explored being single. "On Singleness: Choosing to Be Me," provides both insightful ideas about the experience of being single and some in-depth astrological concepts. Madalyn shares an analysis of the chart and life of Oprah Winfrey and also includes charts of other women who have been able to successfully integrate themselves in a single lifestyle.

"The Impact of Self-Esteem" by Ronnie Gale Dreyer uncovers what is at the core of both victory and defeat in the quest to become whole. Ronnie shares the charts of Nicole Brown Simpson and Hillary Rodham Clinton to illustrate the importance and mechanisms involved in developing, or failing to develop, self worth.

Kim Rogers-Gallagher tackles the question of career. In "Who Should I Be When I Grow Up?" she uses basic astrological concepts to illustrate how to find your life work. Her easy style gives way to an informative discovery of the energies a woman must use to make her way in the world.

Finally, Roxana Muise takes us on a mythic journey into "The Sacred Sisterhood." Women friends, circles of friends, teachers and guides are a special part of achieving a true sense of completeness. Through other women, we are taught mysteries. Roxana even explores the evolution of this sacred sisterhood into modern times, and the importance of making and maintaining this connection among ourselves.

As you read this book, I hope you will recognize yourself and come away with knowledge, insights, and a few smiles, too. Working together with the women involved in this project has been a pure delight, and each of us has undergone significant changes because of our participation in it. You, the reader, are the most important part of this book, because it is your journey toward wholeness which has brought this book to life.

Gloria Star
January 16, 1996

Astrology for Women

Jan Spiller

Jan Spiller has been a full-time practicing astrologer since 1977. As a nationally syndicated columnist in *Dell Horoscope, Globe Midnight Horoscope,* the *New Age Retailer, New Life* and *Visions Magazine,* her monthly articles regularly reach an audience of hundreds of thousands of people. In her line of credits, she has had a nationally syndicated daily radio program in addition to two weekly television shows. She is a regular speaker at national new age conferences as well as astrology conventions.

Jan has been listed in *Who's Who in America* and *Who's Who in American Women.* She is co-author of *Spiritual Astrology: Your Personal Path to Self-Fulfillment* (Simon & Schuster), now translated into Spanish as well as English and in its twelfth printing. Her new book, *Astrology for the Soul,* published by Bantam, will be released in the fall of 1997.

Jan Spiller

The Total Woman

A total woman is a person who has true confidence in herself in all circumstances and conditions. Confidence is a by-product of authenticity . . . being who you are with no pretending, nothing hidden away or shielded from others. When we aren't hiding anything, there's nothing to defend or protect. When we are truly being ourselves, we respond intuitively and accurately to whatever comes our way in the moment. Calm confidence reigns because we are not distracted by thoughts telling us who we ought to be to try to appease or impress others. We are simply being ourselves, authentic and true to our own unique natures.

The confidence we need in order to risk this kind of authenticity is a natural by-product of self-knowledge. Our astrological birthcharts serve as road maps for each of us as unique individuals. It is not someone else's opinion of who we are, filtered through their own biases, hopes, and fears. It is an objective, mathematical picture of the inner workings of each person's unique self. When we know who we are, from an objective point of view, it's much easier to be ourselves without confusion or self-delusion. With a clearer view of our strengths and weaknesses, we are better able to choose how to work with the various parts of ourselves to achieve wholeness.

An individual birthchart isn't duplicated for over 25,000 years! From an astrological point of view, each of us is wholly and totally unique. There is no one else on the planet who can activate the energies in your birthchart as well as you can . . . and when you are openly, honestly being yourself in a non-combative way, no one can dispute you. By the same token, you can't be anyone else as well as they can be themselves. So it is always best to just be yourself, because you can emerge as a total winner every time!

In order for each of us to be herself as a total woman, both the unique feminine and masculine aspects within us must be recognized, appreciated and claimed as our own. Only then can we truly be who we are on the individual level. The specifically feminine aspects within us are represented by Venus and The Moon in our birth charts; the specifically masculine aspects are shown by Mars and the Sun.

In the balance of this chapter, all four planets will be explored in each of the signs from the perspective of being ourselves in a wholistic way. The total woman is one who has claimed and integrated both the female and male parts of her nature. Because she has allowed full expression of her own Sun and Mars, she doesn't need a man to "act out" the parts of herself she has repressed. From this position, it is easy to attract and maintain happy relationships, as there is no sense of desperation or fear of losing part of herself. It becomes possible to enjoy others without sacrificing herself or demanding that others sacrifice themselves for her.

Venus: The Concubine Within

Life would be so dull and boring without The Concubine Within continually finding active expression! The position of Venus in your chart shows what inspires your love, your personal taste, what you feel is valuable, and your most genuine mode of being in social and romantic situations. It is a strictly youthful energy—happy, irrational, and extravagant—which allows you to experience pleasure and enjoy life without having to think about it. It shows your natural tastes and desires in food, decorating, and choosing romantic partners. Venus is beauty, and no one can dispute what you find beautiful. Beauty is a question of personal taste, and is largely determined by the position of Venus in your birthchart.

The sign position of your Venus also shows your natural social style, your own brand of charm, and what you consider attractive. When your actions stem from an authentic attraction, you magnetically pull appropriate people and situations into your life. It's natural! However, sometimes in the process of growing up and taking on rigid social conditioning, you can get the idea that it's not okay to be yourself, or to find pleasure and joy in what personally appeals to you.

For example, if your Venus is in the sign of Leo, and your mother or father had a harsh Saturn aspect to your Venus (conjunction, square, or opposition), then you got a clear message that it wasn't okay to be yourself—to be a Venus in Leo: exuberant, fun loving, open, generous, and trusting—and so you tried to censor yourself, as your parents censored you, with the idea that it would help you adapt to society and be liked and accepted. The only problem with this is that a Venus in Leo doesn't know how to act out any other Venus sign but Leo! So when you pretend to not be exuberantly in love when you are, when you try to hide all the drama in your heart, when you try to dampen your enthusiasm and confident creative intensity, others become confused because what you are expressing is not what they *feel* is the truth—you're not authentic. Thus you may attract people who are not right for you, and you may lack confidence in social situations because you don't know how to express yourself in ways that will be accepted.

When you are being yourself, however, you feel comfortable because you know there is inner substance backing up your external behavior. Venus in the birthchart shows what you value, and when you openly display and act from your true values, self-worth is a natural by-product: you have been true to yourself.

Venus in Aries

To bring love into your life, be the leader that you are! Take the initiative and independently go after what is important to you. You enjoy competition, so exercise that competitive edge in constructive activities that makes you happy. Openly follow the pathways of high energy that lead to self-discovery and a greater sense of your own self-sufficiency. As you let others see your vital, energetic, ardent, independent spirit, you will naturally attract those who can match your excitement about life with equal fervor!

Venus in Taurus

To bring love into your life, allow the strength of your loyal, supportive, dependable nature to flow freely out to others. You have a tremendous capacity to appreciate life, and when you let yourself enjoy the sensual side (good food, good company, comfortable surroundings), your disarming, uncomplicated nature attracts like-minded others. You have a unique gift in being able to build solid and lasting relationships through the steadiness of your affection. In romance, respond to others with your own brand of consistent confidence and work to build what you feel is valuable in the relationship. Those with more ardent or restless natures will either adapt to the steadiness of your truth, or they will leave your life and make room for someone who can more deeply appreciate you.

Venus in Gemini

To bring love into your life, allow yourself the freedom to be the social butterfly that you are! You enjoy interacting with a variety of people, sharing information and understanding the way that other people's minds work. You enjoy seeing life from other people's points of view, and in that process, you gain much understanding. You have an incredible ability to bring a lighthearted attitude into social situations, not taking life too seriously and always looking at the bright side. When you are sharing your happy, positive outlook, those who have affinity will naturally gravitate to you to share and contribute to your positive, uplifting energy. Pursue your natural curiosity about people and ask questions that give you the insight and information you are looking for. Keep your "Huckleberry Finn" attitude alive and you will magnetically attract others who are compatible.

Venus in Cancer

To bring love into your life, allow others to become aware of your concern for their welfare. You truly want to support other people, and when you allow yourself to overtly demonstrate your sensitivity and support, it allows them to reciprocate with appreciation. You enjoy people with whom you can become involved in activities, exchanging the energy of nurturing by getting things started and helping them grow in constructive directions. Allow yourself to have a feeling of "family" with those who come into your life. This will openly display one of your greatest talents: the ability to use sensitivity to create a personal emotional connection through understanding and rapport. By consistently being yourself in this way, you will attract the right people who are truly capable of sharing with you.

Venus in Leo

To bring love into your life, allow your generous spirit to flow out to others, giving them center stage and inspiring them with your confidence in their abilities. There is a part of you that needs parties and fun and romance on a regular basis! Dancing is a great avenue for getting your romantic, creative juices going. Follow the bright lights, the laughter, and all the activities in life that are fun for you! Allow yourself to openly have a good time without censoring your childlike joy, and your example will inspire others to take part in life more enthusiastically. Also, you will magnetically attract others to play with you who can support your exuberant, happy energy!

Venus in Virgo

To bring love into your life, allow yourself to openly and enthusiastically get into your work! When you have a job, a project, or other work-related purpose in life that you feel is of service to others, your enjoyment of life is enhanced. You like helping others by doing "little things" to express your love and caring. You help keep the household in order by doing chores, running errands, and looking after details to be sure the special people in your life feel loved and appreciated. Problem solving gets your affectionate juices going. When you participate in situations where you can be of service by helping to restore order, you magnetically attract others who want to work with you and who will appreciate your conscientious awareness.

Venus in Libra

To bring love into your life, allow yourself to dress up and feel the art and beauty of your own femininity. Grant yourself permission to spend money on clothes and jewelry that bring joy to your heart and peacefulness to your being. You enjoy lovely surroundings and harmony in the environment and have a special ability to create that harmony with others through your interest in them and your naturally supportive nature. When others are out of sorts, you instinctively know how to help them regain their inner harmony by sharing a point of view that helps them see their situation from a different perspective. This is an unselfishly loving and giving aspect of your nature, and when you share it freely you will attract those with whom you can have joyous relationships because they share and appreciate similar values.

Venus in Scorpio

To bring love into your life, allow yourself to choose change over the status quo. You love to "live on the edge"—to experience excitement, intensity, purification, and change in your life! Yet you, more than any other Venus position, can have a difficult time in letting go of relationships that have become destructive or stagnant. Be true to the deepest part of your nature and honor your desire to purify your capacity to love. By going through intense experiences you are able to transform your love nature from being personal, limited, and conditional, to being transcendent—a powerful force for healing yourself and the wounds of others. You need to be willing to go through the fires of passion in order to emerge as the phoenix, free of the burden of trying to possess the other. As you openly embrace the power of love as an intense agent of growth and renewal, you will magnetically draw others to you who can provide the energy for your next transformation! By openly revealing your enjoyment of intense bonding, you can also attract those who share this understanding and can bond with you constructively on a more lasting basis.

Venus in Sagittarius

To bring love into your life, allow yourself to be the "hail fellow, well met" spirit that you are! You love new adventures, conversations with lots of different people, Mother Nature and freedom! You also enjoy helping others who are in trouble, acting spontaneously, driving on an open road, and freedom! Your spirit soars when you contemplate a success that will yield expansion, growth, and more freedom! Romance can be confusing for you, as you seem to most wholeheartedly fall in love with people who are "unobtainable" in some way. Subconsciously, this assures your bottom line—"don't fence me in"—giving you the combination of love and freedom that you need to stay in love. Therefore, don't seek to possess or control the people who inspire your love. Allow love to flow freely in your life, providing a gateway to your next adventure that will lead to personal growth, expansion, and new discoveries. It is important to be honest and direct with those you love. Others may have a more limited agenda and not understand your need for freedom. Therefore, draw on your openness and generosity to be sure that their needs are getting met and they feel loved as well. They may well be the "underdog" in a romance with you, and you always rally to support the underdog!

Venus in Capricorn

To bring love into your life, allow yourself to openly pursue goals that are important to you. Capricorn rules success, and no one loves success more than a person with Venus in Capricorn! Why not be open about it? When you have a goal that you want to accomplish, you love the process of climbing the ladder- taking the steps that are necessary to win the prize! You have an incredible ability to use every obstacle that confronts you as the next stepping stone to get to where you are going, and your enjoyment of this process can inspire others to pursue their goals with the same zest! In fact, you gain pleasure when you are encouraging those around you to achieve the successes that will help them to gain self-respect—and to earn *your* respect. As you allow yourself to openly enjoy the process of being successful, your magnetism attracts others to you to eagerly participate with you in accomplishing mutual goals.

Venus in Aquarius

To bring love into your life, allow yourself to openly pursue your own unorthodox ideas and humanitarian dreams. You enjoy listening to a "different drummer" and creatively expressing your unconventional, vibrant, and exciting tastes in decoration and dress. Equality in relationships is important to you. Your best bet is to openly display your love of friendship. You are genuinely curious about other people, interested in their lives and in discovering what is interesting to them. Approach others with a natural, friendly spirit of openness, and show your willingness to listen to the details of their lives and to give honest, objective feedback. You love to be helpful and to learn through an interchange of knowledge. It's also important for you to spend time with groups of like-minded people who share your humanitarian values.

Venus in Pisces

To bring love into your life, allow yourself to openly be the "marshmallow" that you are. You are sensitive, and "melt" with other people's distress. You truly want to help—not for personal gain, but simply to relieve the suffering of others. Some people may take advantage of your unconditionally loving nature and temporarily lead you down an unhappy path. Even if you are taken advantage of, your compassion easily understands and forgives them, and you emerge intact. Turn away from others values and openly expound your *own* ideals of unconditional love. In the process of letting others see the beauty of who you are and the wisdom of your motives, you will attract those who can respect and resonate with your loving nature and who operate from the same values.

The Moon: The Nurturing Mother Within

To become a total woman, we must accept all the varying parts of ourselves. This includes our need to nurture and to be nurtured by others. Among the planets, nurturing is represented by the Moon. This is one of the most important planets in the birthchart, especially when it comes to intimate relationships, as it represents the feminine need—in both women and men— to feel secure. To become deeply satisfied and fulfilled on every level, it is essential that we embrace our needs as depicted by the Moon, and take responsibility for seeing that those needs are met.

The Moon is where we feel vulnerable, where our deepest needs are shown—including our needs to feel understood, cared for, and deeply accepted and loved on a non-verbal level. This can be scary stuff, especially since the Moon represents an area within ourself that feels incomplete unless there is an interchange of energy with another. That means trusting, not objectively, but personally and emotionally, with a fully open heart. It means being accessible.

Part of being a woman is our capacity to exchange nurturing energy with others, and to feel ourselves nurtured in the process. There is no stereotyped "nurturing image" that will work for everyone, since every woman has her own unique style of caring for others. This style is determined by the sign the Moon is in, as well as the house containing the Moon and aspects to the Moon in the birthchart. (For a complete view of nurturing, also look at the Fourth House and planets in Cancer).

A woman's basic style of nurturing is shown by the sign the Moon is in. The house in which the Moon is located determines which area of her life needs her full participation in order to activate her nurturing energies. For example, a woman with her Moon in Gemini nurtures best through a lighthearted exchange of information that is stimulating for her. If her Moon is in the Eleventh House, she can best activate her caring energy by spending time interacting with friends, or participating in humanitarian causes she believes in.

It is also important to remember that Aspects to the planets strongly affect their expression. For example, if your Saturn is conjunct, square, or in opposition to your natal Moon, it may be more difficult for you to experience being vulnerable than it is for others. It may take you many years and the "karma" of traveling through a lot of difficult emotional experiences to understand how you can successfully be vulnerable without attracting hurtful experiences. It may take you longer than others, but once you "have it down" it will be conscious, solid, and dependable.

To feel supported by others and to evoke supportive energies from life, we must be willing to care about and support others. The trick is to nurture in a way that is congruent with our own needs for being nurtured—to give others the energy that we want coming back to us. It's also OK to ask that others give back to us, especially in intimate relationships, and to let others know the kind of energy we need in order to feel nurtured and secure. When a person's basic needs are met, they're happy—and it's much more fun to live with a happy person! When we give another person the energy represented by our Moon, and openly communicate that we need that energy coming back from them as well, we can tell who really belongs in our life by the way they respond. It is a waste of time and heart energy to try to hold someone in our lives who is unable or unwilling to exchange the style of nurturing we need.

The following Moon positions depict our unique style of caring. Magically, when we seek to nurture others by drawing upon the qualities of the sign our Moon is in, we begin to feel more secure and the nurturing we need comes from within ourselves.

Moon in Aries

You provide nourishment for others through your ability to motivate them and give them confidence in themselves. Deep within your soul you see yourself as a warrior—self-confident, independent, and fully capable of winning any battle you take on. You are also able to spark this instinctive self-confidence in others, activating them to go out and successfully accomplish their goals. This is the special gift of nurturing that you have, and when you bolster others in this way, you feel secure and connected with your own inner strength. To feel nurtured, you need those around you to support your desire for independence, so you can follow your own impulses toward self-discovery.

Moon in Taurus

You have the ability to provide nourishment for others through your special intuitive awareness of their needs, including their physical needs for comfort and their need for security in the area of money. Deep within your soul you are endowed with a sense of stability that most people don't have. Your natural connection with the earth and with mother nature gives you a sense of the proper unfoldment and timing of life, the steadiness of development, and the necessity of taking things one step at a time. When you share your awareness of the enduring nature of things with others and allow them to see your willingness to build in a slow and steady way the things that you consider important, you feel confident and are in touch with you own inner strength. This allows you to further nurture others and help them gain the confidence they need to reach their goals through the steady application of positive energy.

Moon in Gemini

You have the special ability to provide nourishment for other people through your intuitive understanding of the way they think. This natural, instinctive awareness allows you to know how others see life in various daily situations. Your unique gift of nurturing is to show them alternative ways of looking at those same situations that give them a greater sense of security and help balance their emotional bodies. When you focus on sharing a point of view that gives others a more lighthearted attitude, you feel an unshakable sense of security within yourself. By the same token, you need those around you to be light, cheerful, and willing to see your point of view.

Moon in Cancer

You have the special ability to provide nourishment for people through your emotional sensitivity to how others are feeling and your natural instinctive desire to mother them. Food in all forms is your specialty! When you tend to others by "feeding" them, either with physical food or with your intuitive gift of empathy, you heal them through letting them know that you understand and that you care. This allows you to become more secure and fulfilled in your own nature. As you call on your inner resources to nurture others, you nurture yourself in the process, and you also need others in your environment to relate to you with sensitivity.

Moon in Leo

You have the special ability to provide nourishment for others through your capacity to inspire them with enthusiasm and a general sense of happiness and play. When you indulge your childlike nature, allowing yourself to be happy and have fun, you inspire others to do the same. Through your own natural lack of inhibition, you can help others to express themselves more freely and flamboyantly. You see yourself as a queen or as royalty, and when you conduct yourself accordingly and share your absolute confidence in others from your own regal point of view, your encouragement supports them and also fulfills your desire for approval. You need to have your special talents recognized, and one of these talents is your ability to recognize and applaud the talents of others.

Moon in Virgo

You have the ability to provide nourishment for other people through your instinctive desire to be of service—to help others in the small, considerate ways that give them a sense that life is unfolding in some kind of an orderly way after all. When you take care of the details for others, or give them an idea of how something can be done in a practical way, you give them a sense of stability and emotional confidence. Your empathy and helpfulness allows them to put their lives in order and gives them a practical direction: nurturing others in this way gives you a feeling of belonging. Your willingness to do errands for others and take care of the details of life endears you to them and makes them feel taken care of and loved. Simultaneously, you need to be with others who appreciate the services you perform and who will also be conscientious in their relationships with you.

Moon in Libra

You have the capacity to provide nourishment for others through your natural sense of diplomacy, graciousness, and good manners. You see yourself as balanced, just, and socially adept—able to get along in any social situation due to your instinctive awareness of etiquette and good taste. When you nurture others by sharing this social sensitivity, you give them confidence in their capacity to handle themselves appropriately in any situation. You seek harmony and balance in relationships, and your natural tact and willing cooperation bring about a feeling of "togetherness" for others. Simultaneously, you need to be in a refined environment with people who are cooperative and who respond to your need for harmony and fairness.

Moon in Scorpio

You have the ability to provide nourishment for others through your personal courage in taking creative actions that radically transform your life. You see yourself as powerful and willing to take chances that other people are not willing to take. By sharing this brand of courage with others, you support them in overcoming oppression by making radical changes in their own lives. You help them to believe in their own personal freedom and power to make change. Your needs include being in an environment where your own power is recognized and your urge for bonding can be satisfied.

Moon in Sagittarius

You have the ability to provide nourishment for others through your natural buoyancy, your optimism and your innate faith in the positive unfolding of events. You can be a cheerful friend to all, nurturing others by sharing your natural sense of adventure and giving them the confidence they need to take risks that can lead to greater insight and a freer experience of life. As you encourage this sense of freedom in others, you become more free within yourself. You need to be with those who support your desire for freedom and who encourage you to follow your heart in pursuing those adventures that keep you vital and emotionally satisfied.

Moon in Capricorn

You provide nourishment for others through a steadiness in your own nature. You see yourself as fully capable of achieving whatever goal you set for yourself in life. When you share with others your confidence in them and your certainty that they will reach their goals, they feel nurtured and supported in their own capacity to take charge of their lives. You need to be in an environment where your accomplishments are recognized and admired, and others give you the respect and acknowledgment you need to flourish.

Moon in Aquarius

You have the ability to provide nourishment for others through your natural sense of fairness and friendship, and your ability to view things in an objective way—with a sense of humor! You see yourself as a friend to others, and are thus able to see situations in ways that work for the good of everyone involved, rather than just for yourself, personally. When you share this capacity with others, helping them to see situations in a more objective way, you nurture them by creating a perspective that allows them to not take things so personally. This sharing of friendship and equality also gives you a sense of confidence and security. You need to be in an environment where others relate to you as an equal and a friend, as well as whatever role you play in their lives.

Moon in Pisces

Your special gift of providing nourishment is your ability to unconditionally love and accept others. You want to see life and other people through "rose-colored glasses"—believing the best about them and seeing the "bigger picture" that allows you to be truly nonjudgmental. You know that others are only doing the best they can, and this understanding allows you to overlook behavioral foibles. You seek to emotionally connect with love and support with everyone, rather than being selectively loving. When you actively use your sensitivity to reach out with empathy and healing, others feel the purity of your intentions and resonate with appreciation and openness for your caring. Your awareness of our "oneness" give you confidence in relationships and facilitates healing in others at the same time. You have a need to spend time in quiet, restful surroundings where your spiritual yearnings can be satisfied.

Mars: Claiming Our Power to Initiate
The Warrior Within

Mars represents that aspect of the masculine part of ourselves that is "outer" directed: it is our power to initiate and assert leadership, our sexual desires, and our desires for conquest, competition, and victory. The astrological symbol for Mars expresses its meaning: a circle (symbolic of the fullness within ourselves) with an arrow attached, pointed upward for action in a specific direction.

Mars is an important part of our sexuality, and when we actively initiate in areas where it is valuable for us to gain a victory (by our standards), we become more sexually attractive to those who are authentically aligned with our energy.

Appropriate activity feeds energy, and when we are fully expressing our Mars we have plenty of energy and vitality, and a feeling of inner strength and vigor. We have accessed (and are expressing) the masculine part of ourselves that we can count on to do what needs to be done and to weather whatever storms may come our way. We have opened the way to self-discovery by actively moving in the direction of the goals that are important to us. By expressing the Mars in our birthcharts, we have activated that part of ourselves that can assure our survival.

It should be noted that when any of the outer planets (Jupiter, Saturn, Uranus, Neptune, or Pluto) strongly aspects an inner planet (the Sun, Moon, Mercury, Venus or Mars), it greatly affects the expression of that inner planet. For example:

If Jupiter strongly aspects a personal planet, you may fall into a "more, different, better" syndrome—going beyond the boundaries of what is healthy for you in order to *really* experience the energies of the planet involved!

If Saturn strongly aspects a personal planet, there is a need to take responsibility for consciously learning the mechanics of how to express that planet. This can result in your needs being met on a satisfying level that is far deeper—because it is more conscious—than what others experience. For example, if Saturn strongly aspects your Mars, you may feel awkward in taking the initiative, which can result in a fear of inadequacy (because it looks like everyone else seems to know how to do it). Until you take the time to "figure out" how the mechanics work, you feel limited or clumsy in the area represented by the personal planet. However, once you *do* "get it," you have a deeper, more aware, and more fully satisfying experience (in the case of Mars: independently going in your own direction) than others do.

If Uranus strongly aspects a personal planet, the need for freedom, excitement, unexpected change, and vitality is part of your femininity (if Venus or the Moon are the planets aspected by Uranus), or part of your masculine nature (if Mars or the Sun are aspected).

If Neptune aspects a personal planet, the yearning for one-ness, for having no boundaries, for feeling uninterrupted bliss greatly influences the expression of the planet involved.

If Pluto strongly aspects a personal planet (by "strong aspect" I am referring in this work to the conjunction, square or opposition), that planet would first be suppressed until through *expression,* the power of the planet is evoked. For example, in the case of Pluto aspecting Mars, your sexual nature and your power to initiate will be sources of transformation and personal growth, as well as where you gain experience in using power.

Outer planets strongly aspecting the personal planets are an indicator that, in a particular area of your life, this is not a "vacation lifetime"—you are destined to grow beyond the boundaries of what was socially considered "the norm" when you were born.

Mars in Aries

Take the leadership and initiative in actively going in your own independent direction. The impulses that motivate you to action come from within—an inner prompting to rush headlong into a situation with courage and enthusiasm. If conditions around you begin to go against your grain or begin to compromise the individuality of those involved, it's up to *you* to give others (and yourself) the confidence they need to follow their own inner impulses so that vitality can be restored. You can always look to your own independent nature as the key to your survival.

Mars in Taurus

Take the leadership and initiative in building those things that you consider valuable. Once you have decided what is important to you, it's up to *you* to initiate and stay with the process step by step until it is achieved. You are motivated to establish comfort in your world: good food, sensual enjoyment, and comfortable surroundings. If circumstances change and become disruptive, you need to assert yourself in a way that restores serenity to the situation. You can always look to your ability to create comfort as the key to your survival.

Mars in Gemini

Take the leadership and initiative in creating the exciting informational exchanges that you seek. You enjoy sharing ideas with a variety of people, mentally connecting to share points of view and then going your own way. You love teaching and learning, and are energized by all forms of mental stimulation. If your immediate environment becomes dull or routine, it's up to *you* to stir up new ideas that get things in motion! Or you can move on to a new situation that offers the mental stimulation you seek. You can always look to your way with words as the key to your survival.

Mars in Cancer

Take the leadership and initiative in creating a bond of empathy in your relationships with others. When situations around you are becoming too businesslike and dry, lacking in nurturing and emotional fullness, you take the initiative to restore a more personal touch and feeling. It's up to *you* to initiate the closeness you seek in your home environment, and you can do this successfully when you take the lead. You can always look to your gift of empathy as the key to your survival.

Mars in Leo

Take the leadership and initiative in creating situations that contain the elements of fun and playfulness. You love to be vitally involved with life, and when situations around you become too objective or lifeless, you are the one who can take the initiative and restore excitement and enjoyment. It's up to *you* to keep the energy of romance, play, and recreation alive in your life. You can always look to your confidence and creativity as the keys to your survival.

Mars in Virgo

Take the leadership and initiative in your work and in any projects you are involved in. When there is a mess, if *you* take the initiative to straighten it out and clean it up, your energy and confidence will soar! Your work and pet projects are very important to you, so it's best to have a job where you are in the leadership position. You have plenty of energy for work, and if your self-confidence begins to lag or your sense of identity dims, get involved with a project that is important to you! You can always look to your willingness to work as the key to your survival.

Mars in Libra

Take the leadership and initiative in creating the harmony that you value in relationships. Balance and fairness are important to you, and it's up to *you* to take the initiative in situations where injustice exists. You can restore the harmony by presenting resolutions that are fair because they take into account the individual responses of everyone involved. When you put your energy into creating beauty, art, or public relations, you become energized and self-confident and gain a stronger sense of your own identity. You can always look to your talent for diplomacy as the key to your survival.

Mars in Scorpio

Take the leadership and initiative in creating emotional closeness and bonding with those you feel an affinity with. Others don't know how to do it, so it's up to *you* to lead the way and actively create the intimacy and mutual empowerment you seek. As you take charge to do this, your energy will soar and your own sense of personal power will blossom. You can always look to your ability to create bonded relationships as the key to your survival.

Mars in Sagittarius

Take the leadership and initiate the spontaneous adventures that occur to you as possibilities in your life. You don't want your life to be dull, and it's up to *you* to create the excitement you need to keep your energy high. If situations around you become bogged down or depressing, you are the one who can find the optimistic outlook and the faith in positive outcomes that can regenerate hope and vigor for all concerned! You can always look to your faith in positive outcomes as the key to your survival.

Mars in Capricorn

Take the leadership and initiate the discipline that is needed to bring circumstances around you under control and have conditions be manageable for all concerned. When you see situations that are emotionally "out of control" or are wasting energy due to a lack of goal-orientated direction, it's up to *you* to take charge and correct it. This also brings you to a position of being "on top" in that area of your life. You can always look to your ability to "get to the goal" as your key to survival.

Mars in Aquarius

Take the leadership and help others gain awareness of humanitarian concerns. You are naturally conscious of the divergent wills of others and you are motivated to find resolutions that enhance the good of the whole. If the people around you become self-absorbed, insisting on getting their way without thinking about others, it's up to *you* to offer an expanded perspective that will be fair to everyone involved. If your energy lags, actively pursue humanitarian concerns and your vitality will soar once again! You can always look to your ability to create friendship as your key to survival.

Mars in Pisces

Take the leadership and help others to gain an awareness of the private dream that you see. Your style is not aggressive, as you are motivated by a desire to pursue your own vision rather than to attain worldly rewards. If situations around you become bogged down with rules and regulations that are strangling life and joy, it's up to *you* to remind others of the larger spiritual or emotional picture. Then the tension will dissipate and the flow of energy you seek will be restored. You can always look to your connection with the Universe as your key to survival.

The Sun: Being The King Within

In many ways, the Sun is the only "non-karmic" planet in the chart. It is a position of innocence; the place where we "knew" before incarnating, we could use extra energy to extricate ourselves from past patterning. One of the benefits of Western astrology is that, by emphasizing the sun sign, it highlights that aspect of ourselves that is inherently free and innocent, unfettered by some distant past (if we choose to use it in that way).

The Sun in your chart is connected to your "source" of being—the solar battery that keeps the rest of your systems vital and energized—so full of life that you have the energy to shine on others and generously revitalize them as well. The question then becomes: what charges your solar battery? What gives you a sense of well-being and completion within yourself, a sense that you are charged, that you are happy, content, and fulfilled? The specific circumstances that you need to charge your solar battery are represented by your Sun sign. When you fulfill the needs of your Sun sign, you are able to give generously to others because you have tapped into the endless source of solar energy.

Sun in Aries

Aries needs a series of short-term goals that you can accomplish on your own to exercise your independence in order to recharge your solar battery. Any time you risk going in a direction that leads to self-discovery, you become more energized and more self-confident. Then you are able to give energy and impetus to others who need a "push" to propel them into doing what they need to do in order to be true to their own intrinsic nature. The Sun in Aries lady needs to experience the energy rush of independent action, freedom of motion, and unhindered creative activity. If you start to feel "low energy," it's time to put some of your healthy impulses into action!

Sun in Taurus

Comfort and being involved in building something (that is going to lead to comfort) is what charges the solar battery of a Taurean. When Taurus is building, going one step at a time to manifest something you have decided you want, your solar battery is charged. You have a tremendous capacity to appreciate and enjoy life, and when you honor your sensual nature—with a good meal, a massage, or spoiling yourself with comfortable surroundings—your solar battery charges. Then you are full of life and want to fill the needs of others. If your solar battery begins to run down, it's time to acknowledge your basic needs and actively pursue getting them fulfilled.

Sun in Gemini

Gemini needs an endless arena of people you can communicate with. You need a group of people around you, or within easy access (i.e., co-workers, a country club, schoolmates), with whom you can share and exchange ideas and information. When you have a large supply of people you can connect with, your solar battery charges. If life starts to get boring, it's time to expand your horizons and start getting out and about. Enroll in night school, go on a vacation, sign up for a lecture series, or join a club. On some level, the energy of positive mental exchanges needs to occur for Gemini to stay happy and keep your solar battery charged.

Sun in Cancer

Cancer needs a feeling of security. You can obtain this through getting a home, decorating it, and feeling that it is impenetrable because you can financially support it. You need the solid security of a shelter you can count on as your foundation. When that need is filled, your solar battery is charged and you have plenty of energy to give to the world. If you're feeling moody or insecure, take charge by concentrating on money and put yourself in a more stable financial situation. Or take charge of your diet and properly nurture yourself and those you love. If your moods become too intense, join a support group of women with whom you can "problem solve," or initiate contact with family members or close friends for mutual empathy and support. By actively doing things that increase your sense of security, you can recharge your solar battery.

Sun in Leo

Romance, and the constant need for involvement in romantic or creative activity is what charges the solar battery of a Leo. The romance can be expressed directly, through keeping romantic relationships going in your own life, keeping the element of romance going in on-going relationships, or by enjoying romance vicariously, through romantic novels, books, movies, or just by enjoying other people being in love. This need to experience the vitality of love can also be filled through heavy personal involvement in creative projects, drama, or by spending time with children. On some level, the energy of play, romance and pure enjoyment needs to be in your life to keep the Leo solar battery fully charged. If you're bored or depressed, start spending more time with people in situations that are stimulating and inspire your sense of fun.

Sun in Virgo

The Virgo needs work—a sense of purpose, of being important, of being needed on the job—and work charges your solar battery! This desire for meaningful work can be expressed through purposeful mental activity: analyzing the inner working of a person or situation, or problem solving to find and apply practical solutions. It can also be the project of helping to organize and take care of loved ones, seeing to it that the lives of those around you run smoothly. Active participation in being of service to others is what charges the solar battery of a Virgo. If you are feeling lethargic or at "loose ends," it's time to take charge and begin a routine that will give you a sense of purpose and order. Work out on a regular basis, go to lectures, or take classes that will help you develop an area of life that interests you: creative abilities, financial knowledge, or self-improvement courses.

Sun in Libra

Sun in Libra needs to feel you have a partner—someone to do things with, to share with. You need someone around you to enjoy who gives energy back to you. When you share with another person you can count on, your solar battery is charged. Your need to experience teamwork applies not only to marriage. Partnership in all forms charges your battery: a partner for shopping, going to the movies, or working on a project toward a common goal. Too much time alone leaves you feeling drained of energy, like you're "missing" a part of life. Then it's time for you to pick up the telephone and connect with someone you can share an activity with. Even the process of initiating contact with another person will help to charge your solar energy.

Sun in Scorpio

Sun in Scorpio needs to feel the intensity of bonding with other people, or with another (it may be in various forms), in order to have your solar battery charged. You need the mutual empowerment that comes from feeling a full sharing of intense energy with another person. Situations that give you the feeling of living on the edge, taking chances, and risking with another in a way that leads to new kinds of empowerment also help keep you fully charged. Sometimes you want to become invested in situations that are almost over your head in order to feel the vitality of being in the middle of a crisis. If your Sun is in Scorpio and you're feeling listless and bored, think of some action (or constructive goal or activity) that would require a new habit on your part—a change for the better—and then go for it with 100 per cent commitment. Your solar battery will soar!

Sun in Sagittarius

A sense of adventure is what charges the solar battery of a Sagittarian. You need to feel you are on some kind of adventure that has a noble purpose and adds excitement to your life. When you can see that "holy grail" that you are pursuing on your quest and connect with that sense of adventure, your battery becomes filled and you are able to contribute to others. Nobility and honor are important to the Sagittarian. You need to feel that you are acting with honor and integrity, and that those close to you are doing the same. An active sense of faith and a consistent optimism about life are also needs that keep your solar battery charged. If your faith in others is disappointed, or if you're feeling bored with your life, put the past behind you and look into the future. What activity would spark your sense of adventure? Foreign travel, sports, being outdoors with Mother Nature— all these activities regenerate the Sagittarian!

Sun in Capricorn

Sun in Capricorn needs to be pursuing a goal. When you have a sense of responsibility, a purpose in life, and a clear idea of the goal you are working to actualize, your solar energy is charged to the maximum. As a Sun in Capricorn woman, if you wait for a man to come along to take charge of your life and give you a sense of direction, you'll wait forever. You are the one with the inborn capacity to take charge and create success in any situation. All it takes is for you to decide what you want, what you want to achieve at this particular time. Once you have made a commitment to a goal, there's no stopping you! Your vitality soars and you are filled with the energy of success and the joy of accomplishment!

Sun in Aquarius

The Aquarian needs a cause—some humanitarian cause to pursue, a dream to bring into reality, people to help. When you feel involved with humankind in this way, working for unorthodox causes that bring advancement to the world, your solar battery is charged. Spending time with friends, like-minded people who also have unorthodox orientations toward life, charges the solar battery of the Aquarian lady! If your vitality begins to droop or your zest for life disappears, take a class or join a group that interests you, or pick up the telephone and get together with friends to catch up with what's going on in the world from their point of view. Your solar battery will recharge in no time!

Sun in Pisces

The Piscean needs a dream—a spiritual connection so you can feel at one with the universe and focus on your own private vision of a reality that is more meaningful than the day-to-day knocks and bruises of ordinary life. When you are in touch with that reality, your solar battery is totally charged and you are able to give lovingly to others. In the process of giving to others from your sense of self-fulfillment, you experience more healing energy coming into your own life. If your vitality is low or you're feeling blue, it's time to actively *do* something that unites you with the fullness of life. Get yourself moving, enroll in a class that interests you, or take up art, yoga, dance, creative writing, or a musical instrument. If you already have developed a talent, spend regular time alone, peacefully working on creative projects that connect you with your vision, and your solar battery will soar!

The Houses

My research, using the Placidus house system, has led me to the opinion that the astrological *houses* where the planets are located are at least as important as the sign positions of the planets in terms of understanding the inner workings of an individual. Therefore, in interpreting the above planetary meanings, consider the *houses* in which these planets are located. (These interpretations have the potential to work with any house system.)

First House

The energies of a planet found in the First House are best activated through your innate impulses and innocent self-assertion. A sense of self-trust is the energy that stimulates the expression of the planets found in this house.

Second House

The energies of planets in the second house are best activated through consistently building in those directions that you consider worthwhile. The energies need to be expressed according to your own values—the things in life that make you feel comfortable and equipped with a solid foundation to participate in life.

Third House

The energies of planets found in this house are best activated through an open desire for exchanging information with other people. Planetary energies can be accessed by listening and learning where others are, gathering and giving gems of knowledge that enhance the individuals involved.

Fourth House

The energies of planets in the Fourth House are best activated through feeling grounded and centered within yourself. It is from your roots, your basic sense of security, that the energy for expressing these planets emanates.

Fifth House

The energies of planets found in the Fifth House are best activated through play and a romantic style of interacting with others. Act on your desire to create enthusiastic, positive results that stimulate others (and yourself!) with a zest for life.

Sixth House

The energies of planets in the Sixth House are best activated through work—a desire to bring order to a situation of chaos. The need to be of practical service to others by helping to clear-up the confusion in their lives stimulates the expression of the planets found in this house.

Seventh House

The energies of planets found in the Seventh House are best activated through a sense of partnership with an entity or entities outside of yourself. This gives you the energy and balance that prompts expression of the planets involved.

Eighth House

The energies of a planet in the Eighth House are best activated through combining your efforts with others for a mutual enhancement of power. It is this synergy that fires the expression of the planet involved.

Ninth House

The energies of planets found in the Ninth House are best activated through higher knowledge from the intuitive realms. In seeking and accepting a connection with Truth, you attain the peace of mind that allows these planetary expressions.

Tenth House

The energies of planets in the Tenth House are best activated through the process of seeking to attain a goal that is bigger than your own personal life, and serves society in a way that gives you a sense of self-respect.

Eleventh House

The energies of a planet found in the Eleventh House are best activated through promoting goals or ideals that you feel are in the best interest of everyone concerned. The good of the group and a sense of fairness are part of what needs to be considered to fully express these planets.

Twelfth House

The energies of planets found in the Twelfth House are best activated through your private connection with invisible, spiritual forces. It is your relationship with the cosmos itself that is the nurturing foundation for expressing these planets. (For example, with Venus in the Twelfth House you accept love from the angels, or invisible spiritual forces, and then are able to share this love with others. With Mars in the Twelfth House you are motivated from spiritual prompting, rather than from the desire to gain material goals).

We can experience enormous self-confidence, completeness, and self-sufficiency by consciously including and expressing both the feminine and masculine aspects within our nature. However, we can never fully experience our wholeness until we have embraced that factor within us that is greater than personality: the Being behind the birth chart.

As we begin to consciously and fully explore our true potential on the personality level—being ourselves without the "static" created from trying to be that which we are not—we become more peaceful inside. This allows our true Being to emerge and become more consciously part of our daily experience. Then the search for wholeness is complete: we have made room for that which we were looking for to find us. In order for inner Integrity to come forth and claim us and make us whole, we must first have the integrity to be ourselves—fully and constructively—on the personality level.

Demetra George

Demetra George, mythologist and astrologer, has been a counsellor, teacher, writer, and researcher since 1972. She is the co-author of *Astrology For Yourself,* author of *Asteroid Goddesses, Mysteries of the Dark Moon: The Healing Power of the Dark Goddess.* and *Finding Our Way Through the Dark.* Her pioneering research synthesizes ancient mythology and history and archetypal psychology with feminine-centered astrology. She is the past President of the Asteroid SIG of the NCGR, on the AFAN Steering Committee, and a member of ISAR. Demetra also facilitates women's mysteries groups and leads pilgrimages to sacred sites in the Mediterranean. She lives on the Oregon coast and teaches internationally.

Demetra George

Women's Evolving Needs: The Moon and the Blood Mysteries

ince ancient times the Moon has been worshipped as the Queen of Night. Dating to at least 35,000 years ago, artifacts from the upper Paleolithic era, consisting of sequences of notches carved into bone, stone, and ivory have been determined to be the earliest lunar phase calendars.[1] By gazing at the Moon and tracking her phases, early peoples regulated their lives according to the lunar rhythms. They watched the Moon change place, color, and shape, disappear and reappear each month. She gradually unfolded from a slim silvery waxing crescent, increasing in light until she was totally illuminated at the full Moon, and then decreasing in light until she became altogether invisible at the dark of the Moon.

This lunar rhythm presented an image of a creation, symbolized by the new Moon, followed by growth as seen in the full Moon, and then a diminution and death during the three dark, moonless nights. Historian of religion, Mircia Eliade, said that it was very probably this image of the eternal birth and death of the Moon that helped to crystallize the earliest intuitions about the alternation of life and death.[2]

In Mesopotamia, during the processional age of Taurus—around 4,000 B.C., the sign in which the Moon is exalted, nestled in the fertile valley between the Tigris and Euphrates rivers (present-day Iraq) one of the earliest cradles of civilization arose. The discovery of agriculture led to the development of an agrarian economy that allowed people a settled lifestyle and enabled them to create the first villages. Ancient Mesopotamia, in the third and fourth millenniums B.C., was also the seedbed of astrology. The first written astrological records inscribed on clay cuneiform tablets record Mesopotamians' observations and earthly correlations of the Moon and of Venus.

Today we define the Sun as the source of life. However, for the early peoples of the ancient Near East, who lived in a very hot desert climate, the Sun was the enemy against which they had to protect themselves. The Sun was associated with hot, inflamed air, parched land, and exhausted, heat-prostrated bodies. They much preferred the Moon whose gentle light illuminated without menacing, and, in the night, would give forth dew and moisture to water the seedlings and nourish the crops. It was the Moon's brightness at night that guided caravans moving across the desert.

The Phases of the Moon

Everywhere in the ancient Near East it was obvious to all eyes that the phases of the Moon served to measure time before the exact duration of the year was discovered. The Moon's phases became the basis of the sacred calendars regulating both religious ceremonies and agricultural planting and reaping cycles.[3]

Early people saw how the Moon affected the growth of plants as well as the health of women. It was a very simple observation to notice that the twenty-nine and a half days of the lunar cycle replicated a woman's menstrual cycle of twenty-eight to twenty-nine days. Therefore, early peoples assumed that the Moon must be feminine. As such, she was personified as the Great Goddess, and was then perceived as the fertile matrix out of which all life is born and into which all life is reabsorbed.

The story that the Moon tells is one of birth, growth, fullness, decay, and disappearance, with rebirth and growth once again. The cycle of the Moon's phases displays the model that the essential movement of all life is cyclic in nature. All life forms, everything that is alive, has a cycle of birth and growth and death as mirrored in the progressive phases of the Moon's cycle. The Moon turns from new to full to dark, and likewise all living things resonate to her instinctual rhythm of emergence, fulfillment, completion, followed by renewal.

We know that the phases of the Moon are not simply a manifestation of the Moon herself. They are the display of the changing relationship between the Sun and the Moon as the Moon circles the earth each month. The Sun and Moon embody the principle of polarity, both in our physical world and in our psychological nature. In our daily lives, the alternating rhythms of the Sun and Moon regulate our day and night cycles. The Sun rules the daylight of consciousness and the outer objective world, while the Moon rules the night of the unconscious and our inner instinctual life.

Together the Sun and the Moon represent the basic archetypal principles of the God and the Goddess. The phases of the Moon are a display of the Moon's dance with the Sun. They reflect the pattern of her increasing and decreasing light as she separates from the Sun and then returns back to him, and in that process, tapping out the rhythm of how it is that life is created, sustained, and renewed.

In humanity's attempt to conceptualize the holistic meaning of the Moon's cycle, various cultures have subdivided it in terms of two hemispheres, three phases, four quarters, eight cross-quarters, and twenty-seven or twenty-eight mansions. Each lunation phase, or division of the cycle, represents a certain quality and kind of energy that is called for and utilized during each of the successive stages of this cyclic life process in the growth and development of any organic form. Every time the cycle is further subdivided, each additional phase reveals a more subtle and refined level of meaning of the process.

The cycle can be divided by three, into the new, full, and dark phases of the Moon, which correspond to the three phases of the Triple Moon Goddess as maiden, mother, and crone. We will explore this three-fold division in greater detail during the second part of this chapter.

Dividing the cycle by two yields the waxing and waning hemispheres. During the first half of the cycle, when the Moon's light is waxing from the new to full Moon, the life energy is increasing, and the purpose is to build some kind of form, structure, or body. The light, having reached its maximum at the full Moon, begins to wane as the Moon starts her approach back to the Sun. During the second half of the cycle, meaning is infused into the forms that were built during the first half of the cycle.

These two hemicycles, the waxing and waning phases, can be divided again into four quarters. In the lunation cycle, this quartering is displayed as the new Moon, the first-quarter Moon, the full Moon, and the last-quarter Moon. These four lunar quarter phases mirror the symbolic meanings of the four directions, and their corresponding seasons, elements, and cardinal points.

During the first phase of this four-fold sequence, from the new Moon to the first-quarter, the impulse of the evolving life energy is to emerge and initiate action. This first phase corresponds to the direction East, the season Spring, the element air and the rising Sun with all of the implications of new beginnings. The flow of energy during the second phase of the cycle from the first-quarter to the full Moon seeks to build, stabilize, and perfect the form. This second phase corresponds to the direction South, the season Summer, the element fire, and the High Noon Sun. The attributes of power, strength, and will culminate during this part of the cycle.

It is in the period from the full Moon to the last-quarter Moon that the meaning is released into the form and the energy distributed. This third phase corresponds to the direction West, the season Autumn, the element Water, and the Setting Sun. The qualities of relatedness, emotions, and fulfillment infuse this part of the cycle. From the last-quarter Moon to the new Moon, the form is broken down and the meaning is assimilated into a new seed which is prepared during the dark Moon. This final phase relates to the direction North, the season Winter, the element Earth, and the Midnight Sun. Silence, wisdom, and renewal are the characteristics that are associated with this closure phase of cyclic process.

When the fourfold division of the Moon's monthly cycle around the Earth is again halved, it yields eight distinct lunar phases. They are named the New, Crescent, First Quarter, Gibbous, Full, Disseminating, Last Quarter, and Balsamic. This eight-fold cycle of transformation as seen in the increasing and decreasing light of the Moon's monthly cycle is also evident in the increasing and decreasing light of the yearly solar seasonal cycle as depicted in the eight seasonal holidays celebrated in the Wheel of the Year.

In *Finding Our Way Through the Dark* (ACS, 1995), I have detailed the meanings of the eight lunation phases. For the purposes of this chapter on women's blood mysteries, I will briefly summarize them, giving the correlations between each lunation phase and the corresponding seasonal holiday in terms

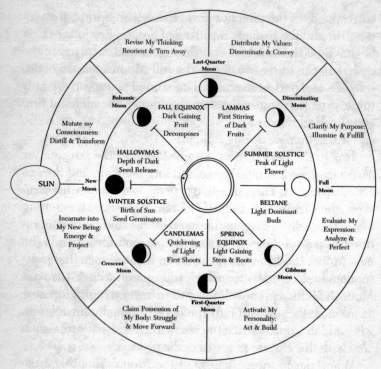

Diagram 1
The Lunation Phases: An 8-Fold Cycle of Transformation

of increasing and decreasing light. Using the image of the growth cycle of a plant, we can draw an analogy to the stages of the soul's evolutionary journey, and the kinds of energy that are utilized at each successive stage of cyclic process by which life forms unfold, fulfill, complete, and renew themselves.

New Moon Phase

The Moon is 0 to 45 degrees ahead of the Sun. The first phase of cyclic process is depicted by the birth of the light at both the new Moon and the Winter Solstice (Yule). The process begins when the seed, containing a new vision infused with an intention, breaks free from its capsule and germinates in the darkness. At this first stage, the evolving soul initiates a new cycle of experience by incarnating into a body, allowing a subjective sense of new possibilities to surface, and projecting an identity into the world. The energy emerges out of the void and projects itself forward.

Crescent Moon Phase

The Moon is 45 to 90 degrees ahead of the Sun. The second phase of cyclic process signified by the Crescent Moon is analogous to the cross-quarter day of Candlemas (Imbolc), February 2[4] when the light quickens. Now the first tender shoots of this vision have struggled against the force of gravity to push themselves above the ground. At this second stage the evolving soul is enfolded with matter and likewise struggles to overcome the backward pull of the past in order to move forward. It must claim possession of the body, gradually focus its vision, and develop new talents and skills. The flow of energy at this stage of cyclic process is a confrontation against resistance and inertia, trying to push through it and establish one's fledgling identity.

First-Quarter Phase

The Moon is 90 to 135 degrees ahead of the Sun. The third phase of cyclic process is depicted by the First-Quarter Moon where there is an equal amount of light and dark, corresponding to the Spring Equinox (Oestarra) when there is the balance between daylight and nighttime hours. Now the light force steadily increases. At this stage, the plant sends its roots downward and its stem and leaves upward, creating a strong structural foundation to support the flower and fruit that is to come. The life force of the evolving soul activates the personality by taking direct action to anchor the vision and to build a similar structural foundation to support the larger purpose that is waiting to be revealed. The flow of energy is forceful and direct, clearing away obstacles in order to build strong forms.

Gibbous Moon Phase

The Moon is 135 to 180 degrees ahead of the Sun. The fourth phase of cyclic process represented by the Gibbous Moon corresponds to the seasonal cross-quarter day of Beltane (Mayday) when the light force is rapidly growing. Our daylight hours are getting longer, and we see the Moon swelling toward her fullness. At this stage the plant is putting forth buds with the promise and expectation of the flower that will bloom. The evolving soul looks back to the structures it has created in order to evaluate and improve upon them. The flow of energy is geared toward analyzing one's expression, finding ways of perfecting one's structures so they can be worthy containers of the coming meaning, and integrating them into the reality of the environment so that they can be of use to others.

Full Moon Phase

The Moon is 180 to 135 degrees behind the Sun. The light peaks at the fifth phase of cyclic process shown by the maximum amount of reflected light at the full Moon phase and the longest hours of daylight at the Summer Solstice (Midsummer, Litha). Now, halfway around the lunation cycle, the flower opens and blooms. The vision is fully illuminated and the evolving soul becomes "conscious," clearly seeing its purpose, and beginning to infuse the meaning of its life into the structures that were initiated, built and perfected during the first four incarnations. In the same way that the flower has to be pollinated in order to bear fruit, the soul at the full Moon phase must open itself to receive someone or something from outside of itself into itself in order to fertilize the cycle and bear the fruit.

Disseminating Moon Phase

The Moon is 135 to 90 degrees behind the Sun. The sixth phase of cyclic process opens at the Disseminating Moon, when the Moon is still full but the first stirrings of darkness begin to occur. This corresponds to the seasonal cross-quarter day of Lammas (Lughnasadh) on August 1 when the daylight hours begin to shorten. The flower begins to fold in upon itself as it forms the fruit. This stage marks the apex or fruition of the cycle when the vision is acted on and lived out through the lives of humanity, thereby fulfilling its purpose. The evolving soul embodies this meaning and lives out its purpose, spreading what it has found to be of value and conveying its message and wisdom.

Last-Quarter Moon Phase

The Moon is 90 to 45 degrees behind the Sun. The seventh phase of cyclic process is marked by the half/light, half/dark last-Quarter Moon that mirrors the time of the Fall Equinox (Mabon) when daylight and nighttime hours are once again in balance. The dark force begins to gain in both cycles. In the plant cycle the crop is harvested and whatever has been realized throughout the cycle is ingested and assimilated. The fruit that is left on the vine begins to wither and decompose. Once the purpose of the cycle has been fulfilled, the destructuring process begins. What was built up must now be broken down. The evolving soul begins to revise its thinking, based on the new awareness gained from the previous phases, and it begins to reject limiting belief systems, reevaluating and reorganizing its ideology. The flow of energy turns away from the old and begins to reorient to intimations of the future.

Balsamic Moon Phase

The Moon is 45 to 90 degrees behind the Sun. The eighth and final stage of cyclic process is symbolized by the waning Balsamic Moon dissolving into darkness. The cross-quarter seasonal holiday of Halloween (Samhain) on October 31 also ushers in the shortest days of sunlight as the dark force triumphs. In the plant cycle the seed is released from the old fruit and is buried underground in the depth of the dark. The evolving soul likewise distills the wisdom essence of the past cycle and intuits the visions of the future, creating seed capsules that will germinate at the next new Moon phase. The flow of energy is to withdraw deep inside oneself, releasing, purifying, healing, regenerating, and preparing to be reborn.

The Moon Phase in Your Life

Each of us is born during a particular lunation phase, and we reflect the characteristics of that phase of cyclic process. Our lunation phase is determined by the angle of separation between the Sun and Moon at the time of our birth.

For example, if your Sun is at 5 Gemini and your Moon is at 10 Leo, the Moon is 65 degrees ahead of the Sun, which would make you a Crescent Moon phase. If your Sun is at 5 Gemini and your Moon is at 10 Sagittarius, the Moon is 175 degrees behind the Sun making you a full Moon phase. The Sun at 5 Gemini and the Moon at 28 Taurus makes you a Balsamic Moon phase as the Moon is 7 degrees behind the Sun.[5]

In astrology the Sun and Moon each have a wide range of individual meanings. However when we look at any two planets in terms of a cycle of relationship with one another, the slower and faster planet each have a distinct meaning. In the cycle of relationship the slower planet signifies the shaping or determining action, while the faster planet shows how this action will be carried out. In the relationship between the Sun and Moon, the Sun is the slower planet, and as such represents our conscious life purpose. The Moon, which is the faster planet, represents the body, the soul, the vehicle through which and in which we will actualize our purpose into our daily lives. The successive phases of the Moon display the stages of the flow of energy moving between the Sun and Moon as their cycle reflects the expression and actualization of some purpose.

The lunation phase at the time of our birth is a major significator of the core of our personality, because it describes the flow of energy between these two primary symbols of our being—our solar consciousness and lunar instinctive awareness. It indicates the kind of interactive energy that we can best utilize to express and actualize our own individual life's purpose. We experience the process of the eight-fold lunation cycle on a monthly basis through Moon transits, and several times within our lives through Moon progressions, as well as over the course of many lifetimes through cumulative cycles of death and rebirth.

Each month, when the Moon is in the same lunation phase as it was when we were born, we are more highly sensitized. Whatever we are feeling (Moon) tends to come closer to the surface of our conscious awareness (Sun), particularly concerning the relative meaning or lack of meaning in our lives (lunation phase).

This phenomena of a brief period of acute sensitivity each month has a distinct biological correlation. Dr. Eugen Jonas, a gynecologist and astrologer from the former republic of Czechoslovakia, discovered that a woman can be fertile during her lunation phase each month, as well as midpoint in her menstrual cycle. Called the cosmic fertility period, there is the possibility of spontaneous ovulation at this time. This accounts for many unexpected pregnancies when women thought that they were carefully keeping track of the fertile midpoint days of their menstrual cycles. This sensitive period can also be used for the successful conception of a child or to help determine its sex and the viability of the fetus.

This is not only a biologically fertile time for women, but also a period of creative, mental, or spiritual fertility for both women and men. The reoccurrence of our birth lunation phase each month is our personal lunar power time when we can engage in any meaningful activity and get productive results. Whatever seeds we plant at this time can yield a rich harvest.

We are all born into one particular phase, and the major part of our awareness operates with this kind of energy. However, life is not a static process. A timing system in astrology called secondary progression measures the movements of the planets in the days after our birth, and it symbolizes the unfolding of our birth potential over time.

The progressed Sun and the progressed Moon move on after our birth, and via their changing angular relationship, called our progressed lunation phase, we also experience the qualities of each of the other phases as well in twenty-nine/thirty-year cycles. Approximately every twenty-nine to thirty years the progressed Sun and progressed Moon come together at a conjunction point which astrologers call the progressed new Moon phase. This occurs at different ages, depending on the phase of the lunation cycle at a person's birth. We then initiate, fulfill, and complete one entire turning of our life's unfolding meaning as we move sequentially through each of the lunation phases. Each progressed phase lasts for approximately three-and-one-half to four years, and we respond to the prompting of each stage of cyclic process. We have the opportunity to utilize the various Sun/Moon energies at the critical periods of actualizing our life purpose.[6]

Finally, from a reincarnational point of view, it is suggested that we incarnate successively into each lunation phase during an eight-fold sequence of lifetimes in the development of a certain experience or lesson. Our birth phase does not indicate how evolved or unevolved we are, but it does point to the stage of development within one particular cycle. We may be a new soul completing a final phase of experience, or an old soul initiating a new cycle of experience. In either case, our lunation phase suggests the particular lessons and qualities our evolving soul consciousness is being called upon to develop in this lifetime as it relates to a larger process and goal that will be realized over a series of lifetimes.

The Blood Mysteries

The rhythm of the Moon, whose phases resonated to women's menstrual cycles, held a special place in the myths, religion, and symbols of the ancient religions that worshipped the Moon as the Goddess. Early people perceived the Moon, which displayed the ebb and flow of birth, life, and death, to be a feminine goddess who ruled over these three great mysteries.

There exist two major feminine cycles in the physiology of women's bodies. Both cycles are physically and symbolically related to that of the Moon. The first one is a monthly cycle, marked by ovulation and menstruation, that reflects the twofold alternation of the light and dark phases of the Moon. The second is a lifelong developmental cycle whose threefold stages of (1) menarche, (2) pregnancy, birth, and nursing, and (3) menopause correspond to the new, full, and dark phases of the Moon.

A WOMAN'S MONTHLY CYCLE

The principle of polarity that operates in our world as sets of complementary opposite forces (masculine/feminine, yang/yin, light/dark) expressed within the female sexual cycle as the two poles of ovulation and menstruation. The average menstrual cycle is twenty-nine and one-half days, which is exactly the length of the Moon's cycle. The words for Moon, month, and menses are all derived from the root "mens." When we overlay

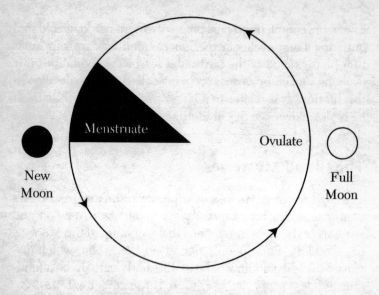

Diagram 2
Woman's Monthly Menstrual Cycle

the lunar cycle upon a woman's monthly sexual cycle, the light phase of the full Moon corresponds to ovulation and the dark/new Moon is analogous to menstruation. We will now discuss the physiological stages of a woman's monthly menstrual cycle as they relate to the symbolism of the lunation phases.

Various hormones rise and fall in a woman's bloodstream each month and affect changes in her uterus. These monthly fluctuations flow according to the same rhythm of increase and decrease as the Moon's cycle. Estrogen rises in the blood stream during the waxing half of the cycle when the Moon's light is increasing; while progesterone predominates during the waning half when the light is decreasing.

The hormonal cycle begins with the waxing Crescent Moon. At this time the pituitary gland secretes follicle stimulating hormone (FSH) into the bloodstream. This stimulates the eggs

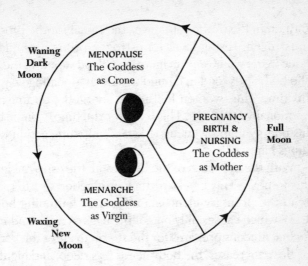

Diagram 3
Woman's Lifelong Blood Cycle

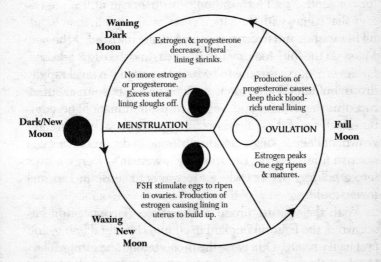

Diagram 4
The Menstrual Cycle and the Lunar Phases

to ripen in the ovaries and gives the signal for the production of estrogen. Rising levels of estrogen prompt a build-up of tissue in the womb and an increased blood supply to the uterus. The body uses food in a building and assimilating way during this time; thus women feel more energetic, optimistic, and emotionally expansive. This is a powerful time; women can use this energy high by taking risks and initiating action to make things happen.

With the approach of the full Moon, the estrogen level begins to peak. This blocks further production of FSH, and instead the pituitary gland manufactures leutening hormone (LH), which causes only one of the eggs to ripen and mature. Vaginal mucous prepares for the sperm to enter the body. The sex drive increases, the body needs less sleep, and night vision becomes sharper. These changes are linked to the instinctual nocturnal mating urge. A woman's receptivity and openness also peak at this time, as her body and emotions are prepared for conception and fertilization. A woman can utilize the energy that comes with the Moon's maximum illumination to fulfill her wishes and to accomplish what she initiated at the new Moon. At the full Moon, ovulation occurs and the egg is released.

Several days after the full Moon the estrogen level rapidly drops, but another hormone, progesterone, is then manufactured in the ovaries and begins to predominate. The combined effects of these two hormones produce an even greater growth of deep, spongy, blood-rich lining in the uterus that can nourish a fertile egg. Emotionally a woman's energy moves into a holding pattern when she wants to settle in and feel more stable.

With the waning phase of the cycle, if conception has occurred, the egg will implant itself into the uteral lining, and pregnancy begins. Otherwise the progesterone and estrogen levels abruptly decrease, causing the uteral lining to shrink and decompose. A woman may likewise feel an emotional letdown, as if she was all prepared for an event that didn't happen. Depression, sadness, anxiety, and irritability, all classic premenstrual symptoms, often occur at this time.

With the dark phase of the Moon, progesterone and estrogen reach their lowest levels. Menstruation occurs as the body sheds the sloughed-off excess uteral lining. The blood's flow is a sign of dynamic transformation; what was built up is now being broken down and released. At the dark of the Moon a woman turns inward, emotionally and physically. She craves sleep, has less interest in outer matters, and feels the urge to pull into the still and quiet renewal of her bleeding time. With the waning Moon, a woman's psychic abilities are heightened. This is a prime time for her to engage in all kinds of inner work, as well as a time for her to complete, release, and let go of the old cycle.

The twin poles of ovulation and menstruation in a woman's sexual cycle correspond to the peaks of maximum light and maximum darkness depicted by the full and dark phases of the Moon's cycle. A woman's emotions and the kind of sexuality that she desires also fluctuate according to this rhythmic pattern.

The full Moon is most receptive to receiving the maximum amount of the Sun's light, and during a woman's corresponding full Moon ovulatory time, she feels most open, magnetic, and nurturing to others. Her sexuality expresses itself as a desire to surrender to the overtures of the partner and to enjoy vaginal penetration. These feelings, which are influenced by hormonal activity, are conducive to sexual union. This is the most fertile period of the month, when sexuality can result in conception and thereby facilitate the continuation of the species. In the goddess lore, these qualities of the feminine nature were personified as the White Goddess. The white ovulatory goddess in women, who uses her sexuality for attraction, impregnation, birth, and nurturance, is most acceptable in Western culture.

By contrast, at the dark Moon menstrual time, a woman's energetic flow is no longer turned outward toward union with the other, but rather it is turned inward. She feels more of a need to nurture herself, and wants to pull away from the demands and expectations of other people in her life. Her sexual desire peaks just before menstruation. She can be multi-orgasmic and is more likely to masturbate at this time. Her sexuality is initiating, fiery, assertive, whether by herself or with a partner. Clitoral stimulation, rather than vaginal penetration, is a more intense, enjoyable, and satisfying sensation, and this kind of sexuality does not lead to procreation. At the menstrual time, the power of a woman's erotic sexuality can be used for transformation, renewal, divination, healing, and magic rather than procreation. All of these qualities of the menstrual pole of a woman's cycle, when she is self-directed, non-compromising, powerful, and impersonal, became embodied into the concepts of the Dark Goddess.

The patriarchal mentality that equates light and increase with good, and black and decrease with bad, created a schism in our perception of the dual aspect of a woman's emotional-sexual cycle. The receptive, surrendering ovulatory feminine became a symbol of the desirable qualities of an ideal femininity. However, the fiery, assertive menstruating feminine who was self-oriented and non-gestative encompassed all that was objectionable and threatening to men. As the patriarchy grew to fear the erotic sexuality of the dark Moon time, they sought to separate women from this source of their power. Menstrual woman were maligned as bitchy, hysterical, angry, furious, irrational while they had the disgusting, impure "curse." Let us now look more deeply into the women's menstruating mysteries that are connected to the Dark phase of the Moon.

Our word blessing comes from the old English—*bloedsen*, or "bleeding." The majority of words used by the ancients for menstruation honor it, and it meant such things as sacred, supernatural, and deity. The earlier people thought that the mystery of creation resided in a woman's menstrual blood that flowed in harmony with the Moon. When she retained this powerful life force, it congealed to form a baby. For this reason, the dead were often anointed with red ochre, symbolic of the life-giving menstrual blood of Mother Earth, that could guarantee a bodily rebirth. The menstrual blood was also called the "supernatural red wine" given by Hera to the gods to ensure longevity and immortality. Women would mix their menstrual blood with seed grain to fertilize it and protect their crops by walking around the fields when they were bleeding. The blood from a girl's first menstruation was considered a potent healing elixir, and was claimed to be able to heal incurable diseases such as leprosy.[7]

The ancient Goddess-worshipping cultures understood that the menstrual time is a woman's most powerful time of month when her psychic and spiritual energies are most highly sensitized. The priestesses of the great oracular center at Delphi (the Greek word *delphus* means womb) would prophecy once a month during their Moon time. Hysteria, now thought of as an out-of-control state of irrationality and madness that is attributed to menstruating women, comes from another Greek word for womb consciousness—*hustera*. In earlier times hysteria was the condition of shamanic possession and ecstatic trance that women cultivated during their menstrual time in order to receive the vision or prophecy. The blood at the earliest altars was menstrual blood, not the sacrificial blood of animals or humans, and was used in rituals for healing, magic, and prophecy. The sexuality that takes place during the menstrual time was considered sacred, and ceremonially practiced to induce ecstasy, regeneration, and spiritual illumination.

When the Moon disappeared each month, she was rumored to be having her period. The word Sabbat originally meant a day of rest, when the Goddess was menstruating. Following her example, human women would retire to menstrual huts during their bleeding times in order that they might commune with the deities through meditation, prayer, and ritual—seeking healing, truth, and renewal.

How did the blessing of menstruation come to be the "curse," dreaded, despised, and tabooed, a source of shame and embarrassment to women? The menstrual mysteries lay at the core of the Goddess religion, protected and concealed from the prying eyes of the uninitiated. Women did not use the upsurge of powerful sexual energy that resulted from menstruation in the service of men nor for procreation. As the social system of patriarchy solidified its power, men displayed an almost hysterical fear of menstruating women, and of menstrual and childbirth blood. Menstrual women were defined as unclean, dangerous, and a threat to society.

A host of taboos were instituted to protect men from the fiery, assertive, auto-erotic nature of the dark feminine, and to deprive women of the sexual, psychic, and magical power of their dark Moon times. It was said that if a man had sex with a menstruating woman, he would become ill, especially with venereal diseases; and a child conceived in this way would be born deformed or as a demon. All kinds of sickness and disaster were attributed to a chance encounter with a menstruating woman. In the Middle Ages, many church laws forbid a menstruating woman to enter a church lest she defile it with her filth.

As a result, a woman during her now-dangerous times was forced into seclusion, ostracized from society, and limited in her contact with the outside world. She was forbidden to touch any food lest she contaminate it. She was not allowed to wash nor comb her hair, as the power of her magic was thought to reside in her hair. Menstruating women were cast out of the villages into the brush where they had to fend for themselves. Called impure, unclean, and an abomination, they were a threat to man, his laws, and his gods.

This collective conditioning has succeeded in obliterating women's memories of the magic of their Moon times. Woman now feel ashamed, resentful, and disgusted with the pain and humiliation of their menstrual blood, originally known as the source of all life.

Now when a woman menstruates, she is pressured by society to hide and deny this central aspect of her nature. All of these messages encourage a woman's and society's denial of the natural and periodic body functions, and this leads a woman to believe that menstruation is something bad, negative, dirty, and undesirable. She is rejected sexually at this time of month and told she is disgusting. Her self-confidence and self-acceptance are undermined, and she associates her period with restriction, a lack of freedom and fun. Society has transformed women's natural power at menstruation into a self-destructive psychology.

This very denial and rejection of menstruation is central to the excruciating pain and discomfort that many women experience prior to and during their period. The suppressed rage over the rejection and debasement of an intrinsic aspect of a woman's nature, in fact the seat of her personal power, becomes directed inward. This violence is then inflicted upon oneself, and it hurts. Women experience this unconscious self-directed anger as physical pain, cramps, bloating, lethargy, emotional irritability, depression, bad temper, and hypersensitivity.

Esther Harding suggests that one of the reasons for women's menstrual disabilities and PMS today is that modern culture does not provide any kind of menstrual rituals. Menstruation is just each woman's private affliction where she suffers alone; it has no positive value or meaning.[8] Women have been deprived of retreating to the ancient menstrual huts where they could commune with their inner beings, attune themselves to cosmic cycles, and share in the secret knowledge passed on in the community of other bleeding women.

In order to reclaim their menstrual power and liberate their bodies from menstrual pain, women must follow the cycle of the disappearing dark Moon and enter into a voluntary retreat during their sacred time of month. The instinctual pull of the dark Moon phase is to deliberately withdraw from the demands of others and worldly expectations so that a woman can nurture a deeper communion with her own self and the inner world

During the menstrual time, a woman can most easily access the workings of her inner life and the powers of the psyche. The heavy sleep-like qualities of the menstrual time help a woman to reach deep meditative states. Through her dreams, she can gain information about her body and mind. The body's craving to draw inward into quiet and stillness is a movement toward accessing the wealth of inner creative energy that peaks at this time. Women have the opportunity to transform this psychic energy into a flow of creative inspiration. This withdrawal from the outer world is conducive to creating the sacred space whereby a woman can receive the gifts of menstruation: meditation, dreams, prophecy, body wisdom, healing, regeneration, and sacred sexuality. This action takes awareness and effort in a society that is constructed in such a way to deny and invalidate women's special needs during their menstrual dark Moon times.

A WOMAN'S LIFELONG CYCLE

In addition to a monthly cycle of ovulation and menstruation that mirrors the two-fold alternation of the Light and Dark phases of the Moon, a woman has another major sexual cycle that operates over the course of her lifetime. This lifelong cycle is a reflection of the triple nature of the Moon's phases as new, full and dark. The ancients personified these three phases as the Triple Moon Goddess who manifested as the

Virgin, the Mother, and the Crone. The three aspects of Moon Goddess correspond to the three stages of a woman's life that are marked by menarche, the triad of pregnancy, birth and nursing, and menopause. These are the great blood mysteries of a woman's life.

The waxing new Moon was personified by the ancients as the Virgin Goddess, such as Artemis, Athena, and Hebe whose nature was akin to that of a maiden. This new Moon phase mirrored the growth of a young girl and culminated in the first of a woman's blood mysteries, that of menarche—the onset of a girl's first menstruation.

Menarche symbolizes the innocence, hope, and optimism of a young girl who is now beginning to come into her menstrual power. In ancient cultures and those today which remember fragments of the old ways, the occasion of a girl's first blood was celebrated by a ceremonial ritual and she was then feted and gifted by the community. As an initiation ritual, the young girl often retreated into voluntary seclusion, where she awaited a vision. Menarche, as a rite of passage, marked her transition from childhood and her initiation into the secrets of womanhood.

Menarche indicates that the cycle of ovulation and menstruation has begun to operate in a young woman's body, which now has the capacity to conceive a child. It also signals that she has "come of age" to be sexually active. The flow of her blood also signifies that the currents of her psychic energy are now activated and can be developed. Today this great event in a woman's life is generally ignored. It may be whispered about in the bathroom as an embarrassed mother tells her bewildered and often-frightened daughter the hidden location of the menstrual pads.

With the growing of the Moon toward the fullness, the slim young maiden likewise matures into the full-breasted, full-bodied sexually mature woman. The full Moon phase, as the Mother Goddess, depicted by goddesses such Demeter, Isis, and Hera, was most influential during the middle years of a woman's life when her body is geared toward giving birth and feeding her children. The full Moon corresponds to the next developmental phase of a woman's life in which the functions of her body and emotions are geared toward the second of the female blood mysteries, the cycle of pregnancy, birth and nursing. In this mystery, woman was perceived as nothing less than miraculous as she chose to create new life, transforming her life blood into a child, and then into the milk to nourish it.

A woman may enter into the full Moon mother phase of her life cycle without having to give birth to a physical child. She may instead leave behind the carefree, self-determined innocence of the maiden as she assumes the responsibility for a career, committed relationship, co-parenting her partner's child, or purchasing a home. She dedicates the next phase of her life to nourishing and sustaining the mental and creative children that she brings forth.

While the patriarchy idealized the image of the pregnant mother, the reality of her bodily functions brought up their irrational terror. In modern times, the entire spectrum of pregnancy, birthing, and nursing has been maligned, shamed, and hidden away. Women have been denied full access to information and even given harmful and erroneous advice concerning their reproductive organs. The discouragement and embarrassment associated with breast-feeding; the denial of womanly midwife support during a mandated hospital labor that promotes the use of drugs, stirrups, bindings, surgical episiotomies; the proliferation of often unnecessary cesarean sections, hysterectomies, mastectomies; and the restriction of abortion—a woman's right to reproductive control depict some of the ways in which patriarchal cultures denied women a natural relationship with their own reproductive organs—the core of their feminine empowerment.

And the waning dark Moon, envisioned as the Crone Goddess, such as Hekate and Kali, was seen to be the predominant force during the final years after menstruation ceases and a woman enters into menopause, the third great blood mystery of her life. The ancients believed that after menopause a woman retained her wise blood and reached her pinnacle as a power holder of wisdom. In earlier cultures, this rite of passage initiated women into their role as community elder sought out for advice, as seer called upon for prophecy, and as healer asked to tend the ill. The Crone assisted the new to be born and the old to die.

For most women this "change of life" begins around the age of fifty, and due to increasing longevity, women can expect to live another twenty-five years—almost one third of their lives. Biologically a woman enters into the crone phase of her life when she is past her childbearing years. For some women, however, the movement into cronehood is not necessarily determined by the onset of menopause. This stage can also occur as a psychological frame of mind, when a woman begins to reap the harvest of wisdom that arises from all of her varied life experiences. Whenever a woman is finally able to think of her own needs after years of being primarily focused on those of her children, family, relationship, or career, she moves into the third great mystery of her life cycle.

Until recently our information concerning menopause has been even more limited, inaccessible, and tabooed than that of menstruation The patriarchy feared the power of the feminine in connection with her role in dying, as solar cosmologies separated her from her powers of rebirth The wise crone became transformed into the ugly hag, the death-snatcher, the modern bag-lady. It is this horrifying image that has conditioned our attitudes in patriarchal culture toward the older woman in her menopausal years, viewing her as a repulsive and undesirable creature. As her body shows the signs of aging, the menopausal woman is mocked, cast off, ignored, shut away, fired, divorced, and abandoned. It is no wonder that a woman confronts this stage of her life with trepidation and fear.

In this way humanity was deprived of the crone's natural wisdom, a belief system that constituted a threat to the patriarchal religions. This negative self-image associated with menopause also served to cut off women themselves from a source of their creativity that was not geared toward mothering. As women confront the changes in their bodies that are not validated by society, it is important to remember that there is no growth without change. The body's natural aging process stimulates the biochemical maturation of the older woman's psychic currents. As we begin to rehonor the dark crone goddess of menopause, her teachings will help to liberate us from our fears of change and transition, aging, and death.

THE PROGRESSED MOON AND A WOMAN'S LIFELONG REPRODUCTIVE CYCLE

In the same way that the rhythm of the monthly cycle of the Moon is reflected in the monthly flow of a woman's menstrual blood, the lifelong cycles of the progressed Moon reflect the timing of the lifelong changes in a woman's reproductive system.

The progressed Moon which moves approximately one degree per month, spends about two and one-half years in each sign, and takes twenty-seven years to return to the zodiacal degree of the natal position. The Moon's return, by progression, to its natal position is called a progressed lunar return. If a person lives to be eighty-one years old, he or she will have three progressed lunar returns. The first return will occur at approximately twenty-seven years of age, the second at fifty-four years, and the third at eighty-one years.

We see the threefold rhythm of the seasons of a woman's life as maiden, mother, and crone also mirrored in the three progressed Moon cycles of a woman's life span. The progressed lunar cycle is especially relevant in speaking to emotional urges women experience as a direct result of the changes in the physiology of their reproductive organs. The halfway point of each cycle when the progressed Moon is opposite the position of the natal Moon is also a key point in the timing of the biological functions of her fertility cycle and corresponding emotional responses.

The first progressed Moon cycle spans from birth to twenty-seven years of age, and corresponds to the maiden stage of a woman's life span. The halfway point occurs at thirteen years, which is the average age of menarche, a girl's first menstruation. At this time a young girl begins to confront the womanly changes in her body such as the swelling of her breasts, the growth of pubic and underarm hair, and witnesses the periodic flow of her blood. On the emotional level she begins to resonate to the emotional swings and moods timed by her monthly menstrual cycle and feels the first stirrings of her sexual awakening. The first progressed lunar opposition brings a young girl into a biological awareness of what it means to be a woman.

While menarche on a physiological level indicates a woman's readiness to be a mother, psychologically many women continue to remain maidens until their late twenties. Up to this time there still exists for them a sense of open-ended possibilities for the future, and relative freedom from long term responsibilities and commitments. Some women become mothers during this time, and others focus on continuing their education, initiating careers, or exploring alternative lifestyles. Whatever choices one has made up to this point can often be easily reconsidered and changed.

At the age of twenty-seven, predating the Saturn return by a year or two, the progressed Moon returns to the birth position, and begins her second cycle. This second turning corresponds to the mother stage of a woman's life span. While the Saturn return forces the necessity to make decisions defining one's role in society, the progressed lunar return marks the ticking of a woman's biological clock. If a woman has not yet had children, she often feels the pangs of "baby hunger" at this time. The physiology of her reproductive system is urging her to make the decisions concerning whether or not she will give birth to children.

A woman must look at how her current lifestyle and values support the possibility of including children into her world. This pressure can provoke an emotional panic to find an appropriate mate with whom to have children, to precipitate a discussion with an unwilling or uncertain partner regarding the conception of a child, to consider the option of single motherhood or artificial insemination. She may come to terms with a decision not to have children, and instead devote her nurturing energy into building a career, a relationship, some kind of social action, or creative self-expression.

The halfway point of the second progressed lunar cycle occurs at the age of forty-one. For most women the progressed lunar opposition in the early forties closes the door to conception and the possibility of giving birth. The vitality of the reproductive system is winding down, and there exist greater risks in childbearing after this age, such as an increased rate of miscarriages, birth defects, and Down's Syndrome. On an emotional level a woman may regret her choice not to have children as she deals with the grief that she will not have known motherhood in her lifetime.

From the progressed lunar opposition at forty-one until the next progress lunar return that occurs at fifty-four years, a woman often culminates her role as mother and comes into her fullest power and influence in her career, community, and creative self-expression. She is also encountering the first changes in her body that will move her from a mother to a crone. While a woman is menstruating, estrogen continues to rise and fall in the bloodstream, peaking at ovulation and ebbing at menstruation. After the age of forty, the estrogen level begins to even out and stabilize at a decreased level. Ovulation becomes less frequent and periods tend to occur at irregular intervals. At about fifty years of age, the ovaries halt almost all estrogen production, and ovulation and menstruation cease.

The third progressed Moon cycle begins around fifty-four years of age and initiates a woman into the crone season of her life span. The gateway to cronehood is menopause. In the same way that the flower then folds in upon itself to form the fruit, a woman's life begins to fold back in upon herself. Her body begins to adjust to the decreased estrogen level and other hormonal changes in her system as she enters the final third phase of her life. It is difficult to distinguish between signs of menopause and signs of aging; menopause itself is a sign of the aging of the female reproductive system.[9]

A woman experiences many biological symptoms with the onset of menopause. Hot flashes, night sweats, the thinning of the vaginal walls, facial hairs, wrinkles, liver spots, moles, thinning and graying hair on the head and pubic area, deeper voice, loss of muscle tone, weight gain, bone shrinkage (osteoporosis). As women confront these changes in their bodies that cause them to be mocked, pitied, ridiculed, and rejected by society, their emotional reactions can often plunge them into a despair of insecurity, shame, powerlessness, and victimization.

During the final progressed Moon cycle, the lunar goddess as crone blesses a woman's life with grandchildren, whom she can love without being responsible for all the work. Anthropologist Margaret Mead is reported to have said that the greatest creative force in the world is a menopausal woman with zest.[10] The Moon as crone enables a woman to harvest and assimilate her crop of wisdom, symbolically found in her retained menstrual blood.

In conclusion, the cycles of the Moon are intimately related to the cycles of a woman's sexuality and to her reproductive organs. This flow of energy is depicted in the phases of the cycle of the Moon, embodied as the Great Goddess, which also pulses through the bodies of women. The Moon as Divine Feminine was worshipped by the ancients in her new, full, and dark phases as the Triple Goddess who ruled over the mysteries of birth, life, and death.

The symbolism of the dark phase of the Moon, domain of the Dark Crone Goddess as the muse of menstruation and menopause, holds the greatest secrets of all: that of regeneration. The serpent which sheds its skin and renews itself, like the waxing and waning of the Moon, was seen to embody the truth of death and rebirth-the transformative power of the feminine energy. The power of the feminine signified by the Moon is not patriarchal defined power, which is the "power over." Rather it is the power to transform, to change one thing into another.

This power to change and transform is carried in the flow of women's blood through her reproductive organs. It is the flow of her blood that nourishes and builds the child while in the womb, and which is then transformed into the milk that flows from her breasts to sustain this new life. It is the flow of her blood that also contains the psychic, healing, ritual, aspirational, and regenerative gifts. When a woman's wise blood ceases to flow, her wisdom is made known to us all of the time, not only several days a month. It is during a woman's menstrual time each month and after menopause that she can most fully contact what Vicki Noble calls the "kundalini (serpent)-shakti energy"[11] which can be used for deep insight, healing, sacred sexuality, and spiritual illumination

This is the teaching of the Queen of Night to women. The way to claim our power and to maintain a state of well-being, enhancing our capacity to be in the flow and in a state of grace is to honor our blood. We should honor our daughter's first blood by celebrating. We should honor our monthly flow by ritualizing the experience, pulling inward to mediate, to dream, to commune with our source, and to regenerate within ourselves. We must honor the blood when it swells in our bodies with new life, and honor our blood when it pours out of our breasts as manna, and honor it when it ceases to flow. Our call is to honor woman's blood as the source of our wisdom and to activate its power in order to bring healing and renewal to ourselves, to our relationships, and to the world.

NOTES

1. Alexander Marshak, *The Roots of Civilization: The Cognitive Beginnings of Man's First Art, Symbols and Notation* (New York: McGraw-Hill, 1972).

2. Mircea. Eliade, *Images and Symbols* (New York: Sheed and Ward, 1961), 71–73.

3. Franz Cumont, *Astrology and Religion Among the Greeks and Romans* (New York: Dover Publications, 1960), 70.

4. There exists a slight discrepancy between the dates on the cross-quarter days of Candlemas, February 2, Beltane, May 1, Lammas, August 1, and Hallomas, October 31 and their astrological counterparts. The cross-quarter days are halfway between the solstices and equinoxes, placing them at 15 degrees of the fixed signs of Aquarius, Taurus, Leo, and Scorpio. These dates fall closer to the 6th or 7th of the month. It has been suggested that the confusion arises because of the switch over from the 13-month lunar calendar to the 365-day solar calendar.

5. My books *Astrology For Yourself* (with Douglas Bloch, Wingbow, 1987) and *Finding Our Way Through the Dark* (ACS, 1995) contain the templates with which to construct a Moon phase and aspect wheel that simplifies the procedure to a turn of a dial.

6. Instructions for determining your own natal and lifetime lunation phase cycles are contained in *Finding Our Way Through the Dark*.

7. Barbara Walker, *The Woman's Encyclopedia of Myths and Secrets* (San Francisco: Harper & Row), 1983).

8. Esther Harding, *Women's Mysteries* (New York: Harper & Row Colophon, 1976).

9. Boston Women's Health Collective, *The New Our Body Our Selves* (New York: Simon & Schuster, 1984), 446.

10. Genia Pauli Haddon, *Body Metaphors: Releasing God-Feminine in Us All* (New York: Crossroad, 1988), 157.

11. Vicki Noble, *Shakti Woman* (San Francisco: Harper San Francisco, 1991).

M. Kelley Hunter

M. Kelley Hunter has been studying astrology since 1967. She holds a degree in drama from Middlebury College, and a master's degree in depth psychology and creative communication from Norwich University. She blends mythology, psychology, and experiential education into her astrological work with individuals and groups. Director of Helia Productions, she founded the *ROOTS* of Astrology experiential conferences and creates mythic dramas with Dragon Dance Theater. She has performed at Bread and Puppet Circus, and at the United Nations. She has been a mother since 1976, and now lives in Vermont and the Caribbean.

M. Kelley Hunter

The Mother–Daughter Bond: A Brief Exploration through Myth and Astrology

She looked into the obsidian mirror held before her. The shiny black surface flickered in the torch light. A dark shadowed face was reflected back to her, haloed by rings in the grain of the gemstone. She smiled and nodded in recognition of her deep secret self, honed from many years of inner reaching, searching, living, feeling. The dark face smiled in return and so did the old woman holding the mirror. "The truth of your inner being is revealed in its full strength and beauty," said the elder.

As women, we have a particular need now to redefine our lives and retell the old stories to match our renewed visions. Sharing our experiences, we reweave the fabric of our lives, drawing together the multi-colored threads that bind us, hold us, and carry us forward. Supporting each other in our mutual growth, we reflect back to one another the beauty of our essential beings.

Myths, in their telling and retelling, reflect the evolution of the human psyche. In the mythic realm we meet the archetypal, underlying currents that flow through time and space and connect all humanity in the web of life. Myth is a feminine expression of history that is concerned with subjective meaning rather than facts and dates. Today, at a time when the divine feminine is re-emerging all around us, the stories of our ancestor goddesses hold particular wisdom that can help us remember our unique creative and recreative power as women.

Astrology is a form of myth, a language of symbols and images through which we can speak of the life of the soul. Through such a language we connect our personal stories to the eternal stories, for the grammar of astrology and the characters of myth convey the core experiences of human life, bringing us in touch with the deeper layers beneath the everyday surface reality that then illumine the mundane with spiritual significance. This is the gift of the feminine spirit.

I'd like to weave together threads of ancient myth, personal story, and the language of the stars to explore one of the most sacred bonds—that of mother and daughter. The art of Motherhood is shamefully undervalued in much of our world today. Mothers are not honored as they once were in ages past when the Great Mother was the universal and supreme deity, giver and sustainer of life. Let us raise this holy service back to its central place, to heal ourselves, each other, and the Earth, our Mother Planet. Thus we reclaim our true inheritance and build a legacy for a healthy future.

> . . . mothering is powerful. We wanted to suggest that mothers recognize the role that they have been asked to play as conduits and, thus, perpetuators of the dominant culture. We wanted to help them see in a new way that mothers can transmit a different culture—heritage more than history. [1]

As the primary relationship of woman to woman, the bond between mother and daughter is a special one. The mother is the giver of life; she shapes not only the body but the early imprints in the psyche of the child. As we know from experience and from the growing body of psychological literature on the subject, it is universally true that the mother is the most important influence in the development of the child and her sense of selfhood. When this is a girl child, the essence of womanhood is passed on in a way that spans generations from the past and into the future. We learn from our mothers about being a woman, through our relationship to her and from her feelings about herself and her way of expressing her female nature.

In astrology, the Moon symbolizes the matrix of the mother-child bond. Moon=Mother and the Child. The Moon carries some of our most deeply personal issues, as it is the closest astronomical body to the Earth. In fact, the Earth-Moon relationship is a symbiotic relationship, like the Mother and Child. There is systemic interdependence, a mutual effect between Earth and Moon. While the Sun, as the center of the solar system, is also the Divine Child and represents the central quality of one's self-awareness, individuality, and life purpose, the Moon reflects this growing light of self-consciousness into the daily rhythms of life. The Sun sign takes growth and development to be consciously expressed; the Moon is active even before birth.

The Moon describes the basic personal grounding that is so intimately bound to our experience of mother. While growing in the womb, the child is receiving impressions and nourishment from the mother, living life inside her, participating in her rhythms. The daughter is a part of the mother; at first there is no differentiation. The quality of these lunar impressions is further deepened after birth as the child continues to experience the mother's feelings and through the way the mother relates to her infant in the early stages of development in those first crucial days, months, and years. The Moon sign and planets in aspect to the Moon will give us information about our relationship with the mother, early family patterns that shaped us, the way we automatically react to circumstances and the rhythm of our growth cycles. The Moon, and the Sun-Moon relationship, describe the quality of the mother-child bond and the path to growth and self-care. How fully did our mother respond to our needs? How did her feelings, thoughts, memories, and even the food she ate affect us while she was carrying us in her womb? The Moon tells us much about our security needs, our deeply imprinted ways of seeking nurturing and support.

There are many stages to motherhood and the growth of the child. One of the most important and difficult stages is the separation process, a long-term process that is necessarily different with a boy child or a girl child. The boy must separate from the mother to become a man, an individual of a different sex. The girl must separate from the mother to become herself while remaining a woman like her mother. There is a return to the mother that is inherent in the feminine experience. Perhaps it is not so much as matter of separation as of changing the relationship.

Thus it is important for mothers to know the stages of child development so they can respond appropriately to the child's changing needs. How many mothers have this knowledge? How is it taught? From mother to daughter, generation to generation, the ways of motherhood are passed on. Family patterns are repeated unless a conscious choice for self-development is made. In community-based cultures, a mother once had a great deal of support in raising her children. The older, experienced women would often be involved in child-rearing and the "training" of the younger women. In modern society, the isolated family unit does not provide the same extended family support. Mothers today are often on their own, uninstructed in child care and under a great deal of stress from other responsibilities. Women's support circles, a natural part of many cultural systems, had largely disappeared and are now being recreated. There is a growing body of literature on parenting and the mother-daughter relationship (see the reference list at the end of this chapter).

Personal therapy work can help uncover and heal unmet needs from our own childhoods that now interfere with effective mothering. Psychotherapy today is an avenue of self-development that may be our modern version of such teachings as the Eleusinian mystery school. Self-realization precedes God-realization, as wisdom teachers throughout the ages have always known. Psychological work is an adjunct to spiritual work; the two are intertwined and often confused.

The Moon is subjective and personal, and yet it also carries a larger dimension. The Moon is the Great Mother, the Earth-Moon Mother of us all. We have two mothers in our lives—our personal mother and the Great Mother, the goddess of creation, birth and death. While we are in the mother's womb and in her arms as an infant, she is the universe, our first experience of the Great Goddess. As we gain a sense of being a separate self, the process with the mother contains the first experiences of the pain of separation that are activated again and again at major transition times when we are again leaving a level of safety and security and growing into further stages of self-awareness. Having an image of the divine feminine gives us a universal mother image that is not constrained by the limitations of the personal mother and can guide us toward fulfillment as women.

Our relationship with both our personal mother and the Great Mother contains inevitable paradoxes as we seek security and also individuality and growth. This paradox is felt in our personal as well as in our collective human experience of the mother.

> For I am the first and the last.
> I am the honored one and the scorned one.
> I am the whore, and the holy one.
> I am the wife and the virgin.
> I am the mother and the daughter . . . [2]

The ancient feminine divinity was almost universally represented as a triple goddess, her three faces reflecting the cycles of nature and the phases of the Moon in her aspects as Maiden, Mother, and Crone. Each stage of life emphasizes particular attributes of the all-powerful Goddess. As Maiden of the waxing Moon, she represents youth, creativity, the freshness of spring and new growth. The Mother, in the fullness of the Moon, bestows abundance through nurturing and sustaining life and the glory of her sensuality and sexuality. The Crone of the waning phase brings endings, wielding her crescent Moon sickle both to harvest the wisdom and fruits of a life at its close and to cut the life cord and free the soul to pass through the veil of death. The waning Moon thins, dies, and passes into the darkness of the new Moon. Then the maiden returns.

The three aspects of the Goddess are one, flowing into each other, and yet distinct. The phase of the Moon under which you were born will indicate your affinity with one of these three aspects. Yet it is also true that women carry the whole cycle within themselves. In the life cycle, the transition from one phase to another may be marked with specific events and experiences that are personal and impersonal at the same time. At one time these transitions were honored as rites of passage in a formal manner that was an acknowledgment and initiation into a new dimension of one's feminine capacity. Today women are beginning again to mark and honor these passages privately through personal rituals and in community circles.

> I begin my song of the holy goddess, fair-haired Demeter,
> and of her slim-ankled daughter. . . . [3]

> In the first days when everything needed was brought
> into being,
> In the first days when everything needed was properly
> nourished. . . . [4]

My solar return chart for my twenty-sixth birthday had Pluto opposite Jupiter on the ascendant-descendant axis. The month my daughter was born my lunar return chart had the same dynamic. An important new relationship entered my life that would deeply change me.

The myth of Demeter and Persephone, often used to explain the seasons, is one of the best-known myths from classical antiquity. These Grecian goddesses presided over the Eleusinian mysteries, one of the major religious and initiatory traditions in that part of the world for over two thousand years. No doubt these mysteries were passed on from even older wisdom traditions. The teachings and rites of these mysteries demonstrated the particularly feminine dimension of life and the natural cycles of life, death, and rebirth. In our lives we go through this cycle over and over again, as we grow, mature, and develop self-awareness and spiritual consciousness.

One of the oldest myths yet translated, from 2500 B.C.E., the story of Inanna, Sumerian goddess of Heaven and Earth, is based on the astronomical cycle of Venus and tells how the goddess grows from her girlhood, through queenship and marriage, to descend to the underworld of her own free will to seek and confront her dark sister, her other self.

It is important to remember that in myth the characters portray the impersonal rather than the personal dimension. If we become too identified with mythic characters, or, in astrology, with any particular planet, we are limiting our capacity to embody our true wholeness. Any mythic figure has a kind of flatness if taken out of the context of the whole story, as any planet taken out of context of the whole chart will not give a complete interpretation. The myths themselves are brought alive through our personal life experience.

Keeping that in mind, we can then wholeheartedly enter the stories and learn a great deal from the goddesses as aspects of ourselves. At times we can easily see these archetypal figures move into and through our lives. Some goddesses remain only briefly to "initiate" us into a new aspect of our potential, while others may play a stronger part in our life story and visit to "teach" us again and again. Such is the potential of the greatest myths, like the stories of Demeter and Persephone and of Inanna. These myths have endured as testaments to women's rites of passage, and therefore call strongly to women in their spiritual awakening. Each goddess passes into a new life stage. Inanna shows us the transition from one stage to another in her own journey. In the Greek myth, mother and daughter do this at the same time, yet each in their own way, as a natural part of the mother-daughter dynamic. The transition process is not an easy one, as it stretches each woman beyond her previous experience and requires a letting go of each other that brings a sense of loss and then a reunion as their relationship changes.

Demeter and the maiden represent the mother-daughter bond and embody the aspects of every woman as both maiden and mother. The maiden represents untouched youth and innocence, the potentially full woman that we see in Demeter, the fertile mother, nurturer, and sustainer, who has realized her goddesshood. The girl as yet has not; her destiny is still to unfold. In order to fulfill this destiny, however, the maiden must be separated from her mother or she will never find her own identity. A nameless maiden, she does not know herself and is predisposed to follow unconsciously in the path of her mothers.

> A young girl in a meadow of wild flowers. The sun shines eternal spring, high and warm, the blue sky blown across by clouds of birds and of white cumulus shaped by imagination into stories of her future. Her heart sings aloud, urging her to wander from her mother and her companions. She is called by some mysterious inner voice and follows a spring to where it bubbles up from the ground. There at the source a lovely scent fills the air. Here is an exotic blossom she has never seen before. Should she pick it or leave it untouched? She must show

it to her mother; her mother knows the names of all the plants. As she breaks the stem, a red sap stains her finger and drops fall into the spring. It is from the flower . . . no, it is spilling from her own body. She is bleeding from below, something in her is dying.

The earth erupts beneath her feet. A chasm stretches out before her. From the depths emerges an alien being, like herself yet vastly different. She is afraid, yet attracted. He pulls her to him and carries her away on his chariot of fire-breathing horses. "Mother," she cries, "Save me!" Only the Sun hears her plea and, almost invisible under the pale waning moon, an old woman collecting herbs looks up, squints for a moment and nods her head.

Standing dark and silent in her cloak, Hecate watches the girl descend. "Mother of necessity, be with her in her trials," her heart intones, and then she departs. She would serve the girl in the underworld, help her bathe and dress. When it was time, she would come to the mother and help her in her grief to see the truth, to make her own passage.

We meet Persephone first as simply Kore, the Maiden, a lovely, innocent young woman living in perpetual summertime with her mother, Demeter, Earth Goddess, Mother Nature. There are various stories about who fathered the girl— Zeus or Poseidon, both brothers of Demeter, are the usual candidates. Important as the father may be, let us pass over that for now and imagine the mother-daughter pair tending the Earth, performing the daily rituals of life and of worship as women have done throughout time. In art, from ancient to modern times, we can see women raising their arms together to invoke the life force.

The maiden or virgin goddess is a major theme in Greek mythology and before. The word "virgin" is used here in its original meaning of a woman who belongs to herself alone, not identified through her relationship to a man. The word does not

have the same connotations of sexual chastity commonly associated with the word today—many virgin goddesses were very
sexual—but rather indicates female autonomy apart from men.
The constellation of Virgo shines in the night sky, reminding
us of the purity of this goddess; the symbolism of Virgo as a zodiac sign is only beginning to be understood in its true quality
in this age as we remember the truly feminine nature of wisdom and the wisdom of nature.

Experiencing the Myths

In the Greek myth Persephone's destiny comes in the shape of
the god of death—Pluto. He has seen her dance in the flow-
ering meadows and desires her. He is given permission from
Zeus, king of the gods, to take her, since Demeter is not likely
to agree to the match. In some versions, her grandmother Gaia
also colludes in this abduction. In her Crone wisdom she knows
it is time the daughter must follow her own destiny and leave
the mother. Kore is gathering flowers when she is attracted by
an unusually beautiful narcissus bloom that Gaia has caused to
grow there. It has hundreds of blossoms, its exquisite scent
intoxicating.

There appears in the life of each young girl something compelling that leads her toward her destiny. As she plucks the
flower, Pluto erupts from the underworld and takes her away.
This may come as an irresistible attraction or as a traumatic oc-
currence. However it takes place, it is part of her entrance into
womanhood. Puberty is a time of new awakenings in both body
and emotions. The hormonal changes that happen during these
years are challenging and may not be welcome. For women,
the world of childhood is abruptly over when the blood flow starts
and one is initiated in an immediate, physical way into mysteries
of death and rebirth.

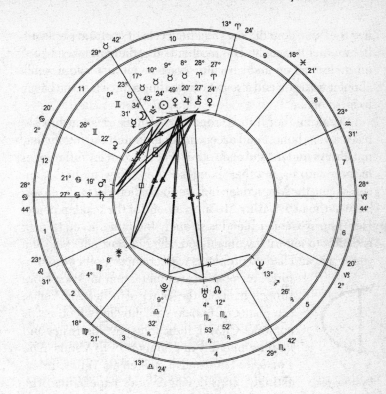

Chart 1. Nora

THE MAIDEN: COMING OF AGE

One young girl, Nora (chart 1), experienced a mythic entrance
into menses at the young age of ten years. Her class was studying mythology. That day she was dressed as the goddess Artemis,
wearing a white sheet draped as a tunic and carrying the bow
and arrow of the Huntress. Artemis, a Moon goddess often
pictured with the crescent moon in her hair, is the protectress
of young girls. Nora was very upset when she discovered dark
blood in her underwear and could not believe it was menstrual,
but was rather distressed that she had messed in her pants.
Her mother had to wash out the underwear to show her that

it was blood. Nora did not want her cycle to start and slept with her mother that night. Her mother had earlier given her a book on menstruation and sexuality, because Nora would not talk about it with her, and also put off wearing a bra when she began to need one.

Nora's mother, Linda, reports that their relationship has been a very honest and accepting one, even though they may not always understand each other. There are many differences in their natures, but their bond is strong. They are both Cancer, giving the Moon rulership over both their charts. Nora was born at the new waxing Moon, symbolic of the maiden phase. Her Taurus-Cancer blend is strongly feminine. Even though resistant to entering womanhood, she did start her cycle at a young age and had no problems with cramps or other discomfort. Her planetary combination in Aries more strongly indicates the source of the tension. Venus, the planet of female sexuality and emotions, is conjunct Chiron, indicating past life issues and healing needed in connection to Venus. The square to Saturn also challenges Venus. Interestingly, considering Nora's experience, the asteroid Diana (the Roman name for Artemis) is conjunct her Venus-Chiron as well. There is a many-layered message here about her female identity. The day she began to bleed the Moon was in Aries, activating the complexity of her Venus nature.

Symbol for the asteroid Diana.

At puberty, the Venus dimension of one's feminine nature is more fully awakened—along with our hormones—and the condition of Venus in the chart becomes highlighted. Like the Moon, Venus is a strong indicator of the female nature, but she is a very different goddess than the Moon. Other than the Great Mother of subjective, nurturing, security patterns and daily rhythms, Venus is the Goddess of Love, Beauty, and Pleasure, indicating the feminine emotional, sexual, and relational qualities of women (and men). Venus has a magnetic, attracting energy that brings us into relationship with another level of our feminine nature, as well as into relationship with others.

> *A woman who walked in fear of the word of [God]*
> *Plucked the tree from the river and spoke:*
> *"I shall plant this tree in my holy garden."*
> *. . . The tree grew thick*
> *But its bark did not split.*
> *Then a serpent who could not be charmed*
> *Made its nest in the roots of the Huluppu-tree.*
> *The Anzu-bird set his young in the branches of the tree.*
> *And the dark maid Lilith built her home in the trunk.*
> *The young woman who loved to laugh wept.*
> *How Inanna wept!*
> *(Yet they would not leave her tree.)*[5]

We first meet Inanna as she pulls a young tree from a rushing river and plants it in her garden, the original Garden of Eden. This tree was uprooted during a wild storm brewed upon the underworld clash and union of her ancestors. The tree represents her roots, her karmic family inheritance and her destiny. She tends this tree, intending that when it is full grown, it will be made into her throne and her bed, symbols of her maturity in rulership and sexuality. Before this happens, unwelcome creatures come to dwell in the tree—a serpent in the roots, a wild bird in the branches, and the dark maid Lilith in the trunk of the tree. One interpretation of these creatures is that they are darkly dangerous shadow figures that must be purged from the tree before Inanna can grow, and she calls upon her brother Gilgamesh to rid her of these creatures. Another interpretation, one that I prefer for its richness, is that these creatures come to remind Inanna of her true feminine powers—the wisdom of the serpent, the full-bodied, earthbased sexuality of Lilith, and the higher-minded wisdom of the bird. An image of the triple goddess, this feathered serpent female figure is Inanna's inheritance. Yet, as a young, adolescent goddess in the emerging patriarchy, she is not prepared or ready to claim her full powers at this time.

Inanna grows to claim her power from her father in a delightful beer-drinking challenge and then must defend her right to queenship. She is courted, and encouraged by her mother to accept the shepherd as her lover. They have a passionate, gloriously sensual honeymoon, and then he takes off to sit on the throne and attend to business. Inanna is left wondering if this is all there is to it. She "opens her ears to the great below," and prepares to descend through the seven gates leading to the underworld, the domain of her sister (or perhaps her grandmother) Ereshkigal.

A feminine face of Pluto, Ereshkigal confronts Inanna with her dark side— repressed, denied issues that she was not ready to deal with earlier in the tree. Ereshkigal is the Death Crone power that kills with a look. Stripped of her outer world regalia, Inanna is brought, humbled and naked, before the Queen of the Underworld. Seeing straight through to Inanna's inner self, Ereshkigal pierces her with insight. Inanna is paralyzed, killed, hung from a meat hook to rot. Like a black hole that sucks all the light into itself, Ereshkigal groans in her own labor process. Both goddesses are in a death and rebirth process together. Inanna is confronted with unconscious aspects of herself she was unable to accept earlier, as well as inherited memories, wounds, and powers from her female heritage, from her mother and her mother's mothers. She is suspended in a deep inner process, in a kind of depression, during this confrontation, and every forty months or so, the planet Venus descends below the horizon, down into the underworld, to renew herself. This cyclical journey of renewal and regeneration is a surrender into everdeepening layers of one's inner essence, the soul.

Here, too, we witness the underworld journey and a confrontation with Pluto, as with Persephone. Pluto as a planetary archetype carries the transformational power of destiny moving inexorably through our lives, of unconscious, cellular, and karmic compulsions, and our link with the larger evolutionary context of human development. From its distant position, Pluto completes an orbit of the Sun in 248 years. Its cycle spans several lifetimes. Its orbit brings it closer to the Sun than Neptune (1979–1999) and then back out four billion miles away from us. It moves through the zodiac signs at differing rates, in Taurus for thirty years, but in Scorpio for only twelve, defining different issues to be transformed by each successive generation. It takes us each deep into the dark labyrinth. Pluto qualifies the sign that contains the death and rebirth issues brought to bear on each major life passage. We excavate layer after layer of these issues to uncover treasures that are to be revealed for the revitalization of each person and for the collective human family as well. Pluto is the nocturnal underground sea we all sail to seek the salvation of the soul.

The myth of Inanna and Ereshkigal shows us the feminine, redemptive power of the underworld, the unconscious, an important process for the renewal of female spirituality in our time. Pluto in its feminine face is an aspect of the Crone wisdom seen in Hecate, who guides Persephone in her underworld journey. Hindu mythology shows us a dark-faced Kali, the consort of Shiva, god of destruction. In Hindu mythology every archetype has a feminine and masculine aspect. Kali can be seen dancing on the prone body of her lord. She wears a necklace of skulls and an apron of severed hands. A serpent twines round her neck and her tongue is bloody. She is not a pleasant goddess, yet she is revered in her sacred motherhood, as she cuts away all that is not life-giving and filled with vitality. She is there at the gateway of death and all major life transitions. There is no return to the place we were before the journey, but we can find new life and vitality on the other side.

> On this bright and starry night,
> All nature is still.
> Inanna stands between the worlds,
> All nature is still.
> A bright star appears in the branches of the trees,
> A trellis for her ascent from the world below,
> The land of no return,
> The land of no return.[6]
> Holy Ereshkigal! Great is your renown!
> Holy Ereshkigal! I sing your praises![7]

Along with the inevitable awakening of the Venus energy during the early teenage years, twelve to seventeen, two important astrological cycles occur which further the process of self-maturation and give witness to the presence of the Crone: the progressed Moon opposes its birth position and transiting Saturn opposes its birth position.

Progressions follow the day-by-day movement of the planets after the day of birth, each day corresponding to the next year in one's life. This day-as-a-year formula works like an inner clock, each planet a hand on the clock, ticking at its own pace. The progressed Moon is the fastest ticking hand on the internal clock, timing the incorporation into one's awareness of deeply personal feelings, attitudes, reactions, and responses. The Moon reflects the light of the Sun; its subconscious rhythm weaves new responses to life based on our increasing solar individuation. The progressed Moon takes around twenty-seven years to circle the chart and can be used as a precise timer of experiences that profoundly affect our human development as it touches planets and patterns in our birthcharts and activates their potential in specific ways.

Because the Moon moves at a varying rate, the progressed Moon comes into opposition with its natal position anywhere from around age twelve and a half up to age fourteen and a half. It symbolizes, in effect, a full Moon of self-awareness in relation to the Moon-mother principle. The opposition can indeed feel just like that—one needs to oppose the mother in order to realize that one is a separate self, with needs that may or may not be met by the personal mother. In this phase of heightened awareness of one's emotional needs, the focus may be on the needs not being met, that the daughter is needing to find ways to take care of herself. The unconscious process may give rise to frustration, anxiety, and anger at the mother, who is not the all-providing one. This is a natural process, though often difficult, since the daughter is necessarily starting to define her emotional self as different than her mother.

> Although we may not like it or acknowledge it, when we are in the process of moving away from someone or something that once nourished and sustained us, we often become critical or angry in order to garner enough energy to make the necessary separation.[8]

My daughter had this opposition just before she turned fourteen. I remember that year as being just about the worst time in our relationship. I felt that she was constantly turning me into the wicked witch, a role I did not like or usually identify with. When she had goaded me into a rage, she would say, "I love it when I get you," and then sometimes she would feel so rejected by my anger, she would flee to a corner and curl up into a little, sobbing child, not letting me touch her.

There are many stages to this separation/self-awareness phase and many variations. The relationship with the father, with older siblings, with new siblings, the extended family, as well as school experiences impact this process.

The progressed Moon opposition opens a new awareness that gives Venus more room to enter. The relationship between Venus and the Moon gives us an indication about the dynamics of one's feminine nature, the ease or conflict with which a young woman experiences her emergence into womanhood as well as how well her mother responds to her daughter's process, and in her own way of defining her own femininity, challenges or supports this process. A challenging aspect between Moon and Venus (opposition, square, quincunx, even conjunction) may indicate that a woman may seek to fulfill herself as a woman in a different way than her mother, that her mother's femininity is not the role model she wants to emulate. With such aspects the emotional tension at puberty may be heightened and indicate tension in growing away from the mother. The mother-child bond of the Moon is in conflict with the emerging emotional-creative, self-love qualities of Venus. Venus is the goddess of self-esteem, of the pleasure we take in ourselves, in others, in artistic creativity, through personal adornment and through sexual activity as a passionate expression of the life force.

Venus is the woman in her fullness, as she establishes a broader connection with the creative and procreative powers of life. This is the passage that the maiden is making in her journey to the underworld—to tap into that creative power. This passage is a sexual initiation, through the onset of menstruation, through sexual activity in relationship, creativity, birth-giving—any or all of these experiences. Women experience this initiation in their own individual way. One's sexuality is highly personal; all women do not become biological mothers. The personal passage into and embodiment of deeper levels of womanhood is a constant, life-long process.

For more astrological information on emotional/sexual dynamics, a discussion beyond the scope of this chapter, we would look at Venus in relation to Mars, the principle of strength and assertion. For now I simply want to point out that, as the emotional/sexual polarity, both principles are essential to healthy self-development. As Venus awakens, so does Mars. As their Venus qualities are blossoming, teen girls also need to be given the scope to try out their Martian initiative and leadership drive.[9]

The second planetary cycle that occurs in these years is the first Saturn opposition. Saturn is a task master that focuses and disciplines us to accomplish our life purpose. The often heavy weight of Saturn brings a sense of responsibility, duties that require us to apply ourselves, experiences that mature us. A planet that takes twenty-nine to thirty years to complete a round of the zodiac, it creates a challenge to its birth position approximately every seven years. When transiting Saturn comes to the opposite side of one's chart between ages fourteen and sixteen and a half, it signals a challenging time in the growth process. This is the time of peer pressure and a test of self-autonomy in relation to increased social and relationship expectations. This is the time when one's sense of ambition and effectiveness in the world is tested, and when areas of further developmental work are indicated.

The mother is important as a catalyst in this process, since she is our first relationship experience. Later in life, ideally, the personal mother becomes less important. As discussed by object relations theorists, the image of the mother, drawn from our experience and the inner idea we carry of her, is a transitional image used in the separation process. As we grow in self and Higher Self awareness, we tap into an inner strength that goes beyond the definition of ego boundaries toward individuation of our true Being,[10] not dependent on others. However, in these early years we are in the important stages of establishing ego boundaries.

As Saturn symbolizes wisdom through experience, it is a planet that carries strong Crone energy. At this opposition, the Crone, goddess of death, wields her sickle to sever a certain level of dependency on parental authority. Parental limitations (Saturn) are challenged and tested. Rules and behavioral expectations may be seen as constricting, as a larger social dimension of pressures for conformity from peers is experienced. It is a rite of passage that forces recognition of the consequences of one's behavior in the broader arena of society at large, as one starts to come "of age." The strength of the boundaries defined by the parents throughout childhood is put to the test. These containing boundaries can be experienced as grounding and/or constricting during this time. Certainly the young woman is testing her own ground as well. For young women in our culture, the social testing ground may be more limited than for young men. This is changing as we watch, and many of our daughters will continue to pioneer new territories of accomplishment, yet young women in the nineties still face social role models and constraints that inhibit their choices more than men.

For some people, these two oppositions—of progressed Moon and transiting Saturn—happen very close together. My youngest sister had these two cycles culminate within a month, at fourteen years, seven and eight months of age. However, I had a rather early Moon opposition at twelve years, ten months and the Saturn opposition at sixteen years, three months, a wide time frame repeating the timing of this stage of my mother's experience as a young girl. Though introspective and emotionally self-sufficient within myself, I was a late bloomer in my physical and social development. My second sister was more precocious in her emotional/physical development. She also had an early Moon opposition, at twelve years, eight months, and an early Saturn opposition as well, at fourteen years, ten months. This age range variation would be an interesting area for further research.

Darlene's experience illustrates this Moon/Saturn phase. She had a difficult childhood, which included sexual abuse by her father when she stayed with him under custody arrangements. At her progressed Moon opposition at the age of thirteen and a half, she told what was going on in such graphic detail that her reluctant mother finally had to believe her. Darlene has a Moon (in Libra) square Venus (in Capricorn) that suggests her desire to be different than her mother. She has a need to go beyond conventional roles of womanhood (Venus in Capricorn) in which women naturally tend to accommodate their partners (Moon in Libra) and explore life on her own to develop a sense of her own capabilities (Venus in Capricorn). At this Moon opposition, her progressed Moon in Aries reflected her need for self-assertion and action. Her mother sent Darlene away to visit relatives. She no longer stayed with her father, ending the custody arrangement and the abuse. This was also the time Darlene began menstruation. At the Saturn opposition, between ages fourteen and a half to fifteen and a half, she moved away from home outside the family circle. When she was sixteen, she went back to live with her father briefly; he did not attempt any sexual activity.

Darlene became a mother when she was seventeen. Her daughter, Ayla, had the progressed Moon opposition a month after her thirteenth birthday. She repeated Darlene's pattern, beginning to rebel and get out of control. She had begun menstruation a year before, unusually early for the women in her family. During the progressed Moon opposition, Pluto was also transiting in Scorpio opposite her Moon, bringing the underworld theme into strong focus. This was a highly charged time. The Saturn opposition came soon thereafter, between ages fourteen and fifteen, the same as her mother. Darlene was having more trouble with her daughter's activities, aware of the likely scenario if she stayed in the Los Angeles urban environment. She sent Ayla to live with her father's (Saturn's) relatives in the rural northeast, a dramatic change and a major separation for mother and daughter.

To briefly consider a masculine example of this phase, let me introduce Alex. At his progressed Moon opposition, his mother had her last baby, a boy. As the oldest brother, Alex took on some responsibility for caretaking, a Moon function. Later at the age of twenty-eight, when his progressed Moon and transiting Saturn returned to their natal placements (more on this phase later), his mother died. The younger brother went

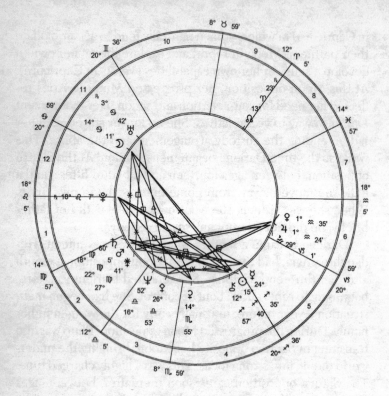

Chart 2. Kelley

to live with an aunt, near where Alex was then living. Alex had more contact with his brother, becoming closer to him and more involved with his life, resuming aspects of a parental guiding role, both Moon and Saturn functions.

The story I know best is that of myself and my daughter (charts 2 and 3). Sanja's progressed Moon opposition occurred when she was thirteen years and eight months old; her grandmother, my mother, was in and out of the hospital and died three months later. Within two weeks of that death, Sanja's paternal grandmother died. Both grandmothers died of the same disease and both carried the same name, Jean, my daughter's

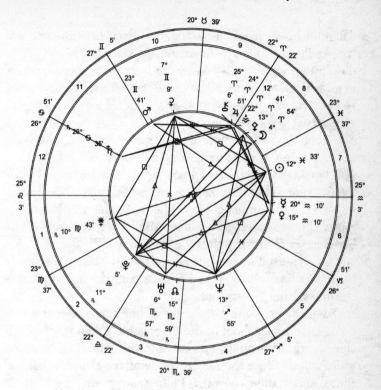

Chart 3. Sanja

middle name. Saturn was stationing very close to the opposition of her natal Saturn at the time of the two deaths. It finished
the opposition when she was fourteen years, ten months old,
an early one. In her fourteenth summer she went to the World
Peace Camp in Maine for two weeks. This experience, funded
by the inheritance from her grandmother, broadened her interest in world issues and gave her a sense of destiny.

We have been a classic Demeter and Persephone mother-
daughter pair for several years, since our little four-member family broke up through death and divorce. With her father living
on the other side of the country, we had a very strong mother-

daughter bond, living alone together from the time she was twelve. Pluto on my ascendant and opposite her Moon brings the Pluto myth into play. We were living in Montpelier, Vermont with Ceres (the Roman name for Demeter) on the State House Capitol. A single mother and her daughter living together have a special bond.

At the time of this writing, she is nineteen. We have been in the process of separating for some time. She has been to visit her Dad in California a couple of summers in her early teens. I remember the challenge of that first plane ride by herself. Then that summer camp in Maine. As a high school sophomore, almost sixteen, she went to Moscow for two weeks with her Russian class right after the break-up of the Soviet Union and found herself somewhat isolated from the rest of the group. She came back changed and restless with the limiting sociocultural setting in Vermont.

Sanja spent the first semester of her junior year at an international high school in the Himalayas, a courageous decision. A friend prophesied that she was going to "dance on Shiva's lake," Shiva the Destroyer being the Hindu version of Pluto. At that time, transiting Pluto was opposing the Moon in our composite chart (chart 4)—a ripe time to significantly further the separation process. (A composite chart blends the charts of two individuals and creates a third chart which indicates relationship dynamics and timing.)

That trip to India was life-changing, exposing Sanja further to the complexity of our world and its peoples. I went to visit her there for a week. It was important to both of us that I be witness to this experience, to share it with her so that she knew I understood when she talked about it. I had been to India three times before; my first trip was a true initiation into life. When my plane was landing this next time, I found myself thinking, "How could I have let my daughter fly off to this place?" with its intensity, poverty, chaos—and, yes, the hidden odor of spirituality, like Persephone's narcissus, in its very dust.

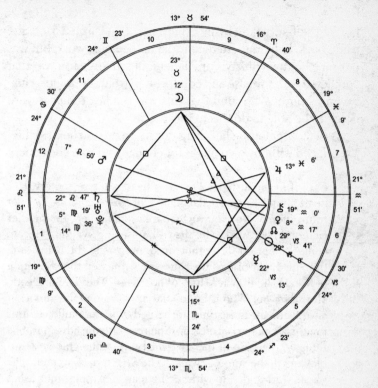

Chart 4. Kelley, Sanja

"Some of my friends wouldn't be able to deal with this," she told me as we walked by skeletal mules and desperately dirty and ragged child living next to a pile of coal. Mother India.

It was even more difficult then to reenter the narrow social environment she had grown up in, with no friend truly able to comprehend her experience. I suggested she try to graduate early. I still congratulate myself for my perception. She barely had the patience to make it through the fall semester, but did finish her courses while earning money to head out on a journey of her own creation. She and a friend flew off to the Virgin Islands, found a house and jobs and stayed for three months, her first self-sufficient living experience. She learned a lot. She came back, helped more than usual in the housework, but was defining her own lifestyle and late night schedule in a way that conflicted with my ease and comfort—in what, I reminded her, was my house. We found that this was the last time we were going to be able to do this in this house.

As a mother letting her daughter move on into her own life, I was faced with my own needs for change and transformation.

Far off in the distance Demeter hears a distressed cry. Her heart jumps. Kore is in danger. Night comes and she does not return home. Not knowing what has happened, the mother cannot do her work. She sits still, unseeing, waiting. Hecate comes to her. At dawn they make prayers to the rising Sun, the Sun-Light of day, the Sun who witnessed the abduction of Kore. When? Why? How? Who? Who!! The Lord of Death. How dare he! Who is he to take my pure one, my innocent one. Demeter is enraged at the gods who have allowed this to be without her permission. She resigns from Olympus. She finds no pleasure in the fragrant flowers, the golden grains blowing in the summer winds. The Sun, too, turns cool. The plants start to dry, to wither. She tears her robes, puts ashes on her face and roams the Earth, heavy-hearted, grief-stricken, seeking, seeking. . . .

> Proud Queen of the Earth Gods. . . .
> You make the heavens tremble and the earth quake.
> Great Priestess, who can soothe your troubled heart?
> You flash like lightning over the highlands . . .
> Holy Priestess, who can soothe your troubled heart?[11]

She passes through the barren countryside, caring not that the people are starving without her food. They share in her suffering. Eventually she reaches Eleusis, where she is invited into the royal household as a nanny. Here she is drawn out of her sorrow by the bawdy humor of the old cook, who lifts her skirts to tease the giggling young women. Demeter, too, smiles and is consoled by nursing the young princeling. Her mother's breast milk ever-flowing, at night she holds him tenderly over the hearth flames to give him her goddess gift of immortality. When the queen-mother sees her at this holy task and cries out, Demeter reveals herself in her full glory and tells her story of loss. The people of Eleusis build a temple for her dwelling, and she initiates them into her mysteries.

> *And God[dess] blessed them, and God[dess] said unto them, Be fruitful and multiply, and replenish the earth....*
> *And God[dess] said, Behold, I have given you every herb bearing seed, which is upon the face of all the earth, and every tree, in the which is the fruit of a tree yielding seed; to you it shall be for meat,*
> *And to every beast of the earth, and to every fowl of the air, and to every thing that creepeth upon the earth, wherein there is life, I have given every green herb for meat: and it was so.*
> *And God[dess] saw every thing that [s]he had made, and, behold, it was very good.*
>
> (Genesis 1:8–30)

Finally, concerned about the barren Earth and starving humans no longer making sacrifice to the gods, Zeus agrees to order Kore to be returned to her mother. Mercury-Hermes, that wheeler-dealer who trades in many currencies, is sent to release her. Mother and daughter take great joy in their reunion, yet each has been forever changed. As they look into each other's eyes, they see reflected both their sameness and their differences. Kore has crossed the borderland and tasted the fruit of Hades, her own terrain. Demeter has sanctified the earth with her tears and opened the gateways of compassion.

Hecate looks on, still holding the mirror.

THE MOTHER: NURTURING

Young women can find much to identify with in the figure of the maiden as she follows inner impulses which lead to her destiny. Kore has eaten pomegranate seeds from the realm of Hades, symbolic of her acceptance of her destiny with him and/or impregnation by him. This union, initially unexpected and traumatic, has been a necessary experience for the development of the maiden's full creative womanhood. She is not the same as she was. She returns not to her mother's world, but rather enters the world of motherhood in herself, as herself. She is now known as Persephone, "Bringer of Destruction," naming her affinity with the Wise Old One who has overshadowed her transformation.

Mother Demeter, too, has changed. Later in life a woman can see how the anguish and grief of this goddess are part of her own trials of motherhood and passage into a new dimension of her being. She has to let her daughter go on to create her life. No longer needed in daily mothering, she must find new ways to express her nurturing capacity, new gifts of wisdom to give the world. There is a necessary grieving as one phase of life ends and another begins. This is the time when deeper soul work takes place. The challenge now is to go beyond ego boundaries toward realization of one's eternal spiritual essence. The mother's relationship with her daughter changes; ideally, she moves into a friendship with this young woman to whom she gave birth. Perhaps she becomes a grandmother to a child of her daughter. At some level, she becomes the Grand-Mother, the Crone.

In Hecate and other images of the Crone, we see the wise older woman who has been through it all and knows how to help guide the transition process of both mother and daughter. The Crone has not been a well-appreciated phase of womanhood in our culture for many centuries, a fact that can make this transition potentially traumatic for modern women. Aging

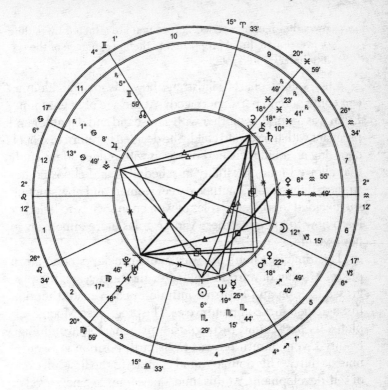

Chart 5. Ellen

carries its particular burdens as well as gifts. For women, the psychosomatic changes of menopause are as significant as those of puberty. In her book, *The Crone*, Barbara G. Walker cites a study of the aging woman in our culture:

> A traditional housewife under patriarchy is left with almost nothing to engage her energy, interest, or ambition at the end of her childrearing years. What she has been taught to think of as her only true fulfillment, the wife-and-mother role, no longer provides satisfaction because it is no longer truly functional. . . . During the period when most men receive maximum reward for their lifework, most women lose even the emotional

> reward of feeling needed . . . women are afflicted by midlife depression in direct proportion to their acceptance of the traditional feminine role. [12]

Ellen's story (chart 5) illustrates how this societal dilemma can contribute to personal tragedy. At the age of twenty-nine, Ellen was a working mother with a husband and daughter and pregnant with her second child. She decided to return to school, choosing an adult weekend program with independent study that allowed more flexibility in scheduling and choosing her studies. Being a wife, mother, career woman, and now student, she decided to study the roles of women in society to help her learn how to integrate these various roles more effectively in her own life.

This time in Ellen's life was another major Moon/Saturn phase. Moving onward in time after the teen years, the progressed Moon and Saturn continue in coordinated motion through their first complete cycles. The progressed Moon completes its first round through the birthchart at around age twenty-seven; Saturn returns to its birth position at twenty-nine or thirty. This double round completes the first full cycle of self-development. At this time, one comes to a new level of maturity. Part of the psychological process of this twenty-seven to thirty-year phase is to consider the impact of the early patterns and conditioning represented by the Moon and the expectations and limitations, the "shoulds" and "do nots" set by authority figures. The foundation of one's life is being completed, the last cornerstone fitted. This is the integration of the first round of recognizing and learning to take care of one's inner needs and responses, to take responsibility for oneself and one's choices in a conscious manner. During this time there is a serious consideration of the conditions that shaped one's life in order to establish a more personally effective ground for moving forward toward accomplishing one's purpose in life. The impact of mother/father/family is perceived from the perspective of experience and often there is a sense of saying "No" to some constrictions that no longer apply or serve in one's further development.

A new level of maturity and responsibility is taken on, willingly or not. Often a woman will become a parent at this time. Whether or not this is a first child, the impact is more apparent that the parent is no longer the child, but the adult. Or a mother may become more conscious of the parenting patterns that she inherited from her mother/father. Whatever the individual circumstances, this phase brings an opportunity for fuller self awareness.

At this stage in her life, Ellen found that her study of the roles of women took on a deeply personal note as she began to think and write about her mother's life and how her mother's choices had impacted her own:

> My mother's life and mine, twenty-five years later, are very different. Not only because of the atmosphere we grew up in but because of our individual views. I have some of my mother's views but I also have others that are there because of my life's experiences. Society has also affected the way that we, as women, do live our lives.

Her mother, Ellen realized, had entirely centered her life around her husband and children. Valedictorian of her class, she turned down a college scholarship to marry her husband, a less-educated man. She devoted her life to her five children, following the same socially accepted pattern as had her mother and sisters. Ellen's mother got a job outside the home when her youngest child entered school full-time, but her family continued to be the central focus of her life. Her husband and children always came first, even before herself, Ellen reports. She raised her children through school, some through college, until all five were married and on their own. At this point, her life changed drastically. Ellen was married and pregnant with her first child when her parents died. Her father was leaving her mother for another woman. With her children gone, not able to envision her life without her husband, her mother killed him and then herself.

> When my parents died, my whole outlook on life changed. I was still very happy with my marriage but I did not want to get into the same rut my mother did. I love my family dearly but I realize that I have myself to think about also. My mother ended her life thinking she wasn't worth anything by herself. I really want to make sure that my life will never end like my parents' did.

Ellen was writing this six years after the tragedy, during her Saturn return. About to be a mother again, pursuing the college degree her mother had encouraged, she found herself dealing on a deeper level than she expected in her studies with the impact of her mother's choice.

> In the end, it was the relationship with her husband that took precedence even over her children and grandchildren. She did not feel that we were sufficient enough to keep living. This is the hardest thing to accept with my parents' deaths. . . . I remember hating my mother for what she did, then for hating my father for what he made my mother do. I have now become resolved to the fact that they were my parents and I love them regardless of what happened. . . . I am still searching for my identity. I cannot come out and say that I am a totally different person than my mother. Yet, I cannot say that I am totally like her either. With her no longer alive, it will be very hard to answer which it is. I am now looking at the relationship I have with my daughter and hope that it grows into a great one. I love my daughter dearly and I want her to be whatever she wants to be, whether it is like me or not. . . . My mother has really had a large effect on how I am living my life today. She really lived the majority of her life according to what society viewed for a woman. She only went against society when she ended two

lives so drastically. I am living my life according to how I want it to be, driven by how I do not want it to be. I know that I am striving to be different than my mom, yet am very satisfied with my roles as wife and mother. I do still have the goal of my mother, to get my college degree. . . . The twenty-five years between us does show some very evident differences but yet we have our similarities. Not only because of society, but because of unchosen and chosen circumstances.

THE CRONE: MATURING

Ellen's mother died at the age of forty-eight, shortly after her second Saturn opposition, which occurs at around forty-five. This phase carries a similar challenge to the teen years, as it requires again facing a deeper level of maturity, now at the later end of life. Saturn contains a degree of depression and a feeling of a lead weight that sinks down to focus on the more serious undercurrents of our experience. Entering the menopausal years and facing old age alone, as she interpreted it, Ellen's mother was unable to cope with this loss and betrayal immediately following the end of active motherhood. She could not imagine how life could go on. She was not able to embrace the transformative darkness of the underworld goddess in a positive way and insteadbecame the death goddess in a literal enactment. In her extraordinary commentary on the myth of Inanna's descent, Sylvia Perera speaks to the capacity of the Crone to accommodate both the light and dark aspects:

> The goddess of the Great Above symbolizes all the ways life energies engage actively with one another and flow together, including connections that are loving and disjunctions that are passionate. Below, and too often repressed, is the energy that turns back on itself, goes down into self-preserving introversions. It is the energy that makes a woman able to be separate unto herself, to survive alone.[13]

This is the power of the Crone. The descent to that place of power and survival is taken by the mother as well as the daughter, as we have seen in the story of Demeter and Persephone. Ellen's mother was unable to face that journey alone. Her experience in the previous phases we have discussed of Moon/Saturn may not have been completed as fully as necessary to adequately prepare her for this time in her life.

Looking at just the Moon and Saturn in Ellen's chart we can see the strong Saturn flavor of her relationship with her mother. The Moon in Capricorn, the sign ruled by Saturn, gives a strong sense of duty, responsibility, and self-sufficiency, even at an early age. Saturn itself is in Pisces in a complex pattern involving Chiron conjunct the asteroid Ceres (Demeter) in the Eighth House. This symbolizes deep issues concerning the healing of the mother-principle, placed in the house of death. The positive sextile between Saturn and the Moon gives Ellen the resilience to learn from her mother's tragic experience to transform her own self-value and her relationships with her children and mate. Any unresolved grief of her mother's or her own will most likely need to be dealt with for a successful separation process when her daughter and son come into the twelve–sixteen year age period. At that time Ellen will be forty-two to forty-five, approaching the second Saturn opposition, the gateway of the Crone years.

SHARING THE EXPERIENCE

In essence we always embody all three goddesses at once. In her Moon-stuff, a mother will still carry her maiden-self, the inner child, and her own mother issues. The separation process with her daughter will bring up unresolved issues from her teen years and unhealed areas in her relationship with her mother.

> Most women struggled alone with the trauma of adolescence and have led decades of adult life with their adolescent experiences unexamined. The lessons learned in adolescence are forgotten and their memories of pain are minimized. Many come into therapy because their marriage is in trouble, or they hate their job, or their own daughter is giving them fits. Maybe their daughter's pain awakens their own pain.[14]

This can be surprising and unsettling. Her daughter, often quite assertive in her compelling need for separation and autonomy, may help the mother break through old patterns. In the simplicity or stark necessity of her vision, the child can sometimes be more like a wise grandmother than her own mother who is in the thick of life activities that call her attention outward so strongly. A young woman begins to see her mother with more clarity as she matures, and she often feels a loss of a kind security as her mother's inadequacies become more apparent.

In psychological work on her mother issues, my daughter explored both the light and dark mother of her experience. Below Sanja shares some of her writing from this work. The first excerpt is about her own childhood memories; the second is her imaginal version of my childhood, an exercise in understanding and forgiving the negative qualities of the mother image she carries. In this writing, she seems to give voice to Kore/Persephone, a strong archetype in her chart as denoted by the Moon opposite Pluto (see chart 3).

On the Positive Mother

Growing up in the countryside I have a deep appreciation for nature and a deep connection to it. I have been taught much about respecting nature and preserving it. I believe it is one of the most important issues of today. I am aware of how every creature and living object is connected and intertwined. I am aware of the many cycles of life and patterns. My mother has always had gardens and I have learned to appreciate nature around me, the beauty of the earth. I have felt at peace when outside and comforted. From especially my mother, I have become very spiritual . . . reaching an understanding of the "more" out there, more than what can be seen, of wanting to return to the source. I am able to see through the myths and veils to the real source, the real meanings behind all this modern, civilized bullshit.

On the Negative Mother

My mother was indulgent a lot, giving us whatever food we wanted and always asking us if we needed anything. She really mothered us. She wasn't strict and usually gave in to our desires. It was her way of showing love, I think. She felt that if she said no we wouldn't love her and she needed me to. She depended on us for that. . . . I think she felt like she didn't do enough for us and this was how she could make it better. It was her way of making sure we were OK. My mother denied herself. I never learned how to be good to yourself. My mother suffered a lot and never complained. I learned that it was good to suffer and that it was OK to do bad things to yourself. I felt vulnerable because of this lack of faith in myself and self doubt. I saw how my mother was vulnerable and it hurt me to see her that way, but I still learned to be like that and wasn't comfortable with or in myself. I learned to avoid conflict very well. It was easier than facing up to the real feelings and issues that were underneath. I learned to deny myself and doubt myself. This is the point I was at when I reached puberty. My family wasn't comfortable and happy and there were a lot of unsaid feelings and emotions that were affecting me in unhealthy ways.

This writing helped her express contradictory feelings and understand many of her own issues and come to a stronger sense of herself in the continuing separation process, which goes on throughout life on various levels:

It feels very frustrating, like I'm not in control of myself, like I'm struggling to get free but I'm not facing it. I'm angry that these patterns have caused so much pain in me and others. I'm angry that she didn't do more to control herself and realize what she was doing, try more to help me out with them, to realize what was happening.

It feels really good to understand where they came from and to realize they are not really me and can be destroyed. I feel lighter and freer. I feel sympathetic for my mom who didn't pass these on to me knowingly. She did what she could but she's not perfect and has a lot to deal with anyway. I understand her better and myself, my emotions. I feel more in control of myself.

Sanja's perspective taught me a lot as well. I was grateful that our relationship was strong enough for her to share this material with me. Some aspects of her experience of me as a mother surprised me—how important the gardens were to her, for instance. Her imaginal version of my childhood, though not factually correct, stimulated insights and a look at shadow issues that were significant to re-evaluate at this time in my life, when I am experiencing the second Saturn opposition. Her perceptions helped me, as well as her, think about the issues that have carried down through the women in our family line now when I am investigating more about our genealogy.

As she has been away having adventures, exploring life, and making her own choices, she has been maturing. When she comes home each time, our relationship changes yet again. When I "regress" into old motherhood patterns that are no longer appropriate, she calls me on it. And vice-versa when she depends on me in ways that I can no longer tolerate, as I am needing to redirect my resources—time and money, energy and talents—to move on in fulfilling new directions for myself. I am also seeking adventures, exploring life anew and making choices for myself again—or at least figuring out what it is

I really want for myself now: a new freedom for us both, and new responsibilities. I left the job that supported us during her growing years, ready to spend more time doing the work that I love and feel is my richest contribution. I also needed more time for myself, to remember how to relax and enjoy simply being rather than doing. That was actually rather difficult to allow myself, but both body and spirit insisted.

I am fortunate to have support from many women friends and guidance from several crones. With a strong Moon in Cancer, I am ever learning to expand and enjoy my Venus qualities and give that goddess more room in my life. The eternal myths have enriched the understanding of my own story. My experience and those of other women encourage me to rewrite the myths, a necessary task to reclaim the spirituality of our experience. Myth continues to live only through our experience of it. The stories are ever re-imagined; as we do so, we change ourselves and the world and leave a more positive feminine inheritance for our daughters.

> O most beautiful flower of Mount Carmel, fruitful vine, splendor of Heaven, Blessed Mother of the Son of God. Inmaculate Virgin, assist me in my necessity. Star of the Sea, help me and show me here you are my mother. O Holy Mary, Mother of God, Queen of Heaven and Earth, I humbly beseech you from the bottom of my heart to succor me in my necessity . . . There are none that can withstand your power.
>
> —from a prayer card to the Blessed Virgin

We still pray to the Goddess, once known as Demeter or Persephone or Inanna or by many other names. Her power is not easy to disguise in male form, for only women give birth. She is the Great Mother, not only of the son of God, but the daughter of God as well.

NOTES

1. Debold, Wilson, and Malave. *Mother Daughter Revolution: From Betrayal to Power* (New York: Addison-Wesley Publishing Company, 1993), xvi.

2. Elaine Pagels. *The Gnostic Gospels* (New York: Vintage Books, 1981), 66.

3. Marvin W. Meyer, ed., *The Ancient Mysteries: A Sourcebook* (New York: Harper and Row, 1987), 21.

4. Diane Wolkstein and Samuel N. Kramer. *Inanna, Queen of Heaven and Earth* (New York: Harper and Row, 1983), 4.

5. Ibid. 5–6.

6. From Dragon Dance Theater and Helia Productions, unpublished script.

7. Wolkstein and Kramer, op.cit., 89.

8. Sherry Ruth Anderson and Patricia Hopkins. *The Feminine Face of God* (New York: Bantam Books, 1992), 61.

9. See Lyn Mikel Brown and Carol Gilligan, *Meeting at the Crossroads* (New York: Ballantine Books, 1992) and Pipher, *Reviving Ophelia: Saving the Selves of Adolescent Girls*.

10. A. H. Almaas. *The Pearl Beyond Price* (Berkeley, CA: Diamond Books, 1988, 221.

11. Wolkstein and Kramer, op cit, 95.

12. Barbara Walker. *The Crone* (New York: Harper and Row, 1985), 32.

13. Sylvia Perera. *Descent to the Goddess* (Toronto: Inner City Books, 1981), 44.

14. Mary Pipher, Ph.D. *Reviving Ophelia* (New York: Ballantine Books, 1994), 25.

REFERENCES AND OTHER SUGGESTED READING

Almaas, A. H. *The Pearl Beyond Price, Integration of Personality Into Being: An Object Relations Approach.* Berkeley, CA: Diamond Books, 1988.

Anderson, Sherry Ruth and Hopkins, Patricia. *The Feminine Face of God.* New York: Bantam Books, 1992.

Apter, Terry. *Altered Loves: Mothers and Daughters During Adolescence.* New York: Fawcett Columbine, 1990.

Brown, Lyn Mikel and Gilligan, Carol. *Meeting at the Crossroads.* New York: Ballantine Books, 1992.

Carlson, Kathie, *In Her Image: An Unhealed Daughter's Search for Her Mother.* Boston: Shambala, 1990.

Chernin, Kim. *In My Mother's House: A Daughter's Story.* New York: HarperCollins, 1983.

——*Reinventing Eve.* New York: Random House, 1987.

Debold, Elizabeth, Malave, Idelisse and Wilson, Marie. *Mother Daughter Revolution: From Betrayal to Power.* New York: Addison-Wesley Publishing Company, 1993.

Meyer, Marvin W., ed. *The Ancient Mysteries: A Sourcebook.* New York: Harper and Row, 1987.

Neumann, Erich, *The Great Mother: An Analysis of the Archetype.* Princeton, NJ: Princeton University Press, 1974.

Pagels, Elaine. *The Gnostic Gospels.* New York: Vintage Books, 1981.

Perera, Sylvia. *Descent to the Goddess: A Way of Initiation for Women.* Toronto: Inner City Books, 1981.

Pipher, Mary, Ph.D. *Reviving Ophelia: Saving the Lives of Adolescent Girls.* New York: Ballantine Books, 1994.

Ruperti, Alexander. *Cycles of Becoming: The Planetary Pattern of Growth*. Davis, CA: CRCS Publications, 1978.

Walker, Barbara G. *The Crone,* New York: Harper and Row, 1985.

Wolkstein, Diane and Kramer, Samuel N. *Inanna, Queen of Heaven and Earth*. New York: Harper and Row, 1983.

Woolger, Jennifer Barker and Woolger, Roger J. *The Goddess Within: A Guide to the Eternal Myths That Shape Women's Lives*. New York: Fawcett Columbine, 1989.

Carol Garlick

Carol Garlick is a professional astrologer, teacher, and lecturer. With her home base in Atlanta, Georgia, Carol has a busy private practice and writes an astrology column for Aquarius newspapers.

She is the former Public Relations Director and staff astrologer for Matrix Software in Big Rapids, Michigan and in that capacity had the opportunity to work with Michael Erlewine on the initial stages of development for both Microsoft and America On-line astrology internet areas.

Long active in the major astrological organizations, Carol is currently a board member and newsletter editor for the Metro-Atlanta Astrological Society. With a B.S. in the social sciences, Carol is a member of the Jungian Institute. She also organizes women's empowerment groups. Her hobbies include art, gardening, and the theater.

Carol Garlick

Daughters and Fathers: The Father's Role in the Development of a Whole Woman

"In childhood a woman is subject to her father; after puberty, to her husband, and after widowhood, she is subject to her son."
Old Tamil proverb

Throughout history, men have held almost all the world power and prestige, women almost none. Within the family structure, fathers have ruled and daughters have obeyed. Traditionally, the good father has been required only to protect his daughter from other men. However, there was no one to protect her from him. For many centuries, daughters could consider themselves lucky, indeed, if their fathers protected and provided for them until they were old enough to be handed over to a husband who continued the job.

First father, then husband, then adult son, made all the decisions about the daughters' life, from childhood through old age. Yes, there have been some notable exceptions, but by and large, this has been the norm. What is startling is not how much, but how little, these patterns have changed until this generation.

A father is the first and often the longest connection a daughter will have with a man. The father-daughter bond, however weak or strong, shapes her future relationships with male friends and lovers and influences how she moves out in the world.

If he is encouraging and inspiring and even teaches her some competency skills, she will more easily develop authentic self-confidence. If he discourages her and undermines her self-confidence, shames her body, or discounts her opinions, self-confidence will be damaged and it may take many years for her to trust and believe in herself. Many fathers are neglectful and are not actively engaged in their daughters' development.

When a father is physically or emotionally unavailable, a daughter may distort who and what he represents to her. An absent father often leads to idealization of him and later other men, giving her fantasies more power than real life. This pattern of longing for the one that got away, or searching for the "prince on the white horse" who never arrives, can lead to affairs with married men or relationships with otherwise unavailable men in order to unconsciously avoid intimacy.

The daughter of an absent father typically feels a terror of abandonment, and has an inability to trust that a man will remain a loving presence in her life. On the other hand, a father who is overbearing and invasive forces a daughter to become defensive to protect herself from him and other men. Her feelings of vulnerability may cause her to build strong boundaries that distance her from him as well as his intrusive behavior, whether physical or emotional.

The concept of boundaries is critical to understanding how daughters and fathers move toward and away from each other. It's as if there is a wall between their bodies and minds, sometimes thick and impermeable, sometimes thinning and, for moments, even transparent. Ideally, a father upholds these boundaries and models limit-setting. He does this by how he says no; how he manages behavior such as physical contact and emotional intimacy; and how he respects the privacy needs of his daughters.

If he violates the boundary through incest, or cannot tolerate her emotional independence and tries to control her feelings through emotional incest, she cannot feel safe or whole in his presence. Later in life, the daughter may continue to suffer from weak boundaries, unable to say no to men and their demands. Or she may develop rigid boundaries that shut all men out and leave her with an inability to be intimate. From an archetypal perspective, a father's ability to uphold healthy boundaries and become a steadying influence for his daughter is associated with centeredness and order. His task is to walk a path between abandoner and over-protector, critical judge and cheerleader. Fathering a daughter is always a dance of balance, rather than an either-or approach.

A father's modeling of the more traditional masculine strengths is the best gift he can give to his daughter. His masculinity assists in the development of her own inner masculine qualities that she needs in order to be a whole woman. A father who acts and speaks from his own grounded masculinity, yet is also vulnerable with his partner and with his daughter, helps to provide her with an image of soft strength as she makes her own way in the world. The greatest impact on a woman's romantic choices and her ability to feel comfortable with her own sexuality is how her father treated her in childhood.

But it is from both parents that a daughter gains her basic identity. One of the greatest values of fathers, especially for daughters, is the very fact that they are partners in the parenting process, for without fathers the mother-daughter bond can become too mutually dependent. Whether a child is male or female, fathers are needed for the "otherness." They are needed to put a healthy wedge between mother and child, to provide a haven from real or imagined maternal injustice or smothering.

Historically, most experts had assumed that fathers were unimportant in child rearing, and traditionally their role in the home environment was extremely limited. After the Industrial Revolution men were seen as the family link to the outer world and that freed the mother to tend to the children. As I was growing up, it was a point of pride for a man to have his wife tending the home. "No wife of mine will ever work," was commonly heard. For those too young to remember, reruns of movies of the 1950s and 60s portray fathers as friendly, but definitely out of place in a home where the full-time wife and mother skillfully kept things running.

It's commonly accepted at this time that the women's liberation movement that arose out of the socially turbulent 1960s and 70s has created the greatest single change in men's lives. As many women declared a life limited to housework and childcare oppressive and fought for entry into the male-dominated work world, men simply were forced to rethink their unquestioned role as distant breadwinner. Today it is common to see new fathers participate in childbirth classes, bonding with and actively involving themselves in their daughters' lives at all stages. The greatest sign of respect that a daughter can see her father pay to the domestic setting is to be a willing participant. As society approves, through custom and law, it becomes easier for fathers to involve themselves as an active part of the family unit.

Astrologically, we can find reasons for these changing role models. The planet Neptune entered Capricorn in 1984 and will remain in that sign through 1998. It's as if Neptune is dissolving many things associated with Capricorn, softening some of the rigidity of the principle that includes, among other things, fathering. Uranus joined Neptune in 1988 and remained until the beginning of 1996, signifying new images and ideals for Capricorn. In 1988 Saturn came along to crystalize these new images of fathering.

The Sun and Moon in an astrological horoscope embody the archetypal parents. In the natal chart, the Sun symbolizes the central archetype of self, both in its superficial reflection as the ego, and its innermost nature as the individual being. This luminary, the Sun, also represents the father. This is no accident, because we can learn the path to selfhood—beginning with separation from the mother, through the father and on to individuation—ultimately to internalize the parental archetype as our own.

We all possess a lunar and solar dimension to our natures. The unfolding self through the development of the Sun is just as relevant to women as the self-nourishing wisdom of the Moon is to men. The terms masculine and feminine do not refer to one sex or another when used to describe a symbolic image, but rather they refer to receptive (feminine) or dynamic (masculine) energy. The mythic conjunction or marriage between the Sun and the Moon describes a potential of inner relationship between these different aspects of the personality in either sex.

The Sun symbolizes our struggle for growth and consciousness, the urge to live our own lives. This is the battle we all face between the need to discover our own identity and the desire to remain in the familiar environment of our parental background. Many women do not take up the fight and prefer to remain unfulfilled rather than to risk cutting the umbilical cord and going it alone. If we refuse the call to live our own lives we can become depressed and lacking in vitality. The Sun symbolizes creative potency and initially it is the personal father who embodies for us the creative masculine principle, the possibility of independence and individuality.

To be an individual and live one's own life, to find one's destiny, means to go from infantile notions of omnipotence, personal preferences, resentments, illusions of good or bad, and the ego's self-interest, to an understanding and acceptance of personal cosmic law, with the ability to see things as they really are, rather than how we would like them to be. The position of the Sun in the birth chart shows where we need to struggle to find meaning and purpose in our life. In other words, it reveals the journey we must make to find our own identity.

The Sun is progressive. The energy develops over a lifetime and we never really finish developing the Sun because this aspect of the personality is always becoming. The Sun also reflects an essential vision that we share with our fathers on the creative level, and that can only mature over many generations of solar striving.

The Sun shows itself unconsciously when it's not developed and sometimes through projection. Richard Idemon defines projection as looking outside of ourselves for material or qualities that for some reason are unawakened, not integrated, or unacceptable within ourselves. We disown parts of ourselves and then see these parts in other people. We can project both negative and positive characteristics. Carl Jung felt that projections are quite natural to us and that we tend to do more projecting early in our lives, but as we move on in years, ideally we have individuated enough so that we can see the projections we put onto other people.

We all have dimensions of the Sun that are unexpressed, because it reflects a process of becoming, and we never finish this process. There are still some cultures where women have little opportunity to express the Sun. What happens to it? It is projected onto their husbands and fathers, onto their male children and onto authority figures in the outer world. It can also be projected onto other women, for women can also carry solar qualities. Because the sense of authority and meaning for the woman then lies outside, she will feel empty and depressed without the qualities that she has projected out, according to Dr. Liz Greene.

In order to feel complete and fulfilled we must give expression to our Sun sign. We must develop ourselves in the area of life associated with the house our Sun is in, and we should try to find constructive ways to use the energy signified by any planet that is in aspect to our Sun. For example, if your Sun is in the First House in the sign of Aries, this is an indication that your main purpose in life is to develop your courage, and the ability to assert yourself in a way that is viable and workable. We can then analyze the chart to see how other factors in the nature will work for or against the healthy development of the Sun sign qualities.

The fullest expression of the Sun requires conscious effort, determination and choice. Because the Sun also signifies the father, we can examine it for indications of what may have passed between you and him. There is a definite connection between ego formation and the kind of interaction you had with your father, We are drawn to him at a time developmentally when we are ready to begin the break with mother, when we first begin to establish an identity that is separate from her. Therefore, what we meet when we move toward father has a great bearing on our sense of individual identity. Howard Sasportas taught that natal aspects to the Sun give one indication of what you meet through father, and because of the connection between father and self-formation, natal aspects to the Sun also indicate "qualities closely associated with your sense of what it means to be an 'I' separate and distinct from mother."[1]

In examining the charts of four sisters, we will use a model introduced at a conference on the personal planets given by Howard Sasportas and Dr. Liz Greene in 1990 in Zurich, Switzerland. I was fortunate to have attended that week-long seminar and have found in my own practice that the material provides an invaluable guide for daughters of all ages in finding their paths to selfhood.

Also, the book, *The Luminaries,* by Greene and Sasportas (Weiser) is a transcript of a portion of that seminar and it gives a more detailed explanation. It is also important to keep in

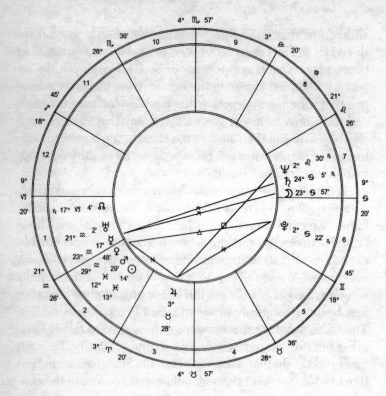

Chart 1. Joseph

mind that though this section stresses the importance of living your Sun for self-fulfillment, it can't be done at the expense of the Moon sign and placement. We have to be the Sun while also acknowledging the Moon. When we begin to separate from the mother and begin to form our own ego identity, we don't abandon what the Moon represents. We cannot deny our past and the inheritance from our mother. Our aim is to recognize and integrate it, thereby giving it an area of expression.

Chart #1 belongs to Joseph, the father of the four sisters and the oldest son of ten children of Irish immigrants. From an early age, Joseph wanted to be a priest. He earned high grades in school and was a favorite of the nuns. He was devastated when he had to leave school in his sophomore year to help support his family. His father was the local bartender and Joseph helped out there while running horse race bets for the local book. A friend convinced Joseph to join the Lithographer's Union. Soon he was learning the trade in one of the largest print shops in the city. He met Darla through a mutual friend and when she became pregnant, they married and moved into a small flat in Joseph's family's building. When he wasn't working, Joseph spent a lot of time upstairs drinking and gambling with his mother.

Chart #2 belongs to Darla, the mother and Joseph's wife, a recent nursing school graduate who moved to the city for her first hospital job. She had always wanted to be a physician and was promised by her wealthy grandmother that she would be sent to college.

Darla earned top honors in her classes all through school, excelling in science and math. At the last possible minute her grandmother changed her mind and said she would send her to nursing school. Feeling she had no recourse, Darla did as she was told.

Chart #3 belongs to Darla and Joseph's oldest daughter, Ann. With her Second House Sun in Cancer, she must learn to nurture herself (her potential, talents, skills, self-worth, values) so that her emotional dependency (Cancer Sun) is not placed on those in her care, partners, or authority figures. Security comes through developing and possessing such qualities as strength, nobility, authority, a sense of being special, and having courage. Developing skills that are valuable in the market place are also encouraged. The Sun placed in Cancer offers a unique dilemma, however, because the ego is not secure with the change and flux that's inherent in that Moon ruled sign. Stress is somewhat lessened with her Sun

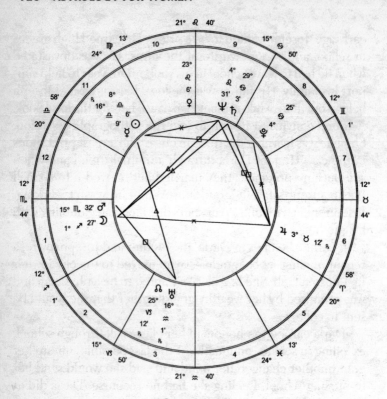

Chart 2. Darla

sextile the Moon, accenting compatibility between will and emotions. With the Moon, ruler of her Sun sign, placed in the Fifth House, Ann feels most at home when creating. She bore six children through two marriages, and was the oldest of six children growing up. As Leo's natural ruling planet, the Sun's actions have a direct bearing on any house with Leo on the cusp. Whatever you create through using your Sun, the result will be strongly felt in any area of life ruled by Leo. Ann has Leo on the cusp of the Fourth House, implying that she has a need to distinguish her own identity as distinct from

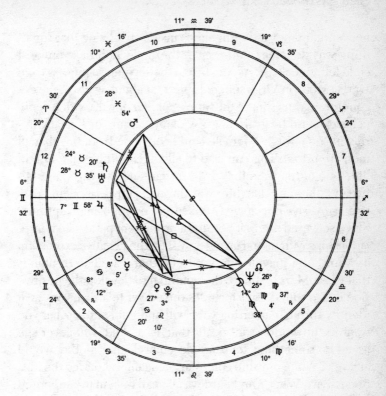

Chart 3. Ann

the family background, without denying that she's also part
of the family.

She has had the idea for several years that Joseph could not
be her biological father and has been to psychics and card readers for confirmation. Joseph died in 1980 and as of this date,
Ann has not addressed the issue with Darla, her mother. Also,
the father may have been physically or psychologically absent.
For a daughter, this could mean a lifetime search for the lost
father. Ann has married three times and divorced twice, hop-
ing each time that she would be supported. She ultimately

needs to find her father qualities inside. Realizing that something was deficient, Ann began therapy when her youngest child left for college. As Ann began the separation process from Darla (Moon in Virgo square Jupiter) at about age two, she encountered Mars square the Sun, a conflict of wills with Joseph. (This can also be gruff, angry, violent, unsafe, or sexually unruly in some way). A female could conclude from this that all men are brutal. This can lead to all kinds of things later on in life. One of the ways that this Martian energy played out between father and daughter was through competition and passive aggressive put-down (Mars in Pisces opposing Neptune). She discovered this as it became a prominent pattern in her relationships with men. Having only seen the negative expression of Mars, Ann may decide not to be that way. The trouble is that when Mars is stifled, the potential to develop the positive side is also stifled. This includes the power to affirm your own identity through asserting your will and going after what you want in the world. Ann recalls that, as a child, whenever she asked for something, for example a bicycle, her mother would answer, "When our ship comes in,"—again, validating the idea of passivity. What Ann heard was, "I can't—a man's supposed to provide." What she also heard was that women cannot count on men to provide. She handled this dilemma by joining the convent after high school.

A devout Catholic from the time she could walk, Ann attended Mass daily and she was active in parish activities throughout all of her school years. She left the convent after a year, stating that she had dreamed of being the bride of Christ, but after she got there, being one of so many brides had not felt "special" at all. Besides her disillusionment, she also admits to having been homesick. In addition, she said she felt as if she had disappointed her father. She doesn't know for sure, because she cannot recall that they ever had a conversation. At that time, transiting Saturn was opposing her Sun.

When she was a child, Ann had a tremendous passion for music, and the violin in particular. She repeatedly begged her mother for lessons. One day, while rummaging through an out-of-the-way closet, Ann found an old violin case with a broken string instrument inside. When she ran to her mother with it she was told that there was no one available in the area who gave lessons. Ann would take out the violin to hold it everyday. As time passed, she saw it less and less—until one day it was no longer there. It had just disappeared. Ann also had a small Jew's harp from her paternal grandfather. It was her most treasured possession and she would practice when she was alone. One day it disappeared also.

Mercury is conjunct the Sun within 5 degrees and so it is said to be combust—or burned up by the Sun's rays. Developing the positive aspects to the Sun (from the Moon, Mercury, and Mars) are the gifts that Ann has received from her father. The obstacles are shown in the chart. It's not easy and takes a lot of work. The Sun quincunx the midheaven (and the Moon is also quincunx the midheaven, forming a yod) show the tension between Ann's views and what her parents taught her. She may not be able to accept her own ideas as valid if they contradict what she was taught. This can lead to trying to live up to others' expectations and trying to suppress her own way of thinking. This causes much tension, leading to confusion that plays right into the strong Mars-Neptune opposition in her chart. Ann earned a college degree and established herself in government service while studying astrology. Though she never had taken an art class, she gathered some materials and began selling her work. She also received a celtic harp as a gift and began teaching herself to play. Now Ann is writing and teaching art and continues with astrology. Her chart supports this path to finding her identity and she has never felt happier and more content. Of her father she says, "I didn't know him, but for many years after he died I thought that my mother sabotaged our friendship.

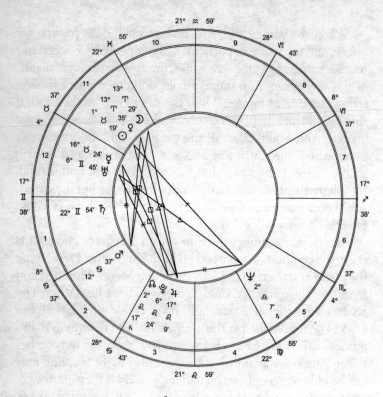

Chart 4. Marie

I didn't want to face the truth. Now I realize that he had much talent that he didn't have the courage to develop. As for myself, just because I couldn't do these things as a kid, doesn't mean I can't now. I'm going for it."

Chart #4 belongs to Marie. With her Sun in Taurus in the Eleventh House, she must learn to build her own value system and especially learn to value herself enough to pursue her own dreams. Pleasure and beauty are extremely important to a Taurus Sun, and what can make one vulnerable is susceptibility to appetites and the importance of possessing things.

It means learning flexibility and tolerance with friends. Because Marie's Sun is less than four degrees from her Twelfth House cusp, we can also look at Twelfth House issues for her. Here we find issues of confusion around the father and sacrifices made as well as issues of crisis and confinement. Various forms of institutions can play a role in their lives.

Upon graduation from High School, Marie desperately wanted to enroll in a program at a local hospital that trained young women to assist in the care of newborn infants in the nursery. Darla would not permit this for her daughter because she said that the training was not of equal caliber to that of a registered nurse. Marie was married at the age of eighteen and had three children within the following ten years. She has never held a job outside the home and as her youngest child reached his teens, she began a series of health crises that continue into the present. She had surgery to remove a large percentage of her stomach because of perforated ulcers. Further stomach surgery was needed that same year, though underlying bothersome side-effects must be endured. This was followed by a hysterectomy performed shortly before the discovery of tainted blood banks and the HIV virus. She contracted hepatitis B from routine blood transfusions so that she has an immune deficiency disorder that remains obscure, but produces symptoms that still baffle the medical community.

Marie has become an expert in the part of the medical world that involves her. She spends enormous time in libraries reading and researching, and constantly amazes her team of specialists with information they don't always have. All of her children have earned advanced academic degrees and are outstanding in their fields, earning salaries at the high end of the continuum compared to peers. Her youngest child and only son started college, majoring in chemistry to prepare for medical school. Much to her disappointment, he switched to accounting in his junior year and now is a C.P.A. Like her older sister

Ann, Marie has the sign Leo on the Fourth House cusp. This suggests that the father may have been physically or psychologically absent, resulting in a lifetime search for a father until those qualities can be found inside. Joseph started working nights when the girls were in elementary school. There was a shift differential and Darla encouraged this change because she felt that they needed the money.

Marie is close with her youngest daughter who is in her early thirties and continues to live at home. Still in touch with one person from her high school years, Marie exhibits qualities of agoraphobia, leaving the house only with a family member and rarely straying beyond the neighborhood. She participates less and less in her husband's social life because he's an avid tennis player and she's not physically able. He visits the racetrack every week and she joins him on occasion. She is an avid reader and when not devouring books, she watches movies. Early in her marriage she began crocheting and needlepoint, but has not touched crafts for years because of her health. When Marie began to separate from her mother, Darla (Moon in Aries conjunct Venus square Mars), she encountered Joseph's Sun square Pluto. There are lots of power issues with this placement. No matter what her father said or did outwardly, Marie was always sensitive to what was unspoken. With Pluto there are dark undertones—violent, perhaps, and sometimes sexual. This doesn't feel safe to an unsuspecting child, so to be separate means that you have to be on guard. Safety can't be taken for granted—life is complex. A rigid style of adapting and coping stems from the need to establish the tightest possible control over self and the environment. This is reinforced by her Saturn conjunct the Ascendant. Also, Venus rules her Taurus Sun and is square Mars conjunct the Moon. Again, there is the juxtaposition of lunar and solar energy that we saw with Ann, showing an insecure ego because of change and flux. That energy was also reinforced by Marie's memory of her mother and father fighting all the time. Commenting about him not long ago, Marie said, "I've been thinking about my father and I've really found it difficult explaining how I felt about him. I guess the best word is uncomfortable. When I was little, he was there, but I was ignored both physically and emotionally. There was no interaction at all. Of Joseph's death Marie said, "In the chapel, sitting looking at what was once the body and soul of my father was total relief for me. When the casket was closed and the ground opened and closed for him at the cemetery, I felt totally comfortable with him for the first time in my life."

Chart #5 belongs to Jean, the fifth child of Joseph and Darla. Children two and four are boys. Jean's Sun is in Leo in the Eighth House. The Sun is the ruler of Leo and is very strong in that sign. Jean must develop her own creative self-expression (Leo) while expanding herself and transcending personal limitations and separateness through some form of union and interchange with other people (Eighth House). In other words, Jean must develop her own creativity and then become transformed by sharing it with a partner. Relationships that expose hidden passions and trigger unresolved childhood complexes also serve the solar processes of growth and unfolding. Jean will also enhance ego-building by noticing how her behavior affects other people and by allowing them to make their own decisions while giving them the credit that's due them. Jean's right eye turned inward from birth and as a pre-schooler she was given large thick glasses to wear in a misguided attempt by her physician to cure the problem. She hated how they looked and when an eye patch was added she was in misery. Her dream was to learn to play the piano, but there was never money for such an expense in the household.

Jean had lots of friends from an early age. While in elementary school, a friend told her that they were giving their piano away. Darla refused the offer, saying that there was no room in the house for such an item. Jean never forgave her. In choosing

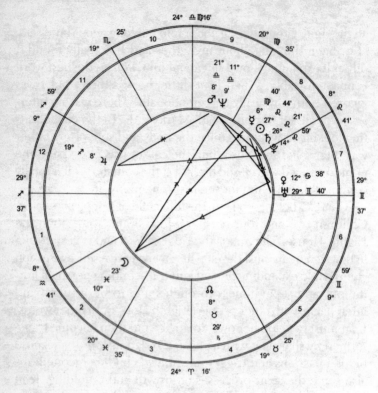

Chart 5. Jean

a track of study in high school, Darla insisted that Jean take all the secretarial subjects—typing, shorthand, and accounting, for example. Again, Jean was unhappy, but acceded to her mother's wishes. After graduation, Jean went to work in the accounting office of Playboy Enterprises. She married at eighteen to a neighborhood boyfriend who was a few years her senior. She went on to a better paying job in the payroll department of an insurance company and dutifully handed over her paycheck to her husband each week. When Jean separated from her mother (Moon in Pisces opposite Mercury), her feelings of stupidity became reinforced by Saturn conjunct the Sun. So Joseph, who came across as cold and remote and authoritarian, reinforced self-doubt and Jean could not be sure about being able to stand on her own two feet or having any fun trying.

Two of her passions emerged in early adulthood—an interest in Hitler's regime and the death camps, and the study of astrology. About this time she gave birth to her daughter. Her husband took a leave of absence from his job to assist his wife whom he didn't trust to adequately care for the infant. As time went on, Jean began formal astrology studies with a teacher, but lied to her husband about where she was going because he thought her pursuit stupid. That was almost twenty-five years ago and even though Jean gained prominence in the astrological field and maintains a large private practice, it is only in the last couple of years that he has come to grudgingly give her and the subject some respect. It is also in the last couple of years that Jean will sit with him and explain generally what she does and share that part of her life with him. In this last year, after a venture into therapy, they have been willing to share more of themselves with each other, including their finances, parts of their home, and the tremendous landscaping project on their property that began as Jean's small flower garden. Jean creates art with herbs, flowers, and vines that she grows and gives as gifts to friends and family. Interestingly, every year Jean digs up a part of her garden to replant and rearrange in other areas. The transformation continues year after year as the layout and design improve and develop. Of her father, Jean said she felt that he left the family for good when she was about seven years old (first Saturn square). She remembers that he picked her up from school—absolutely unheard of—and told her that he was going to start working nights. He was not involved in her life after that—just not available. He didn't go to her high school graduation because he had to work—Darla's idea. Looking at

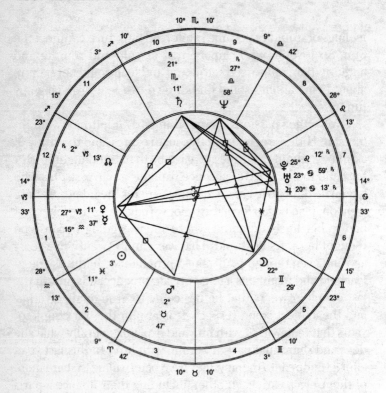

Chart 6. Kathryn

him in the casket, Jean said she felt sadness—because she
didn't know him and because she felt his life was such a waste
of good potential. Jean describes him as quiet, intense, and
very talented with a strong work ethic.

Chart #6, Kathryn, is the youngest daughter of Joseph and
Darla, and seven years younger than Jean. She has an intercepted
Sun in Pisces in the Second House unaspected by any major
aspects. Developing the self for her involves taking the time to
value her dreams and then craft them into shape. She must
gain some understanding of both the mortal and divine sides

of herself and care for them both. A strongly placed and well-aspected Sun shows a healthy ego, a sense of self that supports the needs of the whole person. If placed in a sign where it doesn't work as well, the result can be that the ego's weakness interferes with the overall ability to fulfill desires and achieve success. Kathryn's chart is challenging, and given the inaccessibility of that solar core, one would hope that opportunities offered after the progressed sun changes to Aries, roughly around the age of nineteen, might provide some windows of opportunity for movement. Kathryn's Second House, like Ann's, speaks to the issue of the development of self-sufficiency. Leo on the Eighth House cusp, like Jean's, offers the opportunities to re-examine the connection between present relationship issues and those problems encountered with the mother and father early in life. Kathryn was in big trouble shortly before she was born. The placenta had separated from the mother in utero and the baby was cut off from all nourishment. Kathryn's birth weight was close to four pounds and even though she had gone to term, there were some unspecified oxygen problems that resulted in minor, but significant brain damage. Kathryn is vague about particulars because Darla was vague when any questions were asked and medical records are apparently unavailable. Kathryn tells of early sexual abuse by a retired next-door neighbor and sexual harassment from relatives, none of which parents or siblings were aware of at the time. She also says that at a very young age she realized that she was sexually oriented toward females and while still in elementary school began a series of lesbian relationships that lasted throughout her adult life. Though special education was unavailable as a resource, Kathryn was able to graduate from the public elementary school. Her experience was degrading and she was never able to comprehend mathematical concepts. Also her coordination never fully developed and she had a slight speech impediment with hearing difficulties. She was treated cruelly by the other children and teachers as well. Her high school years went somewhat smoother because she was accepted at the same parochial school that her three older sisters had attended. It was during that time that her talent for drawing and painting emerged and it appeared that she had found her niche. Kathryn enrolled at a prestigious art school, but had to drop out after the first semester because, though she had artistic ability, she lacked the other skills necessary to support the process. For example, she was unable to measure with a ruler or calculate space requirements for a project.

She soon married a man twenty-five years her senior who had a spotty employment history and low skills. She gave birth to a beautiful baby boy who died from a heart defect just two days later. The next year she gave birth to another boy who appeared to be healthy, but who exhibited emotional and behavior problems from very early on. After a messy divorce, Kathryn and her son lived periodically with her parents and lesbian lovers. Her child's continually disruptive behavior fueled conflicts in Kathryn's intimate relationships so that, when the boy was in his teens, Kathryn found her own place for them to live. Darla had gone back to work when Kathryn was seven years old because they needed the money. Though very successful and fulfilled, she took early retirement from her nursing career to raise her grandson. However, his behavior problems led to legal conflicts. Subsequently, he was determined to be disabled for psychiatric reasons and he underwent several years of therapy. After working in a series of entry level positions, Kathryn trained to become a certified nursing assistant so she could work with nursing home patients. Her acceptance into the program and subsequent state certification has done wonders for Kathryn's sense of self. She recently married a man ten years her senior whom she met in a nursing home where she was employed. He had a leg amputated because of severe diabetes as well as some other health issues. With the money he receives from the government and Kathryn's salary, they are able to manage financially without any help from Darla.

When Kathryn began her separation phase from her mother in childhood, there wasn't anyone there. Even taking the minor aspects into account, she encountered Uranus and Neptune by sesquiquadrate. She did not have a positive solar model for that Pisces Sun. At the time that Kathryn was born, Joseph was nearing the advanced stages of alcoholism. His behavior was quite erratic and if he was available, he was ill. It was easier for Kathryn to run back to Darla (Moon in Gemini trine Mercury trine Neptune sextile Pluto) with that promise of having a rudder for her ship. Though the cost was high—lack of opportunity to become a confident self—it was a way to survive. Kathryn recalls that Joseph would come home from the bar very drunk and call her names, and even go so far as saying that he wished she would have died at birth. When she was twenty-four and living at home with her son, Joseph, while drunk, asked her to have sex with him. Terrified, she waited for him to pass out and ran to a sister's house. After that she was never alone with him, but kept wishing for him to die. One year later, he did die. Kathryn's reaction: "I did not cry for him. I felt very calm and relieved that he was gone. I guess it's kind of sad, but to this day I feel the same about him. Dad was dad. He was just there like a lamp would be. He was an object. The only thing I learned from him is that it doesn't pay to drink like a fish."

But what we're realizing today is that we do indeed learn a lot more from our fathers than was ever realized. This family of sisters, each appearing so different on the surface, have a family myth to contend with, and the pattern becomes clear upon further investigation.

Their father didn't share himself with them. As you read about each of the women, it could appear that the focus was on the mother and what she would and would not allow. Indeed, she is a powerful figure. However, Joseph's absence has spoken loudly in his daughters' lives in a much more powerful way. Blame is wasted here and would keep one from becoming empowered. They each have to contend with issues of sharing, dependency, and finance. We are addressing here their Taurus-Scorpio, Second–Eighth House issues that each sister took into relationships. Each is learning that until she takes responsibility for her own issues, she cannot break away.

The aspects to the Sun show the gifts from the father, and the active development of those areas are the work they, and all women, must undertake if we are to become whole. The rest of the horoscope shows how this effort will be supported. It is a lifetime journey.

The examples here highlight the end of a continuum of the daughter-father relationships in which the relationships are distant. The continuum includes healthy relationships near the middle and relationships that are too close at the opposite pole. Father was the one they should have been able to turn to so that they could each begin the separation process allowing them to develop into their own persons. We must each also be able to separate from father and ultimately begin the process of integrating the masculine and feminine, mother and father within. Basically, the Sun's placement and aspects have everything to do with our successful relationship with the principle of selfhood, starting with how we first perceived this principle being enacted by our fathering parent, to how we cope with it ourselves. On a deeper level, the Sun is also the archetype for the process of self-unfolding—becoming who we truly are. The Sun symbolizes both the father and the child, that within us that is in the act of becoming by creating itself out of its own experiences.

NOTES:

1. L. Greene and H. Sasportas. *The Luminaries: The Psychology of the Sun and Moon in the Horoscope* (York Beach, ME: Samuel Weiser, 1992).

2. All charts have been calculated with data as it appears on the birth certificate.

Barbara Schermer

Megan Wells

Barbara Schermer has maintained a vigorous astrological practice in Chicago since 1974. A pioneer in the field of experiential astrology and author of *Astrology Alive!* (Harper-Collins, 1989) as well as many articles, Barbara passionately advocates an astrology that places Soul instead of prediction at the center of its inquiry. Her work integrates astrology with Jungian and archetypal psychology, mythology, Kriya yoga, alchemy, and the arts. She is known for her psychological, enthusiastic, and "hands-on" teaching style.

Her passions for the last four years have included the facilitation of women's groups on Love and Sexuality, and co-leads (with Jungian Analyst John Giannini) Dream and Astrology groups.

Megan Wells is a professional storyteller, writer, theater artist, and coach. Her repertoire includes original stories and story dramas, Greek, Nordic, Native American myths and legends, as well as many classic short stories. Her original story, "Thom's Dream," appears in *A Loving Testimony: Remembering Loved Ones Lost to AIDS*, published by The Crossing Press.

Barbara Schermer

Psyche's Tasks: A Path of Initiation for Women

**WITH A RE-TELLING OF THE
STORY OF PSYCHE AND EROS
by Megan Wells**

At some time in our lives, we all have been seized by love. In that moment the great hand of Eros (limb-loosener, Sappho calls him), falls heavily on our shoulder, and, weak-kneed, we feel a breath at our backs that we know at once could blow us about like a great shattering storm. Listen to what Dante wrote after he caught sight, for the first time across the Piazza in Florence, of his Beatrice: "Ah that moment, I say the spirit of life, which hath its dwelling in the secretest chamber of my heart, began to tremble so violently that the least pulses of my body shook; and in trembling it said these words: Here is a deity stronger than I; who, coming, shall rule over me." (*Vita Nuova II.*) From then on Dante was a lifelong devotee of this goddess, dedicated to love, imagination, and poetic beauty, all three reflections of his *anima*, to use Jung's term—his internal feminine soul figure.

But Dante and his Beatrice give us an image of love in a *man*—indeed an impossible love, which transforms the soul of the man through an encounter with the feminine (and led to perhaps the greatest single literary work of all time, the *Divine Comedy*). But what are images of love, possible and impossible, for a *woman*, and how is love the source of *her* transformation? Sadly, many of these images continue to imprison women in an inner chamber of the patriarch's castle. One such image is of the "Knight in Shining Armor," who will gallop up on his white stallion, honorable of word and deed, will sweep us up to a place far above the pain of living, rescuing us from all wound and sorrow, bring meaning and security into our lives, love us, cherish us, etc., etc. What women have told me in my twenty years as a counseling astrologer bears out that many women are still waiting, weary and wounded by knightly encounters of less than noble outcome.

"Prince Charming" is a variant on this theme. Cinderella gets her Prince—by being a "good girl," not to mention pretty and appropriately humble—but her Fairy Godmother does seem to make her Queen for a Day without any real effort or self-development on her part. Yet love, as we know, makes demands, and we must meet those demands with the kind of courage and effort that make soul, else we will end up like Echo in the Greek myth, whose impossible love for the beautiful Narcissus left her with no more than a voice that resounded with her emptiness.

Joan Didion has said that "the lives we live depend on the stories we tell." If so, then it has become apparent that we need new stories—new myths—for both men and women, through which we can envision and enact new ways of loving. Or perhaps we need to rediscover the old stories, as many feminist scholars have begun to in regard to the Goddess, and retell them with a new understanding of their truth and beauty. "Psyche and Eros " is such an old, true, and beautiful story, and one that is nearly universal in its many forms—versions of it are to be found in Russia, Spain, Germany, Italy, India, and Africa. I believe that it is a story that can teach us what we urgently need to know and that it provides a mythic structure within which we may discover love as a path of initiation for women.

An astrological perspective allows us to see that the quest for divine love, which the Psyche-Eros tale eloquently portrays, should be a compelling theme for most women reading this book, especially for those born between 1942 and 1972, which includes the huge "Baby Boom" generation (1946–1957). Those of us born October, 1942 to July, 1957 have Neptune in Libra, and, along with the younger Pluto in Libra group (October 1971 to August, 1984), we are the women who came into the world with the inherent urge to idealize and to lose ourselves in "the other," transcending the boundaries of our isolated egos through partnerships. On the other hand, those born with Neptune in Scorpio (August 1957 to November 1970), as well as Pluto in Virgo (October 1956 to July 1972), are the generation with the natural urge to lose ourselves in sexual experience and fantasy, searching for a sacred sexuality that also transcends ego. Though the means may be different, the image of a self-transforming love is a pole star for many in these groups.

If astrology points to one source of the current appeal of the Psyche-Eros story, psychology has sought to understand its eternal worth. Jungian psychologists in particular have analyzed the fable, notably Eric Neumann (1956) in his *Amor and Psyche: A Commentary on the Tales of Apuleius*[1] and Robert Johnson in *She*[2]—both of whom examine female psychology—and Marie Louise von Franz[3] (1980) in *The Golden Ass of Apuleius*, who describes male *anima* development. James Hillman's essays in *The Myth of Analysis*[4] use the story in an exploration of the soul's essential creativity.

In this chapter, I will draw from these sources, among others, but will emphasize the nature of the Four Great Tasks that Aphrodite required of Psyche as penance for her presumed arrogance and a prerequisite for her reunion with Love. Thus we will begin to understand the tasks as a process, for women, of *initiation* through the encounter with love. Further, we will examine the underlying structure of the tasks as an initiatory path and will discover a parallel to the symbolic meaning of the Four Elements in our astrological charts—with their close relationship to the yearly vegetative cycle of the four seasons. To make these relationships clear, we will attend to a new telling of the Psyche-Eros story which illuminates just these themes. Before recounting the tale and turning to the tasks, however, let's tend to some preliminaries: What are the origins of the story? What is its cast of characters, and what are they about?

Psyche-Eros: Origins of the Tale

Though it had been around as a folk tale for centuries, the Psyche-Eros story made its grand entrance into Western consciousness in about 170 A.D.[5] in Apuleius' *The Golden Ass*, surely one of our all-time great works of imaginative prose. Besides being an uproariously funny read, *The Golden Ass* is also a sacred text and an energetic piece of propaganda for the Goddess. It is a supremely psychological yarn. Lucius, the young protagonist, is fascinated by the possibilities of magic— particularly erotic magic. To satisfy this craving he sets out on a quest which soon becomes an odyssey of misfortunes that by no means ends when he is turned into an ass! His struggles are great, his agonies many, until at last he eats the rose petals of the Goddess and regains his human form, apparently having been all along drawn in by the Goddess toward his life's true purpose, his sacred calling to serve Her. Throughout, we are regaled by tales told, at one turn ribald, the next refined, with Psyche-Eros as the centerpiece of the account, and the axis on which it turns.

The appearance of Psyche-Eros in *The Golden Ass* was contemporaneous with the spread of Christianity, when many and various sects were vying for the spiritual allegiance of the citizens of the Roman Empire. Thus it is possible to see its mythos as one of *two* great transformation stories embedded in Western culture. Both teach us about love, suffering, redemption. The first is the heroic masculine story of the divine Christ who takes on the form of the mortal Jesus to save mankind through love and sacrifice. The second gives us a glimpse of the heroic Feminine as the mortal Psyche, who transforms through love to become a Goddess—perhaps showing us the way? Whatever their value, of course, patriarchal ascendance banished all such feminine narratives to the margins of cultural concern.

According to von Franz,[6] it would be nearly eleven hundred years before the heroic myth of feminine love would so strongly emerge again—in the traditions of the *Minnedienst*, the wandering minstrels of the Middle Ages who traveled from court to court finding shelter with other lovers of verse and song. They gave a lyric voice to the experience of love, writing in the vernacular so that all could receive the teaching, and created an environment that exalted love as a theory and an ideal. For the minstrel, the *troubador*, true love was *fin amor* or fine love that "carries a medicine intended to heal his companion."[7] The object of his affections was inevitably a fine lady, very much married, but still available to be swept up by his beguiling words, by a sort of divine seizure at recognizing her soul's counterpart—and also to be left yearning at the poet's inevitable departure. Mythologist Joseph Campbell speaks of the troubador tradition as the birth of the Western ideal of love, for it brought forth a new way of experiencing love, a person to person relationship and not one arranged by either Church or parents.[8] Perhaps, but anthropologists have found that something very like romantic love has existed in most cultures and throughout history: "In fact, in a survey of 168 cultures, anthropologists

William Jankoviak and Edward Fisher were able to find direct evidence for the existence of romantic love in eighty-seven percent of these vastly different peoples."[9] Troubadour love seems to be a form of feminine love-myth that is much entangled with Patriarchal elements—the likely birthplace of our "Prince Charming."

If Marie-Louise von Franz is correct, we have only just now arrived at a point in history where the Daimon Psyche with her butterfly wings can again draw near us. And it is up to us women who tell our stories of various sorts to bring her forth in her best expression yet. Psyche's story is crucial for women today (whether straight or lesbian, I believe) for *it revives the heroine's story*—giving us a female protagonist, a mortal woman who is transformed into an immortal goddess, not by whim but by her own supreme efforts wed to the grace of creation. In the doing, she also brings about the transformation—at least the maturation—of the God who will continue to govern love.

Cast of Characters

Eros

Eros is, simply, Love—but to say that is to say nothing simple at all! First of all, Eros is one of those gods with more than one birth time and more than one set of parents, which is always a clue that we are dealing with an especially powerful deity. Hesiod first introduces Eros personified as one of the earliest gods. This Eros is sprung from Chaos itself along with Erebus and Night, Tartarus and Gea—thus he is the primal force that makes life possible, the creator of every connection and the precursor of every birth. Sappho, in the seventh century B.C., evokes him: "Eros once again limb-loosener whirls me sweetbitter, impossible to fight off, creature stealing up."[10] Joseph Campbell describes this Eros as the god behind our erotic biological urge and our "zeal of the organs for each other."[11] It is Eros in the form of desire that is the great mediating Daimon, *the impetus and the transforming agent of our soul.* Eros is a force outside ourselves that comes into our lives unexpectedly and unannounced. As James Hillman says, "Eros is never something we have; it has us."[12] You and I may be seized by the God just as Psyche is in our story:

> *Fierce and wild and of the dragon breed*
> *He swoops down all conquering, born on airy wing,*
> *With fire and sword he makes his harvesting;*
> *Trembles before him Jove, whom gods do dread,*
> *And quakes the darksome river of the dead.*[13]

The later Eros is the son of Aphrodite and Ares (some sources say Hermes, others Zeus). He seems to match up best with the images of the beautiful, but mischievous, winged boy that artists since the Hellenic period have shown slinging barbed arrows and causing havoc among unlikely lovers. As the Roman Cupid he is sometimes still handsome and athletic, sometimes reduced to the cherubic "Valentine" mischief-maker. Either way he appears whenever a myth is about love or seduction. In Apuleius, he is by turns young and beautiful, but also mighty and fearsome, and as we shall see, by story's end he has achieved a manly maturity.

In Plato and subsequent philosophers, Eros is a god on his way to becoming an abstract principle; in Freud eros loses his capital personhood, but is still fundamentally important—as a biological-psychological instinct. However we imagine him, love is above all an *experience*, so that poetic language about barbed arrows, piercings and woundings, deep-wild, instinctual-passionate, agony-ecstasy speak about Him best.

Psyche

Now, who is Psyche? She'll reveal herself in story form shortly. For now, let's simply say that the word "psyche" in Greek means "soul"—the animating force in all that lives, and the seat of consciousness. In early antiquity, one could not say "psyche"—soul—without also calling up a "butterfly," another meaning for the word. Later Psyche was personified as a mortal woman. A link between Psyche and Eros was suggested by Plato in his *Phaedrus* with his depiction of Love as the driver of "the chariot of souls," and the two are linked in Hellenic sculptures as well as an abundance of paintings and poems since.[14] Psyche's greatest role, however, is with Eros in the love story told below.

Aphrodite

In Apuleius, she appears under her Roman name *Venus*, but we shall refer to her by the older, revered name she got as the one who was "foam-born" from the sea where the genitals of the castrated Ouranos were cast. In that incarnation she is *the* Goddess, with prehistoric roots in Asia. She comes (through Plato, probably) to later antiquity and beyond as a duality: Aphrodite Urania, the "Heavenly," or Pandemos, the "Popular," suggesting her grittier, more sensual attributes. Sensual, lusty, even rapacious she could be—witness her many sexual encounters though married to Hephaestus, and her frantic seduction of the reluctant Adonis. As will be made clear, Aphrodite's dedication to Love, Pleasure, and Beauty (by which names her attendants, the Graces, are often called) is only rivaled by her vanity.

The Others

These characters will be joined by others whose appearances will be minimal, if not their personages. Zeus, the "Big Boss" of Olympus will be called upon to administer justice and to send a much needed Eagle helper. Persephone, the goddess of the Underworld, will make an appearance, as do Zephyr, the West Wind, and Charon, the creepy ferryman to Hades' realm, a sorry pair of sisters, and various ants, whispering reeds, and ferocious Marsian rams.

Soon I'll turn you over to my friend, Megan Wells, a gifted writer and story-teller, whom I've asked to tell you Psyche's tale. Megan and I have engaged in a year-long conversation about Psyche and Eros. We've shared our own stories of the rose-covered, thorn-guarded paths of love, and we have each come to our own way of teaching love's lessons—hers through performing and writing the story of Psyche and Eros; mine through trying to explicate its meaning in terms of psychology and astrology. She will tell the tale. I will amplify. You the reader will, I hope, find something here that resonates in your own soul and make it part of your own heroic quest to become a whole, conscious, and loving woman. As you read, you may wish to engage the story on three levels:

1. As an enjoyable tale of love and conflict, interesting in its own terms.

2. As a depiction of the typical stages of any love affair.

3. As a model for the transformational encounter of love and consciousness over the life cycle.

Psyche's Journey

It all began the spring my body betrayed me and the world went mad. A lead heavy sap filled my body, sprouting sore breasts until spilling forth, at last, into my first cycle of blood. My sisters taught me the rituals and decorating me with garlands of fragrant flowers, announced, "Psyche! We will celebrate your blossoming at the Spring Festival!"

But the festival betrayed me too. A fawning crowd gathered around me igniting my sister's jealousy. As the exaltations grew my sisters abandoned me. The swooning mob tore the garland from my neck, pulling at my garments crying *"Behold, the second coming of Aphrodite!"* Oh horrible blasphemy, they compared me to Aphrodite, the Goddess of Love and Beauty!

Spring ripened into summer as petitioners besieged our father's castle. I feared Aphrodite's wrath and rightly so, for though love smiled and brought husbands to my sisters, no suitor ever came for me. When my father traveled to seek the wisdom of the Oracle of Apollo, the oracle confirmed this punishment for my vanity. And more, on the first full moon of harvest, I was to be sacrificed to the monstrous snake-like demon of the land!

We walked the long path of the mountain together, my parents and I. Their tears fell with the leaves upon the autumn ground as I gave them what little comfort I could, "Sweet my parents, I am content. Death is the bridegroom I have long wished for."

But, I did not die! Zephyr, the west wind, carried me gently down the mountaintop and placed me on the steps of a wondrous palace. Three invisible spirit voices welcomed me as mistress to this enchantment. They enveloped me in their care, feeding me, bathing me, and assuring me that my new husband was indeed no monster!

The Psyche we are given here is the naive psyche, the consciousness that is untouched by the complexities engendered by an encounter with love—or any of life's challenges. She is a thing of beauty, but the beauty is the "skin deep" kind our mothers warned us about. She is innocent, but condemned to punishment for just being beautiful. Why? To teach us that beauty without consciousness is itself a danger, one must suppose. And to prepare us for the greater teaching that consciousness requires a tempering through love before beauty can be complete. This Psyche, though beautiful, is also passive, shallow—even vapid—and utterly without vision or purpose.

Thus she is fair game for any monster that comes along, and she makes no strong protest when pointed toward that fate.

I suspect that many of you, like myself, can remember such a state of ingenuousness, and maybe can recall a monster or two as well. Is the Other a god or a beast? Like Psyche, we must know, but the knowing is fraught with peril.

> I remember . . . that first night . . . the soft sound of the velvet bed curtains as he parted them. I feigned sleep. I remember . . . the silk sheets sliding slowly down my naked body. I . . . I remember . . . I remember his hands . . . so cold at first . . .
>
> But in the morning my new husband was gone. The spirit sisters comforted me, "Do not despair, Mistress, he will come again in the dark of the night."
>
> The second night, I pinched myself to stay awake. I heard his footsteps and reached to part the curtains but he stopped me, "Extinguish the lamp before I enter." I entreated why. "I cannot bear to love you in the light." I blew out the lamp and my husband entered again through the dark, rocking my fears to sleep in the cradle of his body.
>
> And so it was, the voices cared for me by day, for my husband only came at night. Until my sisters arrived! They came at last from their distant kingdoms to the mountaintop to mourn my death!

Ah, first love—and all loves are first loves in the beginning—when bliss carries us like a great wave, when the Other is at once both perfectly known and perfectly mysterious. We yield, we dissolve, merge, and gain a glimpse of the infinite and the eternal. But, time passes and mysteries beget inquiries. Voices always whisper. The sisters always come.

> At first my husband refused. "Forget them, Psyche. The world must think you dead, or we are lost." But at last I persuaded him. He warned me, "They will beg you to discover my identity. And if you do, I swear that I will leave you." I assured him, "I swear upon Eros, God of Love himself, that I will not!"

In the morning, Zephyr brought my sisters. Beg me they did. "Sister," they said, "Your husband deceives you. What horror can he be hiding?" I confessed that truly I did not know why he was so loathe to be seen. "It is your lust that makes you blind. The beast takes manly form to pleasure you and keep you enchanted. When you are fat with child he will devour you both." Then placing a dagger in my left hand, "When you know he sleeps, re-light the lamp and restore your sight. This dagger will restore your freedom."

I feigned gratitude to my sisters. I filled their arms with jewels. I called upon Zephyr and sent them away. But their words . . . I could not send away. "What horror can he be hiding?"

That night I followed their advice. My fears like wild horses, my heart unseated in its saddle, I held the knife in my right hand, the lantern in my left. With all the courage I could muster, I raised the light to at long last behold . . . my husband . . .

My starving eyes feasted upon his form, his smooth flesh, the curve of his jaw, the thick curls upon his handsome brow. Gossamer wings sprouted from his shoulder blades! The betraying lantern illuminated, the God of Love himself! Eros, upon whose very name I had placed my vow!

My guilty hands began to shake spilling hot oil from the lamp upon his shoulder. He awoke violently, "There can be no true love where there is no trust," After an excruciating silence, he reached for his bow and quiver. I lunged to stop him and wounded my hand upon an arrow. Oh misery, I fell in love with him the moment he flew away.

Betrayal. Remorse. Anguish. Has any great love eluded these voracious three? Love as it is experienced at first flush, as the manifestation of the God, *is* too good to be true, too much for a mere human to contain. Betrayal is not only human and inevitable, but as James Hillman has shown us, it is also *necessary*: "Neither trust nor forgiveness could be fully realized without betrayal."[15] And trust and forgiveness, which are mastered only through experience, are prerequisite for any enduring human relationship, any mature consciousness.

Everything vanished with him. My fresh wound tortured me with fevers. I wandered away into the valley, for I know not how many days, searching in vain for my love, with nothing but images to feed my fever. Finally, I came upon an old shepherd tending his flock. His eyes were pools of kindness and into them I poured my heart.

Feeding me cheese and bread, he shared the town gossip. "Ahh . . . little Psyche, I fear to tell, Aphrodite has laid a price on your life. It was she, ya know, that ordered your death. And Eros, her own son, betrayed her to marry ya his ownself. He hides now, in his mother's palace, lickin' his wounded pride. You'd best go to Aphrodite yourself beggin' her mercy."

The shock of the news drove the fevered poison from my wounded hand. Eros betrayed his mother? For love of me? Oh my beloved Eros, how selfish I have been!

Kind Zephyr carried me to Aphrodite's palace. I found her in the garden. Her beauty filled me with awe and I was quite unable to speak. But she . . . roared at me, "USURPER!"

For hours, she berated me. When her rage subsided, I spoke: "Grand Goddess, I do not ask you to spare my life, for I see how my existence pains you. I ask only that you carry a message to Eros. Tell him, the feverish poison of his ill-fated arrow has run its course and still . . . still I love him."

Aphrodite spared me, "Do not flatter yourself. You are no equal to my son, only the poison of his deceitful arrows could have made him succumb to your counterfeit beauty. But your devotion, though misdirected, is refreshing. I have not heard the like for too many moons. I will put you to the test. We will see how deep is your devotion, how steadfast your love. Only then will I sing your song of affection to my son."

Anguish and Remorse seem most like visitors from the hellish Underworld, itself. Yet we have come to know from hero tales of all sorts that behind the shadowy torturers, beyond the flames and obscuring haze, there is always an invitation from the Divine. When Love is the heroic path, we may by courage and supreme effort at last discern its true maker—the Goddess Aphrodite. For if it is Eros that incites to love, who is its irresistible force, it is Aphrodite that is its immovable object, the One who demands that we learn love's requirements and disciplines before we are allowed to advance. Our poor dear Psyche has come to such a pass. She finds herself before the Great Goddess Herself. At the fateful moment when she lit the lamp Psyche set in motion the whole process of what is to follow. The die is cast, the challenge made, and we as witnesses can only fretfully stand by as she faces the consequences of her choice. She is to labor and to suffer, tending the seeds she has sown—but as we shall see, they are the seeds of her salvation.

It is the Swiss psychologist Adolph Guggenbühl-Craig who has shown us that "Marriage," indeed any committed, loving relationship, is "not for welfare, but for salvation."[16] The salvation he means is *individuation*, in Jung's terms the process by which we achieve a distinct and integrated "middle place" for the complex forces that operate on and through our lives. Individuation is, potentially, a spontaneous, natural movement within the psyche, a process of unfolding and maturing, the psychic parallel to the physical process of growth and aging. But individuation begins in dissatisfaction with things as they are or ought to be; it requires the making of a difference, a disturbance in the flow—an act of disobedience that carries us away from childlike fusion with the maternal-paternal matrix of identity. To make soul, individuation first makes trouble. The trouble on love's path may be seen as the demands of a deeper, more profound image of the feminine, a god/dess, or, in Jung's terms, an *archetype*—an innate form in consciousness through which great patterns of thought, image, and behavior may be drawn. Psyche, Eros, Aphrodite, and the rest may be seen as vehicles for the archetypes, but so may processes or qualities that have the required potency and depth. Thus we will examine the *tasks* that Aphrodite will soon pose for Psyche as archetypal tasks—demands that arise out of the elemental depths, indeed tasks that emerge from the Elements, as discovered by Empedocles and other early philosophers, and as revealed in the astrological chart. These tasks are: Sorting the Seeds, Gathering the Ram's Fleece, Collecting the Waters, and Retrieving Beauty's Potion.

Psyche's Tasks: An Astrological Interpretation

What are the connections between astrology and Psyche-Eros? Two seem obvious:

1. Each task can be directly related to the four Cardinal Points, the four points in space whose yearly intersection by the sun marks the beginning of each season. The elemental nature of Psyche's tasks appears to parallel that of the seasons in the northern hemisphere—Winter solstice (Earth), Spring equinox (Fire), Summer solstice (Water), to Fall equinox (Air). Thus the progression of the tasks appears, at least in part, to depict the yearly cycle of vegetative life on Mother Earth—the eternal succession of life, harvest, death, and renewal. (See Figure 1.)

2. The elements, of course, are represented in our horoscopes, and we may expect that the placement of planets in signs related to each element, and transits to them, will inform us as to our status regarding each of Psyche's tasks.

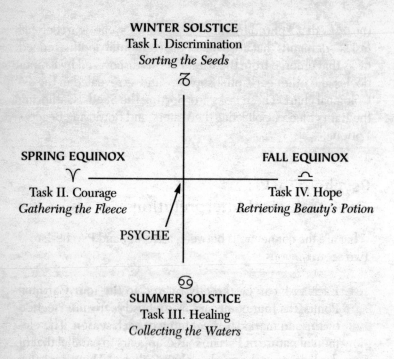

WINTER SOLSTICE
Task I. Discrimination
Sorting the Seeds
♑

SPRING EQUINOX   **FALL EQUINOX**
♈   ♎
Task II. Courage   Task IV. Hope
Gathering the Fleece   *Retrieving Beauty's Potion*

PSYCHE

♋
SUMMER SOLSTICE
Task III. Healing
Collecting the Waters

Figure 1.
Psyche's Tasks and the Cardinal Points

Table 1 relates Psyche's tasks to the seasons, signs, and elements and identifies the functions and processes they symbolize. We will explore these relationships in the next few paragraphs, emphasizing the guidance a knowledge of the horoscope can give in determining your own mastery of tasks that, from this point of view, are critical to a woman's erotic and spiritual development. (Don't worry if you are not an accomplished astrologer. Most of what I say will be easy to follow and to apply to your own life.)

TABLE 1. UNDERSTANDING PSYCHE'S TASKS

	Task	Function	Season	Sign	Element (Process)
I.	Sorting the Seeds	Discrimination and Grounding	Winter	Capricorn	Earth (Sensing)
II.	Gathering the Fleece	Courage and Passion	Spring	Aries	Fire (Initiating)
III.	Collecting the Waters	Healing and Intimacy	Summer	Cancer	Water (Restoring)
IV.	Retrieving Beauty's Potion	Detachment and Hope	Fall	Libra	Air (Imagining)

To discover which of these four tasks you are likely to have greater or less mastery of, study your horoscope, particularly the analysis of the *four elements*. You should determine the placement, by element, of the ten planets (plus your ascendant, if you have an accurate birth time), each of which represent a different psychic component within you—eleven factors sorted into four "categories" of elements. Frequently on computerized charts, which many of us have, you will find a breakdown of your planets by sign and element somewhere on the page. Following are some examples to give you the idea. Suppose for a moment that your planets (and ascendant) fall into signs with the following elemental energies:

Fire: 5   Earth: 0   Air: 4   Water: 2

You have a predominance of the element Fire, what we then might consider your "dominant function." You may find task two, the "Gathering of the Golden Fleece" to be most accessible (but, I would hasten to say, not without challenge). You have fiery energy in abundance and have it more accessible to you. Ideally you are learning the task—to find your courage, your passion, and your inspiration. With nearly as much of the element Air in your chart, you may also find task four, "Retrieving Beauty's Potion" to be quite open to you. With the element Air (mental energy) in abundance, you are able to learn it's task functions, detachment and hope, with some facility. The lower availability of Earth and Water point toward greater challenges. The total lack of Earth in the sample chart would suggest that its owner is least conscious of the "Sorting of Seeds" task, needing to become aware of and to learn discernment, pacing, developing a sense of patience, and focusing on what is at hand. And with the element of Water also in somewhat short supply, task three is the other key task for this chart. This is the task of "Collecting the Waters," mastering feelings and emotions.

Let me give another example: Perhaps you have a predominance of the element earth, for example:

Fire: 1   Earth: 7   Air: 2   Water: 2

Then you might be the opposite of the previous example. You might be over-involved with task one, the endless seed sorter, obsessed with analyzing, and you may need to break out of a cautious concern with details to work on task two—learning to *act*, and to find your initiative, courage, and passion.

Others of us have well-balanced charts, each element divided up equally:

Fire: 3   Earth: 3   Air: 2   Water: 3

Does this pattern mean that you are balanced and need to read no further? I'm afraid not, since each of these tasks are *potentials* for your self-development. Without the work you don't progress. Further, though with this alignment you might *find* your sense of inner balance and wholeness more easily, it might be harder to *keep*, since your attention is constantly being drawn to what is beginning to feel out of balance. In this instance there can be a sense of a constant internal juggling. Those of you with a more advanced understanding of astrology know that this is especially true of women who have a Cardinal T-square or Grand Cross in their chart.

We have kept the astrology simple so far. Advanced students are aware that the chart can shed much more light on these matters when more than the elements are considered and would also especially want to study Venus and Mars, their sign placement and aspects. Venus by sign, house, and aspect tells us about our powers of attraction, what we are drawn to in love. Mars in the various signs, houses, and aspects informs us about our power to initiate action and to act on our desires. If I haven't lost you so far, then you know enough to apply astrology to an understanding of Psyche's tasks, perhaps by examining aspects to other natal planets (i.e., if your natal Sun in Aries is opposite your Neptune in Libra trine your Pluto in Leo), you may find that you need to work on task two—seeking your Aries Sun and "your fiery sword," learning to stand up for yourself and to find expressive power through your trine to Pluto, also in a Fire sign.

Other clues as to what task your psyche might be involved with in a particular time period might come from following your transits (i.e., if transiting Saturn is conjuncting your Moon, you might need to be sorting your emotions, and you will probably feel more of the depressing, heavy ones. Nevertheless this transit can bring order to your emotions, and direct you to feel more grounded in both your outer life and/or your inner process. Or your strategy for dealing with your heavy emotions may be to focus on task two, giving yourself some fire by starting an exercise program, or otherwise getting yourself *moving*.

The transit of Saturn is a helpful indicator of tasks we are *collectively* challenged to master. From February, 1994 to March 1996, Saturn was in Pisces, requiring all of us to be diligent with task three, and drawing upon the watery depths for the energy to heal ourselves and others. From April 1996 to January 1999, Saturn is in Aries, and collectively we are involved in task two, bringing forward our creative and erotic energy, searching for what stirs our passion, and finding the courage to pursue it.

Now enough introduction and analysis. Together let's return to Psyche's story and see how she meets her challenge—and how we may understand her and ourselves in the symbolic languages of astrology and psychology.

Psyche's First Task

Sorting the Seeds

Aphrodite led me to a storage chamber. Once inside, she tore open bags of tiny seeds, barley, millet, poppy, and flinging the seeds wildly around the room, she commanded: "Now, my impersonator, you think that beauty is the power of a goddess? Let's see what beauty will do for you now! All these seeds must be retrieved and sorted. I will return in the morning to see it done." She locked the door behind. Overwhelmed with self-pity I sat staring at the seeds.

As the shadows marked the passing hours on the wall, memories appeared—pieces of my life unfolded in front of me, all a jumble, just like the seeds. I stared at the sea of seeds and memory. Slowly, the seeds began to move. And my memories too, parted and spread, magically sorting themselves. I saw the events of my life as I never had before, all the decisions I had passively given away. As the dawn light crept through the chamber window, both I and the seeds were newly sorted.

As Robert Graves[17] points out, in the *Metamorphosis*, Ovid's presentation of the creation myth, Earth is very nearly first in appearance: Nature emerged from Chaos and "separated earth from the heavens, the water from the earth, and the upper air from the lower. Having unraveled the elements, he set them in due order, as they are now found." Earth, then, is present at the very origins of separation and order, and thus guides Psyche's first task: the sorting, the separating, the ordering of *seeds*. Seeds, as a component of the psyche, are best seen here as *memories*. We are our memories, our history, and "Whoever does not know his own history is condemned to repeat it" is as true for individuals as for nations. Seed-sorting, as an act of Psyche, the Soul, consists of re-*collection*, re-*structuring*, and re-*visioning* of our past, our memories—the images which are the repositories of our experiences of life. It is, of course, possible to lead an unexamined life—Psyche in our story has apparently done so—but not with impunity. The earthy task of sorting our memories, especially our erotic memories, is a requirement for achievement of full feminine consciousness. Its goal is *discernment*, the heightened capacity to determine qualitative differences and to chose wisely among different options.

(Women with little Earth in your chart, listen up!) Seed-sorting begins with *recollection*, the conscious, intentional recalling of events and our feelings about them. Have you ever set about the full recollection and recording of your erotic life? If not, I urge you to do so. Begin with a chronology of every man (or woman) you have ever loved or made love to. Don't forget that boy who kissed you in first grade, or the way you used to curl up on Daddy's lap! Be specific; record as many details as possible. Memory may be dim of course—are there old letters? Photographs? Can you talk over old times with a friend or parent? You may wish to assemble a scrapbook of erotic memories. Mine has everything in it from a tiny cocktail dress worn by my Barbie Doll, to romantic letters from a French lover, to a photo of me and two friends with a nude exotic dancer from Forty-second Street—and a few things I'd tell you about in person but not in print! Savor these memories, draw them out, see whether they are a stimulus for pleasure in your current relationship. They are your achievement and your buried treasure—take them out and enjoy them.

Recollecting can be delicious fun, but it often is a serious, even painful exercise. Few of us have not been wounded by love, or perhaps by loveless sex. Memories may be hellish as well as heavenly. One fact has emerged from my own experience and that of other women: Good memories are often concealed behind disturbing ones. It is here that *restructuring* begins, an alchemical process that separates good memories from bad, experiencing and releasing the pain of recollection, and thus recovering gold from the leaden dross. It can be done alone or with a loving partner or friend, but some processes of recollection are so agonizing and difficult they are best done in psychotherapy. Even at that, I urge you not to neglect the recovery, the celebration, and the savoring of pleasant or even ecstatic moments from even the most problematic relationship.

As a restructuring exercise, I suggest that you *literally* sort seeds. Reflect on each loving or sexual encounter from your "chronology," above. Using "seeds"—black and white beans, place a white bean in a bowl for every pleasant memory, a black bean for every unpleasant one. Many women I've had try this exercise have been surprised to find they have sorted out enough to make a largely white bean soup!

Recollection and restructuring lead naturally to *revisioning*, the process by which we reorganize our recollected and restructured memories into new images and new stories with new possibilities of future action. Have we too often been a victim in our sexual encounters? Then we may need to cultivate a new vision of ourselves as empowered women. Have our wounds made us too timid about striving for what we really want in a relationship? Then we may need to author a new story of ourselves as fierce protagonists intent on success as lover and beloved. As an experiment, take pen and paper and write out a story that reflects the new you. Save it for contemplation, for embellishment—for revision.

Recollection, restructuring, and revisioning hardly exhaust the Earth task. In the earthly realm we are engaged in the process of *sensing*, of the basic encounter between Soul and matter, a process that comes to symbolic completion at 0°

Capricorn, the time for contemplative re-evaluation. It is a task that may require a sort of "ant-like" behavior—patient, methodical, with attention to day-to-day routines and deliberate effort (Earth as expressed through Virgo). Thus the Earth task directs us toward practical matters (Capricorn) and a focus on details (Virgo), but it also points toward the sensual appreciation of the body and of the pleasures the Soul may enjoy in its earthly incarnation (Taurus). Discernment—sorting—is still the key here, since on the one hand we may become too involved with matter (i.e., materialism), or too involved with sensation (vulgar sensuousness), or we may "spiritualize," all to the realm of airy intellect, losing the soulful middle ground, and thus missing the engagement with tastes, sounds, smells, and images—the pleasures that are the gift of the Earth to the Soul. If we do not receive the gift of pleasure from the world, we do not know beauty, and if we do not know beauty, we cannot encounter love. Psyche, as Soul, must sort out the gifts of the Earth, must examine them from a perspective grounded in a cultivated memory, and then may selectively embrace those that are appropriate to the task and to the moment.

At this point, you may want to have another look at your horoscope. This task may be most familiar to you who are "earthy" types, with many planets (especially Sun, Mars, or Venus) in Capricorn, Taurus, or Virgo—or with a well-aspected Saturn or Mercury. If not, this is a good place to start! The Earth task may be more of a challenge for impatient fiery types, dreamy water sign natives, or those whose strong preference for reasoning leaves them "up in the air." This work is perhaps best done when the transiting Moon is in Earth signs, when you have a good Saturn or Mercury transit, when the Sun is transiting the Earth signs, especially when at 0 degrees of Capricorn, the Winter solstice, the natural time of year to reflect and evaluate. But, whenever you engage this task, get grounded, learn discernment through recollection, restructuring, and revisioning, find the proper balance between body and spirit—and one of the four gates of the world of love will open to you.

Seed-sorting is a soul-making process, as are all of Psyche's tasks. Our story will return us to the soul-making possibilities of claiming our *passion*.

Psyche's Second Task

Gathering The Fleece

When Aphrodite found the task was done, she seized my arm, pulled me roughly from the storage chamber and led me out to the gardens of the palace. "So, at least you are clever. Do you think with cleverness you can tame the son of Ares, God of War? You know nothing of the wild and violent side of love. Across that brook live the fierce rams of the sun. Prove to me how mighty is your love." Unsheathing a golden dagger from her thigh, "Bring me the golden fleece from the belly of a male. My robe needs mending," then flung the dagger, impaling the ground between my feet.

When I reached the brook, I dropped exhausted at its edge. I stared at the dagger, imagining its sharp blade piercing my heart. But the swaying reeds whispered, "Even Ares, God of War, must have a time of peace. There is a twilight, when respite falls over all things. In that gentle moment, even the mouse may walk into the mouth of the lion." When I woke the sun had fallen and indeed all the rams were resting. Lying like babies around the brook their bellies exposed. I tied my skirts high and crossed over. Kneeling carefully at the side of a male ram, I shaved twelve curls from his underbelly.

The gathering of the golden fleece is Psyche's initiation by elemental Fire. Typically we think of the direct assertion of Fire as a masculine attribute—"Mars in Aries," but women are no longer quite so ready to concede that territory. Some women are stronger than some men. Women serve around the world as soldiers and fighter pilots. That said, there does seem to be a male disposition (genetic in origin?—testosterone enabled?) toward assertion and a female one toward receptivity, and it is the latter that Psyche must draw upon to collect the Golden fleece—in an interesting contrast to the Hero Jason, who needed a ship, a hoard of warrior Argonauts, and a magic shield to accomplish his masculine mission! Psyche achieves her goal through receptivity, by listening to the whispering reed, heeding the subtle prompting of Nature, perhaps attending to the wisdom of what we have known traditionally as women's "feminine" nature—but not by avoiding the necessity for *courage*. Even if her way avoids direct conflict, she must still take up the dagger and approach the source of her terror. Courage, by definition, is not fearlessness, but the willingness to advance even though shaking in one's sandals, as Psyche must have been. To do so she, and we, must achieve the self-confidence, the "Queenly" (the evidence is in that the *lioness*, who rules every pride and does most of the hunting, is the *real* King of the Jungle) mastery of ego that is the higher expression of Fire through Leo. We must show ourselves to be open, flexibly creative, *willing*, as Psyche has been to accept the friendly ministrations of the ants as well as the counsel of the reed—and the prompting of the wrathful Goddess: Fire as developed through Sagittarius.

As we have seen, Fire has many levels of expression in a woman's character, but we will occupy ourselves with the most basic one, the achievement of passion. The ram in Psyche's tale is of particular interest as one of nature's most obviously sexual creatures. The Spring equinox, 0° Aries (of course named for *the* ram) is the time when the ewes bear their lambs, a time that harkens back to Fall, when the mountains resounded with the clang of horn-on-horn as the male mountain sheep competed for the right of access to as many females as each could manage. I've not been fortunate enough to witness the sheep rut, but have seen one of their antlered cousins, a full-grown bull elk, in full possession of seven delicate females—an awesome sight—and a ranger friend told me of an even bigger bull he saw with a harem of forty-seven, who in five hours fended off eight rivals and mounted four of the females! The females themselves were hardly passive, forever drifting to the perimeter, seeming to invite competitors and to be quite choosy about the time and place to respond to the bull's attentions. Fire is about passion—*sexual* passion.

The Fire task requires a woman to come into her full power, especially her sexual power, possessing the Ram's fleece, the most dangerous part of solar consciousness, her raw instincts, and her own animal nature. Psyche learns to relate to the solar, hot masculine (Eros) energy within herself, having an experience of her own courage and her power of action, and in the process gets turned on, beginning to get in touch with her own erotic passions. Of course, for women in patriarchal culture, sexual passion, any sort of passion really, is problematic. Only Bad Girls have it, or women who are locked into a monogamous relationship with a man. *News Flash*: The patriarchy is crumbling like Ozymandias' statue, and women are seeking safe, responsible, but highly passionate ways of being in the world of love as well as the world of work. There are pioneer women out there making it easier for the rest of us, like sex educator Betty Dodson,[18] for example, whose workshops teach women to love their own bodies—especially the parts we rarely look at and *never* think of as beautiful. Or like Annie Sprinkle, teacher, performance artist, comic genius of sex instruction whose video tape[19] tells us all about the "Sluts and Goddesses" we each carry within us, not to mention showing us a seven-minute orgasm! My own series of "Women's Erotica Groups" has brought a number of women together to speak about the unspeakable, to share knowledge about love and sexuality, to learn spiritual-sexual techniques from the ancient Tantric disciplines, and to experiment with stretching beyond limits and overcoming inhibitions as well as healing from the injuries that relationship and sexual encounter always seem to engender.

Here are a few of the "stretches" I have used in my groups. I suggest you pick one or more that appeals to you—that scares you just enough but not too much—thus inviting your courage to become more passionate and more knowledgeable.

- Women are rarely aware that their external genitalia vary greatly from woman to woman, and are a place of secret beauty. Yes, yes, I know that we were taught not to look or touch "down there," but I encourage you to get a mirror and do just that. If you can get Betty Dodson's video or the (amazing) *Cunt Coloring Book*[20] be sure to do so for the purpose of comparison. Don't just take a peek, really take a close look. Note the subtle shadings of color and texture, see what her (yes, *her*) shape reminds you of— a robed figure? A goddess, even? If you're feeling a little braver, draw or paint her to the best of your ability, or write a detailed description of her many beauties. Braver yet, describe her, or even show her to a lover or spouse. Even more? Start your own Erotica Group? It's up to you!

- Especially if orgasms don't come easily to you, buy a vibrator. Such "massagers" are now readily available at the larger local drug stores, or from the Radio Shack™ outlet or catalog. Take the time to learn to use one, to take more and more responsibility for your own orgasms.

- If there is an "adult shop" nearby that is not too sleazy (yes, they vary), try a visit and see what sex toys, books, and videos might interest you. Take your husband or girl friend if you're just too shy.

- A risky one if you don't know your partner well or either of you is the overly jealous type: Tell your partner your sexual history, all those adventures from before you met. Sometimes this is a *great* turn-on, leading to other things.

◆ Take a new lover. . . .

Fire is not all about sex, of course, or even the warmer side of a loving relationship. Physical activity warms the blood for all creative concerns. So take the exercise class. Study Karate. Or try this experiment: Buy yourself a *sword*. Learn what it is about a weapon that always seemed to fascinate boys. Psyche must take Aphrodite's dagger and face the rams to find her courage. I've found that thrusting and parrying with the three-foot sword I got at a military supply store brings out my Fire. When I pick it up with one hand, the sword overmatches my strength and my whole arm sags trying to hold it, but when I use both my hands on the hilt, I am its match and can wield it with abandon. By experimenting with a weapon in hand, you may gain insight into destruction and protection, both attributes of Mars. You can thrust forward to (symbolically, of course) pierce and wound, or to bestow a blessing on the shoulder of a knight. With its precise and sharpened blade, it can ritually cut away "BS" or slice through confusion.

As the ancient alchemists knew, timing is important to the accomplishment of the Work. The prime time to initiate Fire tasks, then, is at the Spring equinox, 0° Aries, but things also go well when the transiting Sun or Moon are in Fire signs, or when you have a good Mars transit. We all have Fire in our makeup—it's the basic life energy that fires the neurons, drives the limbs, and pulses the blood through the body—but our charts, our personalities, and our life experiences all shape the way we seek passionate expression. So, check your Elements, your fiery signs and planets, and look to the transits for the best times to *light your fire*.

Psyche's Third Task

Collecting the Waters

I found Aphrodite in her bed chamber. At the shock of seeing me still alive she dropped a perfume vial, spilling luscious perfume onto the marble floor. "You survive well Psyche. I must know—are you merely a reflection? Can you see yourself? Without insight you can never love. Take this empty perfume vial and fill it with cool water from the mouth of the River Styx. If you can pass the sentinel dragons and withstand the cruel currents at the cave, I might be tempted to forgive you."

Three days I traveled. When I reached the river Styx, I collapsed against a cold boulder, shivering at the sight of the foul icy water, the treacherous whirlpools bringing fear and pestilence up from the underworld into this one. I saw the two dragons guarding the mouth of the river. They watched my every move, craning lizardlike heads from their scaly necks.

Only one jump, I thought to myself, one small leap into those waters and I am free. Slowly, I crept toward the edge. Suddenly an eagle appeared, swooping down and lighting upon the boulder. He spoke, "None may trespass the Stygian waters, without my knowing, for I am Zeus' eyes. Your willingness to descend into the dark waters of shadow is the only power you need to command these waters. I shall complete the task for you."

The royal bird spread his wings, seized the crystal vial in his razor talons and flew toward the dark cave. The dragons lunged at him in a furious dance. The eagle stopped mid-air, released a deafening screech and the dragons dropped their heads in obedience to Zeus's messenger. He filled the vial and delivered it to me.

"Water is the First Medicine," a Lakota medicine man once told me, "It heals everything." But Water as Healer, as our dreams so often inform us, requires that we plunge down, down into its cool depths in the unconscious. Water has moods, is wet and secret—it dissolves into nothingness and shimmers into vision. As an elemental task, Water draws us down a river to the edge of the Underworld, as it did Psyche. We can get lost there in the realm of feeling and illusion. We can fall in and "die," overpowered by the instincts. Without visiting that domain and accomplishing the Water task, we too are lost—we remain "shallow."

Water heals, *restores*, in part through demanding that we feel what we would rather not. Tears are the Soul's first medicine. Water as unconscious mind is always splashing up something in dreams, in memories, in symptoms and slips of the tongue to invite us into the painful depths beyond ego and personal history. If we accept the invitation, as Psyche did under protest, we will find monsters there and will need both discrimination and courage to acquire the healing liquid. As an aid to the task, we may do well to consider a depth psychotherapy, an experiential growth group, and intensive body-work or spiritual discipline if our work is to be found in the realm of Water. The journey leads through, not across, the water, toward a deeper capacity for compassion and intimacy. How we approach this task has much to do with our basic security issues derived from how we were mothered and nurtured as children, and how since then we have learned to mother and nurture ourselves and others. If we find Father issues when we confront the Fire task, we are sure to meet Mother here.

In the cycle of the seasons, Water begins the Summer as the Sun crosses 0° Cancer at the Summer solstice. Our bones begin to warm after Winter's chill. Our bodies unwind, our muscles become fluid, and our feelings flow outward to embrace an inviting world. Summer invites languorous days and "Midsummer Night's Dreams." It is in dreamwork, I believe, that we find the key to mastering the Water task, for dreams are the meeting of Cancer's feeling and intuition, Scorpio's instinctuality and intensity, and Pisces' vision and mystery. Dreamwork is the practical discipline I'll urge upon you with one simple suggestion: Begin to keep a dream journal. Place a pen and your diary on the night stand, and write before rising, write in the middle of the night, write "no dreams last night," if that's all you can, but *write something every day*, and review the journal often. Draw or sculpt the dream images. Spin them out into a story. Dialog with the characters. Relate the persons and objects to myth and symbol, but don't reduce them by interpretation. Read Jung and James Hillman to broaden your knowledge of dream processes. By this nightly dipping into the waters, you will soon feel the healing that the collective depths have to offer.

Example: I conduct dream groups with Jungian Analyst John Giannini, drawing on both psychological and astrological understandings. In one group a woman reports a recurring dream in which she finds herself on a path to a lake, by which there stands a terrifying shadowy figure. Each time she flees. "Next time, look him in the eye!" John says. Two weeks later the woman comes upon the dark man again, but this time she stares him down, then jumps into the lake from which she rises like "The Creature from the Black Lagoon," and devours the man! In the weeks to follow, the man is gone from her dreams and a long-standing depression seems to lighten.

Psyche's benefactor, the Eagle, gives us a clue about how to deal with dreams and other manifestations of the watery unconscious. A visitor from the Air realm, he is the messenger (like Mercury/Hermes, ruler of Gemini) for Zeus; his vision is from the highest perspective (Aquarius), and his function is to establish the balance (Libra) of conscious and unconscious process in an integrated whole, as Jung has taught us is essential to a life well lived. Air joined to Water forms the stuff of Spirit—the lasting gift of Water work well done, and the spiritual transformation of the base impulses of a primitive Eros begin here.

Of the many rewards of Water work, I will mention three. Each may be sought in youth, but most only find fulfillment in mid-life. First is an achievement of a certain richness and complexity in one's character, a broadening and deepening of perspective that provides not only a basis for tolerance, but for empathy, for compassion. This is work that makes marriage, or any long-term relationship, possible. An essential component of the "relationship as salvation" referred to above, it invites meaning in even the more brief or casual of human contacts. It enlarges the cup that holds Love's potion. Second, Water work washes away the psychic debris that obscures our awareness and encumbers our freedom to act and to create. It is "individuating" and thus empowers our ability to stand apart from our beloved enough to see them as they are, to allow them their freedom as well as our own, and to hold the ground between the twin terrors of abandonment and engulfment that are the scourge of any intimate endeavor. Finally, the gifts of the spirit seem only to rest easily in those who find the underwater passage to the inner chamber of the Temple of Self-Knowledge. Without it we may have a full Spirit, but an empty Soul—no better than the "Realized Masters" who can't keep their hands off the chelas. With it, we can navigate upstream from the Underworld, seeking the Source among the high mountain peaks.

Do this work if Water predominates in your chart, or you have strong aspects involving planets in Cancer, Scorpio, or Pisces, or prominent Moon, Neptune, or Pluto configurations. This task is a greater challenge for you who are unreflective fiery types, "stuck in the mud" earthy types or, "emotions are unreasonable" airy types. How have you navigated through the stormy waters of the past eleven years (Fall of 1984 through November of 1995), with Pluto transiting Scorpio? You may need a bit of healing. Dip into the Water. Drink deeply.

Psyche's Fourth Task

Retrieving Beauty's Potion

Stars covered the night sky when I returned to the palace. Aphrodite was sitting on the steps waiting, "Ah! You've enchanted Zeus too? Good. That is good!" Then taking my hands in hers she scrutinized them as though the fate of the universe rested upon what she found. At last, she seemed satisfied. Tipping the vial on her finger, three times she placed a drop upon my forehead, "I must anoint you for the final task."

I protested, "Aphrodite, you said you would forgive me. I beg you, try me no more. Deliver my message to Eros."

"It is because I have forgiven you that there is yet one more task. Come foundling, there is little time and so much left to be done!" She led me up a spiral stairway to a secret tower chamber. When my eyes adjusted to the dark, I saw that the moonlight traced a pattern upon the marble floor. Aphrodite walked to the center of the pattern and lifting a round tile retrieved an exquisite little box inlaid with shells and precious stones. "Psyche, there is a mystery which has long waited your arrival." Then raising the box over her head Aphrodite filled the tower with her voice, "BLESS THE ONE WHO COMES TO BRING THE TWO TO THREE!"

Then she handed me the box, lowering her voice again, "In the morning, Psyche, you will face your life's most dangerous journey. I must send you to Persephone, Queen of the Underworld. At the entrance to the underworld, open this box and listen carefully to all its instructions. Then close the box and do not open it again. Listen to your deep heart Psyche. It alone will tell you what to do. One thing above all to remember, Psyche, DO NOT RE-OPEN THE BOX."

In the morning, Aphrodite's attendants left me at the entrance to Pluto's dark kingdom. The hot breath from the tunnel made steam in the crisp air. I opened the box and listened. I removed four objects, placing two gold coins in my mouth and two honey-barley cakes, one in each hand. I took a deep breath, closed the box and stepped into the dreary passageway.

Deep in the tunnel, I came upon the old shepherd! He was lost and begged me for directions. I started to speak, but nearly lost the coins from my mouth. My heart was loud, "Do not cripple him with your pity. He must find his own way." I closed my eyes to his pain and walked on in silence.

When I reached the banks of the dark River Styx, Charon the ferryman grumbled for his coin. I lifted my hand, nearly losing a barley cake. Instead, I gestured for Charon to retrieve the coin himself.

Rotting corpses clawed the ferry on all sides. "Psyche help us. . . ." My heart spoke again, "They wish to suck your life. Touch them and you will never escape to see your love again."

At the gate to Pluto's palace, Cerberus, the vicious dog demon stood snarling. I threw one cake. The ravenous beast gave it chase. Inside, Persephone greeted me with fine pillows and cake but my heart bade me refuse both. When the box had exchanged hands, Persephone confided, "Only Death knows the secret to eternal beauty, and the elixir I have placed in this box carries that mystery. Tell my sister Aphrodite how deeply honored I am to share my art in exchange for hers."

I seized the box and retraced my steps, using my last barley cake and coin. With the little strength I had left, I climbed up from the tunnel, then fell exhausted against the trunk of an ancient oak tree. My lungs cried with joy to breathe the sweet air of the earth again!

The box caught my eye . . . the exquisite enchanting box . . . the forbidden little box pulled me close to hear a whispery small chant, "What must be done, shall be done . . . Psyche shall open the box. What must be done shall be done . . . Psyche must open the box."

And I did. I . . . Psyche . . . opened . . . the . . . box.

A foul thick vapor crawled out of the box, spiraled around me paralyzing me within it's encasing grip. I tried to scream, but alas, no sound issued forth.

And then suddenly, Eros was at my side. I saw him scoop

me in his arms, though I could not feel his touch. He covered my mouth with his but his warm breath could not penetrate the invisible casing. I heard him cry, "MIGHTY ZEUS! HELP ME!" And then I fell into a dark dream and could not wake, until . . .

Beauty is Woman's most equivocal endowment. Too little beauty and we suffer self-hatred and are disadvantaged in the politics and economics of patriarchal culture; too much beauty—especially too soon—and we often attract so much male pursuit we scarce have room to breathe and to grow, and we may be blinded to our other potentials. Beauty will serve, but to do so, She must be mastered and Her essentially mysterious nature penetrated. It is her beauty that gets Psyche in trouble in the first place, revealing the truth that Beauty assaults us if we dwell too much on Her, or too little. Women spend billions of dollars a year on beauty care and fashion—a case can be made for dwelling too much. Yet so often we fail to appreciate, to understand, to master the beauty that each of us has as our birthright. Psyche's fourth task is concerned with discovering beauty in its essence—a task which demands a momentous confrontation.

"Only Death knows the secret to eternal beauty." An awful truth resounds in Persephone's words. Her message is as simple as it is devastating: Some portion of beauty belongs, irrevocably, to youth. That form of beauty will at last leave us, and we will experience the leavetaking as a kind of death. Some of you readers are so young as still to experience your youthful beauty as eternal. Some are more like me, at the threshold where the skin is changing in ways creams won't conquer, and gravity shows signs of winning over grace. I have shed enough tears over the loss that Psyche's final lesson has become clear to me: Our beauty must die, so that Beauty may be born!

I do not mean to say that beauty with the small "b" is of little consequence, nor that, young or old, we should abandon its enjoyment. On the contrary, buy the dress! Wear the perfume! Find (or educate) the partner who will see your beauty and reflect it back to you! Celebrate your beauty and embrace the same in others! Yet, oddly, it may only be when we reach an age at which beauty is fading and when we have been diligent in our work on Earth, Fire, and Water that we can truly appreciate beauty. Before that, the love of one's own beauty may be no more than narcissism, where love indeed becomes a potion, an intoxicant with fateful side-effects. But a mature, cultivated self-admiration—self-love—leads first to love of others and then to higher ends. To separate the false beauty from the true requires discrimination, to bring out beauty's full potential demands passion, and to find the truth in "Beauty is only skin-deep" requires a knowledge of the heart and soul that lie deep beneath the surface. The fourth task reveals a truth that was known by philosophers from Socrates to the Neoplatonics to Ficino: Through Beauty we approach Divinity. The *beautiful*, which to the Greeks was synonymous with the *excellent*, the *perfect*, the *satisfying*[21] is our best teacher about the highest states to which the Soul may aspire.

As to the season, we are in the Fall, the paradoxical time when Nature shouts to us of the abundance of her harvest—and speaks in a dry, leafy whisper that prefigures the howl of Winter winds. The Fall equinox, launched at 0 degrees of Libra, the Cardinal Air sign, marks the exact moment at which Persephone was herself first dragged down to the Underworld, and the day she must make her annual return. Psyche's final task begins that day, with her own descent. Our own final task begins in that season, with elemental Air as its overseer. Especially in late mid-life our challenge is to know ourselves as beautiful even as we come to realize that we are now "fair" rather more in the modern sense than in the older meaning of the term. We cannot manage this without feelings, of course—denial, depression, anger (in our story, even the Goddess succumbs to rageful jealousy at the beauty of the young usurper) and the bargaining and, finally, acceptance that follows. All our work on prior tasks will stand us in good stead here, but let's not mince words; what peace we achieve in transcending the loss of mere beauty is preparation for that final privation, death itself.

But, enough whining. There is so much life to be lived through the season of Air, so many blessings to be counted. We have the blessings of Gemini—not only are we in full grasp of our mental faculties in this time, but we have enough of a basis of experience to sometimes manage even to be wise. We count the blessings of Aquarius—we are often the true changemakers and pursuers of humanitarian aims (especially if the kids are finally on their own). We are rewarded with the blessings of Libra, with harmony in relationship within our grasp, and a balance of needs and satisfactions available, if we but apply what we have come to know. Yes, we must cultivate detachment, but that is well within our means and has predictable rewards.

But is this enough? Note that it was not enough for Psyche. Even with all warnings to the contrary, she still yearned for beauty—*she opened the box*. Death was the inevitable consequence, and I would offer that we must all continue to strive for beauty; no matter what the consequences, we must *all* open the mysterious box, for we must have Beauty. As James Hillman has said, "Our soul is born in beauty and feeds on beauty, requires beauty for its life."[22] At any age we must make a study of Beauty, and her Graceful companions, Pleasure and Delight. In practical terms, the principle tool for such a study is the *disciplined imagination*, the Air's magical method. Throughout this chapter I have spoken of the various ways in which the mind uses its image-making capacity: Sensing and memory for the Earth, re-visioning one's sexual self beyond the constraints of patriarchal culture for the Fire task, drawing upon dream and archetype for the Water, and, now, a special kind of *seeing* for the Air endeavor. Yes, I mean something like the *seeing* Don Juan teaches Carlos,[23] and something like Hillman's *seeing through*.[24] It is an imaginal practice that is simple to name, but difficult to convey, though you may know it through the art and poetry of the Romantics. It begins with the act of imagining the World to have a Soul and to be a place of Beauty and with seeing, feeling, touching, smelling, tasting that beauty wherever we turn. It is a practice and a prayer known to the Navajo *seer*:

> *Great Spirit, may we walk in Beauty.*
> *May Beauty be above us so that we dream of Beauty.*
> *May Beauty be in front of us so that we are led by Beauty.*
> *May Beauty be to the left of so that we may receive Beauty.*
> *May Beauty be to the right of us so that we may give out Beauty.*
> *May Beauty be behind us so that those who come after us may*
>   *see Beauty.*
> *May Beauty be inside us so that we might become Beauty.*
> *Great Spirit, may we walk in Beauty.*[25]

These are a few practical ways to experiment with *seeing*:

♦ Learn to see your own beauty as completely and as deeply as possible. Someday, spend a whole hour before a full-length mirror, first in street clothes, then in your best going-out-dancing gear, then in your finest French lingerie (and if you don't have some of that, girrrl, you gotta go get it!), then nude. Study every part of you, every delicious detail. What three things do you like most? Least. When we do this in my erotica groups, we find that we are invariably puzzled at what beautiful parts of themselves women choose not to like.

♦ When you pass a gorgeous hunk of man on the street or an exquisite beauty of a woman, try the Tantric practice of "breathing in their energy," as well as recording their image, and carry both with you to the next encounter with your partner. This is an Air practice of the first degree.

◆ Recover a memory of a beautiful experience in nature. Hold the feeling and imagine an experience in a wonderful place you have never been. Do the same with a sexual or loving encounter—first the memory, then the imagining. In this way you can learn how the practice of memory as a discipline is the key to a vivified imaginal practice.

◆ Read Rilke, who has seen Beauty in the world, and knows Her well.

◆ Pray, chant, meditate; take up or continue upon, the spiritual path.

I'm not sure that "Air People" (Gemini, Libra, or Aquarius) have such of an advantage at this task, since it is advanced work for any of us, but be sure to take it on consciously if you have your Sun, Venus, or Mars in an Air sign or a well-aspected Venus, especially in good aspect to Saturn—or even if you don't. The task may be a greater challenge for watery types as you can easily get lost rescuing others or allowing your compassion to stand in the way of success. Difficult aspects between Venus and Saturn (issues of self esteem, "I'm not pretty," and fear of rejection) make hard work on this task a must. If you have a predominance of Fire, Earth or Water, you might learn to accomplish this task from your airy friends, who seem to have a built-in ability to detach. But, like any of the tasks, this one is optional only for those who prefer to remain unconscious.

But still the mystery of the beauty box remains. For understanding, we must look to the other great appearance of that box—in the myth of Pandora. When she, the First Woman, opened the container and unleashed all manner of darkness upon the world, one item alone remained inside. And that was

Hope. The continued quest for Beauty, Pleasure, Delight—
the active use of imagination to *see* what gladdens the senses—
teaches us to hope, informing us that we may know a life beyond the senses, beyond material concerns. Hope, too, is an
imaginal discipline—the capacity to imagine future possibilities—and thus is learned by the application of memory, self-
revisioning, dreaming, and *seeing*. So, open the box, seize the
hope you find, and look to the possibility of divine rebirth.

   Psyche continues:

> A drop of cool moisture fell upon my left eye. And then another,
> and another upon my cheek . . . then I heard my Eros, "Psyche.
> I love you!" Slowly, the casing melted away. I opened my eyes
> . . . to his. Eros! It was his tears that fell upon my face. His salty
> tears released me from my dark dream!
>
>   Then he told me everything! His warm strong hands cupped
> my face as he poured out the secrets of his heart, " . . . my
> mother sent me to befoul you, but when I saw you . . . I fell in
> love with you instead . . . but Apollo helped me steal and hide
> you . . . I thought to hide myself to protect you but truly I did
> it to protect myself. I was afraid. Oh sweet Psyche, forgive me.
> I did not know how much I loved you until I saw you so near
> to death and then I feared it was too late." I bathed in the lus-
> cious perfume of his love! Oh my Eros!
>
>   At that moment Zeus, God of Olympus, arrived! He raised
> a golden chalice of immortal ambrosia to my lips. "Though you
> are not a God yet you shall be no longer mortal. Psyche, forever-
> more you will go between; between the Heavens and Earth, be-
> tween Gods and mankind, you are the ONE to join the TWO
> to THREE! And then he whispered my new name into my ear
> and bade me speak it to the heavens.
>
>   At once Aphrodite and her attendants appeared giggling
> all around me, fussing me into new attire. When they stood
> back, I was draped in glimmering gossamer, and behind me,
> newly sprouted from my shoulder blades—the wings of a but-
> terfly! I came near my beloved Eros and took his hand. I reached

toward Aphrodite and took hers too. I the ONE joined the TWO! Now we are THREE! My name rose up from my belly swirling around my chest, harvesting the happiness of my heart. As loud as I could, I cried out to the heavens, I sang my new name. "I am Soul!"

We have come full circle, and yet are much higher upon the path, as if we had traveled up the spiral staircase that Aphrodite showed Psyche before her final journey. We have lived through the seasons, Winter to Fall, and stand before Winter again— but now with the knowledge that every Winter begets a new Spring. We have sorted, gathered, dipped and drunk, and even gone to Hell for Beauty's sake. I hope we are better for the journey. Psyche is. I know I am for the similar excursion I've made through life. Psyche's final words are what it's all about, you know—the making of Soul, through the pursuit of Love. To be sure, this is a path of initiation for women. A Sacred Way. But we should not neglect the change the journey has wrought upon Love, Himself. As Psyche grows, so does Eros. He, with the reader and Aphrodite, are the observers, the *witnesses* of her trials and inner struggles. Eros has a particular bond with Psyche and a vested interest in watching her, for he is her own inner masculine, her own maturing animus. In witnessing, he starts his fall into true love with her, realizing who she is becoming—his other half in the search for wholeness. As women we have a vested interest in witnessing the story, for as Psyche grows, so do we, but we also have an interest in joining with men who will re-vision love as Apuleius began to so many centuries ago. Let's get on with the work—and the play—together.

NOTES

1. Eric Neumann. *Amor and Psyche*. (Princeton: Princeton University Press, 1956).

2. Robert Johnson. *She* (New York: Harper and Row, 1976).

3. Maria-Louise von Franz. *The Golden Ass of Apuleius* (Boston: Shambala, 1992).

4. von Franz. Op. cit., 8.

5. von Franz. Op. cit., 8.

6. Maria-Louise von Franz. *Projections and Recollections in Jungian Psychology* (London: Open Court, 1980), 132.

7. Guillem of Aquitaine. In Christopher Bamford. "The Magic of Romance: The Cultivation of Eros From Sappho to the Troubadours." *Alexandria*, 2, 1993, 302.

8. *Joseph Campbell and the Power of Myth with Bill Moyers*, #V, "Love and the Goddess." PBS Television Series.

9. W. R. Jankowiak and E. F. Fischer. *Sex, Death and Hierarchy in a Chinese City* (New York: Columbia University Press, 1992). In Helen Fischer. *Anatomy of Love*. (New York: Fawcett Columbine, 1992), 50

10. Anne Carson, (Trans.) *Eros, the Bittersweet*. (Princeton: Princeton University Press, 1986). In Christopher Bamford. "The Magic of Romance: The Cultivation of Eros From Sappho to the Troubadours." *Alexandria*, 2, 1993, 290.

11. *Joseph Campbell and the Power of Myth with Bill Moyers*. Op. cit.

12. James Hillman. *The Myth of Analysis* (New York: Harper Perennial, 1972)., 69.

13. Apuleius in *The Golden Ass*. In Eric Neumann, *Amor and Psyche* (Princeton: Princeton University Press, 1956), 7.

14. *The Oxford Guide to Myth in the Arts: 1300-1900's* (Oxford: Oxford University Press, 1993), Vol. 2, 940.

15. James Hillman. "Betrayal." *Loose Ends*. (Dallas, TX: Spring, 1975), 79.

16. Adolph Guggenbühl-Craig. *Marriage Dead or Alive* (Dallas, TX: Spring, 1977), 38.

17. Robert Graves. *The Greek Myths* (London: Penguin, 1955), 34.

18. Betty Dodson. *Self Loving: A Video Portrait of a Woman's Sexuality Seminar* (Betty Dodson, 1993).(A Video tape available from *Tantra: The Magazine*. 1-800-341-8272.)

19. Annie Sprinkle and Maria Beatty. *Sluts and Goddesses*. (A Video tape available from *Tantra: The Magazine*. 1-800-341-8272.)

20. Tee Corinne. *Cunt Coloring Book* (San Francisco: Last Gasp, 1981).

21. Jerome Stolnitz. "Beauty." *Encyclopedia of Philosophy*, Vol. I. (New York: MacMillan, 1967), 264.

22. James Hillman. *The Thought of the Heart and the Soul of the World* (Dallas, TX: Spring, 1992), 39.

23. Carlos Castaneda. *A Separate Reality* (New York: Pocket Books, 1971), 10–11.

24. James. Hillman. *Revisioning Psychology* (New York: Harper Perennial, 1992), 115 ff.

25. "Navajo Blessed Beauty Way Prayer." As taught to Harley Swift Deer Reagan by Grandfather Tom Two Bears Wilson. In Kenneth Ray Stubbs (ed.). *Women of the Light* (Larkspur, CA: Secret Garden, 1994).

Gloria Star

Gloria Star has been a professional astrologer for over twenty years. Her clients span the globe, and she also teaches and lectures on astrology, spiritual development, and personal growth. In addition to this work, she has written the book *Optimum Child: Developing Your Child's Fullest Potential Through Astrology* (Llewellyn, 1987), and has written the *Sun Sign Book* for Llewellyn since 1990. She has been a contributing author of the *Moon Sign Book* since 1995, *Houses: Power Places in the Horoscope* (Llewellyn 1990), and *How to Manage the Astrology of Crisis* (Llewellyn 1993).

Listed in "Who's Who of American Women," Gloria is active within the astrological community, has served on the faculty of the United Astrology Congress (UAC) since its inception in 1986, and has lectured for groups and conferences throughout North America and internationally. She is a member of the Advisory Board for the NCGR, has served on the Steering Committee for AFAN and was the Editor of the AFAN Newsletter from 1992–1997. She also writes a regular column for *The Mountain Astrologer Magazine*. When she is not busy with her astrological and family activities, Gloria sings with local choral groups. She has also been seen in community theater productions pretending to be somebody else.

Gloria Star

Creating Healthy Relationships

e are involved in relationships of all types, but family and love relationships take the greatest toll and can require the most delicate finesse. To love and be loved, that poetic quest which has driven womankind to the heights of ecstasy and to the brink of despair, is the force which propels great change and challenge. Deep loving relationships can, indeed, be difficult, and with all the problems involved, it is sometimes a mystery why women continue to desire them. The quest is for more than pleasure. It is the quest for a powerful confirmation of the Self through the opening of the heart. Our lovers, partners and children hold many of the keys to the opening of that sacred door.

Rather than exploring the idea of "successful" relationships (according to whom?), we are exploring the concept of *healthy* relationships. Relationships which allow growth, which stimulate positive interaction and provide support, caring, and tenderness are more healthy than relationships which are filled with excessive conflict, desperation, addiction, or abuse. The path of creating a healthy relationship has many twists and turns, but it begins in one simple place: within yourself.

As society has changed, women's roles have undergone a series of alterations. Women have become increasingly aware of the importance of self acknowledgment and personal fulfillment as a part of experiencing a more satisfying life. Today's woman is just as likely to have her eyes set upon pursuing a career as is her male counterpart. Achievement once equaled finding a "successful" man. In Gloria Steinem's 1995 commencement address to Smith College, she said, "At my graduation, I thought we had to marry what we wished to become. Now you are becoming the men you once would have wanted to marry."[1] Nonetheless, the need to connect to a significant partner remains powerful for women and men alike. Although society is gradually evolving in terms of women's roles, the struggle to move out of the stereotypes occurs a bit at a time as individual women make personal and more diverse choices. Whether a woman is actively involved in pursuing a career as a single or married individual, or is a full-time homemaker, matters very little in the overall context of her ability to create the relationship she needs. The question becomes one of priorities.

The rush to get off the train of codependency spawned a different approach toward viewing emotional needs in relationships during the 1980s and early 1990s, but it was not as easy as it seemed to change the old patterns of relating. One of the offshoots of this movement was the increasing awareness that we each play a powerful role in the creation of our relationships. Relationships do not just happen: they are made.

Through my astrological counseling sessions with clients, I have had the opportunity to explore thousands of relationships. Despite the complexities resulting from individual personalities, there are several factors which have consistently shone through in satisfying, healthy relationships. The factors which arise in difficult relationships have also been highly notable. To begin to unravel the mystery of the healthy relationship, we will start with you, the individual woman.

A Look in the Mirror

DETERMINING WHAT YOU NEED FROM A RELATIONSHIP

In many respects, your astrological chart works like a mirror. It provides information which allows you to see yourself more clearly. The symbols of the planets, signs, houses, and aspects in an astrological chart reflect you back at yourself. Many times in the course of developing a relationship, you will uncover significant information about yourself. A relationship can also function much like a mirror. What you project upon another person is frequently the experience of what you feel deep within yourself. Conversely, what another person sees in you may be a reflection of themselves. If you are honest with yourself about your feelings and needs, you can reflect an image or picture of yourself which is easier for others to read, but it is rarely a simple and straightforward process.

One of the most powerful indicators about your basic needs centers around the expression of the energies of the Moon, Venus, and Saturn. The Moon tells the story of your deep, nurturant soulful self. This is the energy you rely upon to keep your automatic responses going. Much like the autonomic nervous system of the body, which controls the functions necessary to life, the quality of your Moon operates as your most fundamental need. Moon is a predominantly feminine function because it absorbs, reflects, and holds. This level of feminine is not necessarily "womanly," but is part of that process which deals with polarity. Feminine-masculine is as basic a polarity as light-dark. One is not necessarily better than the other, but they are necessary to grasp as a unit in order to understand the true quality of either.

Venusian needs are also an intensely important quality in relationships. Venus is the energy through which you attract what you want. It stimulates your ability to make value judgments, it is inherent in your experience of pleasure and harmony. As archetypal qualities, the Moon and Venus provide the music for the dance.

Your Saturn expression also underscores your basic needs, but differently from the Moon and Venus. This is the part of you which determines your stability, focus, and commitment. Saturn can be a harsh taskmaster or your most inspiring mentor. This is the energy which comes into play when the rules are important, and this is also the repository of your most chilling fears.

The energizing force of Mars operates when you are ready to take action. You're in touch with Mars when you're feeling assertive, and when you are pursuing the object of your desires. Mars is also the expression of anger and aggressiveness. This quality in your personality is responsible for impulsive action and direct confrontation. This is your courage and drive.

When you are operating from the position of your Moon and Venus, you are in the realm of emotion. Then, when Saturn comes into play, you are in the realm of critical judgment, autonomy, and control. Whether or not you are familiar with your astrological chart, you can recognize when these energies are taking a high priority. When it comes to relationships, these are the energies which are frequently dominating your expression. With a little help from Mars, which adds the spark to your ignition, once you get in touch with what you really need from a relationship, you can then fulfill those pressing needs and desires by taking action.

There are other energies within your psyche, too, but it is these qualities which you can most easily identify during the course of your interactions with others. When you gaze into the mirror of your soul with honest eyes, you must first deal with yourself. If you can recognize your own beauty, lovingness, nurturance, power, and stability, then you can embrace those elements of yourself and shine them forth into the world. If you cannot find those qualities in yourself, and unconsciously go about seeking to find them in others, you will only be met with a series of disappointments. Frequently, awareness of the inner self can escape you. After all, life is demanding, and often a struggle. It takes a certain level of effort to maintain contact with your inner needs and to stay in touch with yourself. Sometimes, it helps to remind yourself what lies at the core of your being.

IN SEARCH OF YOUR MOON AND VENUS

To be more in touch with your Moon, try these things:

◆ If you are still menstruating, become more consciously aware of your menstrual cycle. Honor the ever-changing forces at work within your being. Listen to your needs. Pay attention to the similarities and differences you experience each month. Get to know your body and her clock.

◆ Take some time each week to curl up and relax. Read your favorite books or magazines. Write in your diary. Listen to your favorite music. Be with yourself.

◆ If you have a partner, spend time cuddling with each other.

◆ Pay attention to the foods you like to eat. Determine the best ways to nourish your body and spirit through your diet. Occasionally indulge in something you love, but which you may think is not good for you. Total denial can be costly.

- Take luxurious baths.
- Create rituals which mark the passage of time. Reflect upon where you've been. Feel where you want to go.
- Spend time with other women.

To get in touch with your Venusian energy, try these things:

- Know your favorite colors. Wear them. Use them in your home and office.
- Spend a day being indulged: perhaps a local spa or beauty salon. Have a make-over. Get a pedicure. Get a massage. Feel beautiful.
- Take time to enjoy your favorite artistic activities regularly.
- Give gifts to others on your birthday.
- Flirt.
- Surround yourself with what you feel is beautiful.
- Find the place where love resides within your heart.
- Look in a mirror and say, "I love you." Mean it.

Discovering Your Own Pattern in Relationships

Before you can go about creating the type of relationship you hope to experience, it can be helpful to explore where you've been. Psychologists are both chided and revered for suggesting that their clients review their early childhood and relationship with parents and family, but this is where your early patterns begin, and where your behaviors are conditioned and learned. Another function of your Moon is memory of the past, and you can learn a great deal about your current life situation by reflecting upon where you've been. First, start with your mental images of your parents, their relationship and inter-action with one another. What did you learn about the way men and women treat one another from the model your par-ents provided? What do you wish you had experienced? If the two are different, you're connecting with conflicts which are stored in the repository of the energy we define as your Moon. These inner conflicts can drive you to be much the same as or quite different from your parents. Even though you may con-sciously want one experience, your unconscious drives operate through the pattern which has been programmed from your pre-vious experiences, and until you consciously alter those programs or patterns, they will continue to function.

In addition to exploring the model your parents provided, you have been exposed to other models, too. Movies, books, tele-vision, and significant individuals all play a part in creating your pattern. Additionally, you have also stamped out a pattern of your own based upon your previous experiences with rela-tionships. You have learned from your lovers or partners, and your inner self remembers all of it. The complexity of what you've learned all ties together. If you've experienced support and tenderness in love relationships, then you'll want more of the same, because that is what you know. But if you've experi-enced abandonment, abuse, excessive conflict or rage while at the same time feeling love, then sorting through the complex-ity may not be so straightforward. You may wonder if a certain amount of abuse is part of being loved. That may be the pat-tern you know, and your life is only what you know it to be—until you change it!

You can change these patterns, but you have to see them first. Careful analysis of your astrological chart helps you locate the patterns. Each pattern frequently has the "signature" of a planetary energy. If the Sun and Mars are strong, you need to be decisive and the center of attention, or you may attract men who are very self-involved. Power struggles can be a feature of your relationships. If Moon and Venus have great strength, you may be quite comfortable in the role of partner and home-maker, and can feel most satisfied when you have an opportunity to give of yourself. Jupiter's signature illustrates a need for adventure and a desire to explore many realms of yourself and life through activities like education, travel or spirituality. With Saturn strong, autonomy is important, but you also may close yourself away from intimacy. When Uranus plays a powerful role in your chart, you need independence and plenty of room to actualize your individuality. With Neptune strong, you may love being in love, and can lose yourself in a relationship. Pluto's signature can point to obsessive behavior, and can certainly be an indicator of a tendency to become too absorbed in a rela-tionship. Granted, a certain level of emotional maturity provides an impetus for changes in deep-seated patterns, but the sub-conscious is stubborn and does not easily release its grasp on your psyche. Even though you may think you want to alter your patterns, it's much more easily said than done!

The first step toward transformation is often accompanied by a crisis or precipitated by a traumatic experience which functions like an alarm clock. During the process of these al-terations in your inner self, you may feel somewhat lost or con-fused. It is important to continually stay in touch with how you feel, and to recall what you want and need. These checkpoints will help you maintain a sense of integrity and strength, espe-cially during the times which seem most difficult.

There are several patterns which can emerge, and you may discover that you have one pattern for serious relationships and another for those relationships which are more fun-loving. One of the keys to making change could be to merge the two! But you must consistently remind yourself that the more im-portant priority is to honor what you need, who you are, and where you want your life to go.

Determining What You Need from a Relationship

Several years ago, I taught a university non-credit courses focusing on women's needs to achieve prosperity. Although I had been working with many women clients in my astrological classes, I had not yet done work for a women's group addressing our particular needs and issues. One of the startling realities which emerged during the class was the fact that a majority of these women had not taken the time to determine what they truly needed for themselves from their relationships. For those who were either involved in a relationship or married, the concept itself was somewhat difficult to address. One woman expressed a fear that if she started asking for what she wanted or needed that her husband would leave. "I don't want to appear to be demanding!" she said. Another commented that she did not have time to think about her needs, since everybody else had so many other things in mind for her. An attorney in the class shared that between the demands of her work and her children, she had no idea how she could take enough time to figure out if there was anything she actually needed.

For some women, it seems easier to just concentrate on making another person's needs more important, or to focus on a partner's problems and ignore their own. This attitude is frequently associated with the astrological energies of Neptune and Pluto in close aspect to the personal energies of the Sun, Moon, Venus, and Mars. Neptune's energy defies boundaries, and is the quality which stimulates our link to the more subtle realms of consciousness, to the world of imagination, and to the experience of spirituality. This energy also stimulates denial, deception, and illusion. Pluto's energy provides the experience of power, transformation, and healing, but can also be the destroyer. When Pluto is in difficult aspects to personal planetary energy in your astrological chart, there can be a strong power struggle which can undermine the positive strength of self-worth or self-preservation. You'll know you have problems with Pluto if you suffer from feeling excessive shame, guilt, or self-destructive tendencies. The latter sections of this chapter address ways to regain your personal power and redirect these energies.

With the 1980s emergence of the concepts of dysfunctionality in relationships and the difficulties resulting from codependent relationships, a large number of women began to question their personal needs and requirements instead of always putting someone else ahead of themselves. Recognizing these qualities can be helpful, but getting beyond the tendency to allow these old patterns to overtake your needs takes patience, practice, and self-love. Codependency has not disappeared, but awareness of this pattern has increased, and more women are alert to their need to establish boundaries—but the boundaries have to be set around something!

To discover what you need from a relationship, begin by first acknowledging what you expect from *yourself*. Regardless of your sexual orientation, you still need to take an inventory of your personal needs, desires, and hopes. If you've been in the habit of ignoring yourself, then take the time to work with the Moon/Venus Exercises in the preceding section. Also, you might try taking a personal inventory. Make the time to regularly contemplate where you are emotionally. In "normal" situations, there will be some days where you're feeling on an even keel, others when you're at a low ebb, and yet others when you feel like dancing. With regular attention to your state of being and feeling, you'll discover your personal ebb and flow and will find it easier to recognize the signals which tell you when there's something out of adjustment.

These types of inner exercises give you the power of self-knowledge, and will allow you to feel more confident when you are making choices which will change or alter your life in some way. From this position, ask yourself what you really need from an intimate relationship. Do these needs reflect deficiencies you feel within yourself? If they do, can you find a way to satisfy them? The honest needs for companionship, for mutual support and encouragement, for creating a family or other needs which will allow you to grow on multiple levels can be healthy and life-affirming. If your needs arise from feelings of deficiency, fear, or worthlessness, you may, instead, attract a relationship which emphasizes these problems, rather than resolving them!

Security needs are frequently paramount in a relationship, and your awareness that you are part of creating your own sense of security will add strength to your base of stability. If you are familiar with your astrological chart, there are a couple of factors you can focus on which will give you some keys to what you seek from a partner. These same factors tell you what kind of partner you need to become! The astrological sign on the cusp of the Seventh House and the planetary ruler of this sign are excellent clues to your deepest sense of your ideal partnership, and also illustrate the type of partner you need and want to become.

ABOUT THAT PEDESTAL

Getting off the pedestal (or not getting on it in the the first place!) can make a big difference in the quality of an intimate relationship. In dreams, every woman wants to be adored. Is it possible to allow, or even encourage, adoration without falling into a trap? Your self-worth, as well as the value you have for your partner, is strongly linked to this level of need. We are encouraged through literature, movies, and television images to believe that there is an ideal love, and that when your true love walks onto the scene, they will adore you forever. Neptunian romance in all its glory has a painful aftereffect. You may feel that the only form of love which is real requires an unrealistic, dreamlike quality, or that the only love which you can accept is that of a soul mate. Also, if you've been the object of another's unrealistic adoration, it can be devastating to both of you when they discover you are human, after all.

Even if you may not consciously want this experience, you may have a partner who views you unrealistically. Certainly, in deeper levels of intimacy, you realize that there is something beyond the ordinary physical boundaries which connect you to your partner. Many times, it is a deep spiritual yearning which propels anyone to place another upon a pedestal. It is possible to have that spiritual connection with your partner and still be realistic about them, and you can allow your partner to be realistic about you, too. The true respect and admiration which emerges in a healthy relationship is quite different from unrealistic ideals.

Pedestals—who needs them? If you've got to be that high above it all, maybe you need to try getting your feet firmly on the ground and walking in the midst of the reality of life circumstances for a while. After all, that pedestal is a distant, and can be a lonely, place.

ENJOYING THE CHEMISTRY WITHOUT SUFFOCATING IN THE FUMES

In the beginning of a new relationship, something sparks your interest. The energies which draw you to another person—the power of attraction—cause twinges of excitement and anticipation, and stimulate desire. Science has analyzed this experience and connects it to the increase of endorphins, which do elevate when sexual arousal occurs. Beyond the biochemistry, the alchemical, juicy, ecstatic feeling of being in love is difficult to match. Poets may experience high endorphin levels, but they're not giving out the chemical formula!

During this phase of a love relationship, common sense can fly out the window. If the energies involved have the quality of life-altering or revolutionary change, then this period in a relationship can be associated with sudden changes which seem to make little sense to observers. If you have been snugly situated, this may be the perfect stimulus for life change. There are attractions, however, which can have a negatively mind numbing effect, in which you see only what you want to see and cannot connect to the reality of the person or circumstance.

When you experience this high level of chemistry, you're connecting to the energies of Venus, Mars, Uranus, Neptune, and Pluto. Where Venus is the quality of attraction and Mars the quality of action, the interplay of attraction, pursuit, and conquest is continually played out on the stage of life. When the *outer planets*—Uranus, Neptune, and Pluto—are stimulated during the course of a love relationship, the energy intensifies, becoming more hypnotic and life-transforming.

When your natal chart shows flowing aspects or connections between your personal energies (Sun, Moon, Mercury, Venus, and Mars) and the outer planets, you may find it easier to maintain a balance between the chemistry of being in love and continuing to maintain your objectivity about your needs, but if there are conflicting aspects between these energies in your chart, they indicate that you can lose your objectivity.

Uranian chemistry is the high intensity, electrical energy which sends shock waves through your body and rushes through your senses. This is also the energy of breaking away from the ordinary and expression of the extraordinary. But this energy is known to be "flaky" and unpredictable, and can change its focus at a moment's notice. This energy does not like to be controlled.

Neptunian chemistry is mystifying, mesmerizing, and can be addictive. Neptune is pure romance. The flowers, music, fragrances, and magic of love are Neptunian. The dream, the escape, and the illusion of being in a world apart are Neptunian. And the desire to rescue someone in pain, the ability to see what lies at the soul of another and the denial of problems is also Neptunian. Through Neptune you can become the victim, and if your personal energies are connected to Neptune, you may find that you have difficulty maintaining your personal boundaries.

Pluto's chemistry can be all-consuming, filled with profound desire and obsessive longing. Pluto's chemistry lurks in the shadowy space where your power waits to be unleashed and where you await rebirth. When this energy is stimulated in a love relationship, it is difficult to let go of the attachment which develops, If you have Pluto closely connected to the personal energies of your psyche, then you will long for this stimulus more fully, but you can also become more easily obsessed, and may have difficulty avoiding power struggles.

Some women love being in love, but feel disappointment when that feeling does not continue. If you've fallen into Neptunian delusion, you're likely to awaken when you realize that your sweetheart still leaves dirty socks and underwear in the living room; the sparkle dulls. If you're dazzled by Uranian enticements, your sweetie may walk out of the picture as suddenly as they appeared. When caught in Plutonian obsession, you may still hang on long after the relationship has ended, but you are not doomed just because these qualities may be activated in the course of a relationship. By maintaining your vigil, watching yourself, you may find a way to use these energies to bring consistent levels of excitement or playfulness into your relationship. The only requirement is that you remain connected to that part of you which needs to grow and be inspired by the joys of life.

EXPRESSING YOUR NEEDS TO BE NURTURED AND NURTURING

For anything to grow it needs the right kind of nurturance. For centuries, women have played the role of the nurturer, both to children and to partners. This is one of the primary functions of your Moon energy. Although the Moon is concerned with receptivity, it also reflects light. By focusing on the nature of your Moon, the sign and house in which it is placed, you can uncover the ways you need to express nurturant energy toward others. You will also expose the way you feel and hope to be nurtured by others.

If you have a tendency to put everyone's needs first, while you take the leftovers, you will eventually burn out. In fact, you will simply run out of energy. The only person you can blame for this is yourself, because you make the choices about where and how you target the outpouring of yourself! If you fall into this category, you are likely to be dealing with the influences of Saturn, Neptune, or Pluto in aspect to your Moon (or a combination of these influences). There is probably some part of you which has learned or which believes that you will eventually get your reward. Sure, but you may be too worn out to enjoy it!

Now, I am not advocating that you should become totally self-absorbed, but you might start thinking in terms of "self-fullness"—which is the real key to becoming more completely nurturing to everyone, including yourself. The first part of this shift in focus is to determine the types of things which fill your soul. Allow yourself to concentrate on experiences which bring you a feeling of comfort, satisfaction, contentment, or happiness. Make a list if you must, and add to it as necessary. Perhaps you feel more completely alive when you have time to take an evening walk, or when you're working in your garden. Maybe you can cope with the pressures of your life more easily if you allow yourself time to indulge in your creative or artistic leanings. Whatever brings a light into your eyes and joy into your heart will fill you with love for yourself, and allow you to love others more easily and fully.

This shift in focus, which allows your needs to take a high priority, can be quite difficult if you've been used to staying on the bottom of the heap. What you achieve is a way to keep yourself healthy and whole. If you are continually depleted, then you will have very little quality to give to others. If you have children, you will find that you have more energy to attend to their needs and demands. Within the context of a marriage or other committed relationship, the same is true. Every person has a need for contact, touch, support, and tenderness—especially you.

The other side of the self-nurturant coin is learning how to ask for support. Strongly one-sided relationships are more the norm than relationships where the balance shifts from one to the other. There is a difference between asking for support from your partner and leaning on your partner because you refuse to stand on your own. Part of your request may come from practical situations. Simple everyday duties, like cooking and chores, may sometimes overtake your life. Asking for support may mean that you request help in these areas — from partners or other family members, but other levels of nurturance or support arise in more subtle circumstances.

Taking time to cuddle, hold hands, or embrace can affirm your connection and fill both partners. In crisis, instead of assuming that you must shoulder the burden alone, express your needs and concerns. Be open to your partner's requests, too, because the best relationships involve two people who are willing to be open to one another, allowing both partners to become "self-full."

NURTURING VERSUS MOTHERING

While nurturing is a form of mothering, there is a difference. During the course of intimate relationships, nurturant support stimulates stability, growth, and trust. Even some acts which are associated with mother, like protection, care-taking, and tenderness can be positively nurturing within a relationship between two adults. Since Moon energy does come into play through intimate relationships, it follows that some of the same tendencies toward protective nurturing will develop between partners.

Children need nurturance above all else, but they also require guidance throughout their development. Just because you are a woman, you do not innately know how to mother. It is a combination of what you learn and your intuitive sensibilities which allows you to develop as a mother.

Unlike children, who are undergoing a series of developmental stages in quick succession, adults reach a certain level of self-awareness and do not require the same guidance and outside support. During different cycles of Saturn, about every seven years, each person experiences a period of marked growth and stabilization. The first three Saturn cycles—at approximately ages seven, fourteen, and twenty-one—still involve circumstances which are connected to important stages between mother and child. Beyond that, an individual becomes increasingly more self-reliant as they mature emotionally.

In a relationship between adults, these Saturn cycles frequently stimulate a period of crisis, and it is during these times that the true nurturant quality of the relationship is tested. Part of that nurturance involves learning when to step away, or to let go, and allow another person to deal with something on their own. If you fall into the mothering role, trying to make things better, or, if you're tempted to take on the pain of a difficult situation so that your partner does not have to deal with their own feelings, then you may undermine the integrity of the relationship. If you have a strongly placed Moon, aspects between the Moon and Saturn or Pluto (or both), or if your chart contains a number of water elements— then you are more inclined to act in this manner. Re-focus, and try again!

Developing Positive Forms of Communication

Perhaps the most important key to a healthy relationship is good communication. From the moment of first contact, you are communicating in a relationship. How effectively you communicate is likely to determine whether or not the relationship sustains through the course of time. There are many levels of communication. From verbal interaction to body language, communication allows you to connect your thoughts and feelings with those of your partner. Underneath it all must be honesty and integrity. Lies and deception have no place in the healthy relationship.

The energy most often associated with communication is Mercury, whose function within the personality is to provide connection or linkage, and which strongly influences the expression of your thoughts or ideas. Since Mercury's primary function is centered around making connections, you can see why it is important in relationships. To sustain a relationship, that sense of connection to one another is crucial. Through Mercury, your meeting of the minds can become a doorway to an open heart.

Your philosophical contact flows through the energy of Jupiter, which also promotes good will, generosity, and humor within your relationships. By bringing the energies of mental communication and philosophical understanding into a relationship, you can develop a feeling of hope for your future. Optimism adds confidence to your ties with your partner.

Good communication implies that you understand one another, and that you feel understood by one another. It does not mean that you always agree. Similarities mark part of your common ground with a partner, but because you are different people, you will have different viewpoints. To achieve good communication, you must find a way to maintain the contact and connection which allows the flow of energy to continue.

Positive communication models allow room for many forms of expression. Long-term relationships are easy to spot, because you can see the language two people have developed with each other. A certain look, twist of a smile, or laugh has meaning. Special phrases, pet names, favorite music, colors, or gestures are also part of the language of love. One couple I've worked with for a number of years has a special way to deal with tension. After the second year of their marriage, they purchased a new home and added a hot tub. (They each have Moons in water signs.) In the beginning, the hot tub provided ample opportunities for both play and relaxation. They even discovered certain things about their own sexual preferences thanks to their hot tub. The key thing the wife noticed was that when they were both tired after a day at work or a difficult week, they could sit in a hot tub and talk about anything, where before they had a tendency to be rather brusque with one another. After another couple of years had passed, she found that he would sometimes block his thoughts or feelings, especially when difficulties had arisen—like tax problems or trouble at work. After dinner one night following an especially problematic period of crisis, she said, "I think we could use a hot tub." About fifteen minutes later, when she noticed he was not in the house, she peeked onto the deck to see him relaxing in the tub, and joined him. He pulled her close and whispered, "You know, it's been too long since we really talked."

Now, they use the words "hot tub" to signal that they need time out together. That's communication.

Another level of communication involves learning to listen. Active listening is one of the best ways to improve communication in a relationship. If you are taking the steps to express your feelings and needs, it will do you very little good if your partner does not hear you! Conversely, if you really want to grow closer in intimacy, you will pay more attention to what your partner has to say. Hearing and understanding may mean that you have to become more of a participant instead of just passively waiting for the other person to finish what they have to say, so you can have the floor!

The Big "C" Word

Commitment. At some point in every relationship, the "c" word arises. In a world which has been geared toward throwing away what no longer works, commitment is almost foreign, but once you've progressed beyond the attraction and have determined that you want to see what develops, you are making your first commitment. Future stages of commitment might involve moving in together, becoming engaged to be married, or marriage. Despite all these forms of commitment, the primary focus is your commitment to yourself. Never are you truly committing yourself to somebody else — your focus is upon you. Once again, the circle has been traveled, and there you are!

Promises are complex mechanisms. I remember my surprise at my own reaction, when, reading over the marriage vows prior to my first marriage, I realized what the words really said. "Love, honor, and obey." The "love" part, I was pretty sure I could accomplish. "Honor" seemed a reasonable request and held a positive feeling, but that "obey" issue really knocked me for a loop. I told the minister I could not say those words. He replied, "They're traditional, and besides, they're only words." Well, not in my mind, they were not! My husband-to-be must have gotten his first look at my rebellious and stubborn nature, because I would not proceed until we could agree to leave out "obey." Since I no longer hold much stock in the old patriarchal models, this has not been such an issue, but it was an awakening for me at that early age of almost nineteen.

During many counseling sessions with clients, we've met a crisis when discussing how to make a commitment, or if it is necessary. Voicing or openly stating that commitment allows a couple to determine why they are together. Designing the nature of the commitment is a personal thing. One model will work for some individuals, but I always suggest that couples determine what they want to achieve by being together. These hopes and wishes form the basis for their commitment to one another. As time goes by and life brings its inevitable alterations and changes, I suggest that the commitment be re-evaluated and re-designed. Sociologists and psychologists have performed studies which point to the idea that men and women experience different priorities in regard to relationships. Women are more likely to want to "preserve" a relationship, and sometimes place themselves in a form of emotional bondage in order to do just that. Before you consider making a commitment or reaffirming an existing commitment in a relationship, examine your reasons carefully. Find a way to use your Mercurial and Saturnine energies to help you integrate the more emotional energies of Moon, Venus, and Mars.

The energy of Saturn is one of the primary factors in your attitudes toward the promises you make, and the promises you are capable of maintaining. Saturn is focus and discipline, but it is also the energy of clarity and reality. When using your Saturn force in a healthy way, you are standing on a firm foundation with open eyes. This is the perfect position for formulating your commitments. Your vows are sacred mantras which create the structure upon which you build your relationship. Even if you only vow to try something for six weeks, it's still a promise to yourself. Those lifetime promises need a bit of special consideration. Keep in mind that everything changes, and your commitments need to allow room for the changes while providing a stable base.

BUT IT WAS HIS FAULT!

Wait a minute! What do you mean, the relationship is not working? Did you say that you are not getting along, or that you just don't understand one another any longer? Did you say the other person was a jerk? Perhaps it's true, but where were you?

Any healthy relationship will have its difficult moments. Some relationships have a string of difficulties, which may be the only glue holding it together. Problems in a relationship, whether perceived or real, are not the fault of the other person. Your personal responsibility cannot allow you to escape that easily, and if you are continually blaming others, you're probably surprised to find out that the same problems keep emerging over and over again. Taking responsibility allows you to improve your sense of self-esteem, even if part of that action involves admitting your deficiencies to yourself!

Keep this in mind: Scapegoating is a form of denial.

Exploring Your Sexual Needs and Desires

Although men have been the ones to traditionally boast about sex, we women are exceptionally sexual creatures. A woman who accepts and owns her personal sexuality has tremendous power. This power exudes through the essence of the woman, who is more comfortable and confident about her entire being. The role of sexuality within a relationship undergoes alterations, just as every other aspect of an intimate relationship changes. Exploring the physical aspect of an intimate relationship helps to open pathways to greater emotional and spiritual alchemy.

Whereas the old patriarchal models involve woman serving the needs of a man with little regard to her preferences or desires, your healthy relationship involves two people serving mutual needs. Sharing, touching, holding, caressing, honoring, and immersing into the same field of energy draws you into a sacred space—the essence of transformative ecstasy. Ecstasy is easier to achieve if you are open with yourself and freely, playfully in tune with your feelings. Removing any blocks is a highly personal process, and can also be a process which is part of the evolution of a close relationship.

Your sexuality begins in your mind. If you have a chart strong in fire and air signs, words and conversation can be a phenomenal turn-on! Regardless of your elemental make-up, to shift your focus to a more gratifying love life, start with your mind. Examine your thoughts about your sexual needs often. Sometimes, what you know, or what you think you know, can get in your way. Free your mind. Allow yourself to fantasize about sexual encounters. Read a steamy romance novel. Keep a private diary of your desires. Write fantasizing letters. Read books which encourage development of greater sexual satisfaction. Finally, talk with your lover.

The energies most people associate with sexual attraction are Venus and Mars. The sign placement of Venus provides important clues to the things which stimulate your outpouring of affection. Through Venus, love flows within yourself and outward to others. Venus is the way you love. Mars is the expression of passion and desire in a more active form. Frequently what you seek from your lover can be described by the sign in which Mars is placed in your chart. In mythology, Venus and Mars were lovers. In your psyche, the same story unfolds. These energies are frequently expressed physically and emotionally, but they can be more easily expressed if there are no barriers in their way.

One of the blocks toward achieving a fully satisfying sex life is the emotional baggage which so frequently accompanies sexuality. Everyone has received different impressions about what is right or wrong sexually, and many women carry excessive guilt about admitting to feelings of sexual desire. Some women have been abused, emotionally and/or sexually, and cannot allow themselves to open these doors because of the pain from the past. Emotional difficulties or other pressures can inhibit sexual energy during the course of any normal life, and sometimes, if you feel that you are without sexual desire, it may simply be because you are using that energy elsewhere!

Addressing these blocks takes time and patience, but if they go unchecked, you're likely to run into a series of very firm barriers, even when you feel you'd like to get beyond them. Many of the walls and doors in your emotional suit of armor are built to protect your vulnerabilities, and some of them are important and necessary until you reach a secure level of trust with an intimate partner. If you keep running into your barriers, be kind to yourself. Try to open the doors one at a time. You hold the keys to those locks, and might be more comfortable exploring beyond the doors on your own before you open them to your partner. Working with a supportive and understanding counselor can also be helpful.

If you are a younger woman and have little experience with relationships, you still may run into a few barriers. Most of these are cloaked in the fear of the unknown. It is healthy and normal, regardless of your age, to explore and become familiar with your own body, your own feelings, and your own responses. Before you can become openly intimate with another person, you must be comfortable with yourself. Your body is the vessel you inhabit, and the sensations which stimulate and arouse your physical senses also arouse an emotional response. Erotic energy frightens some women (and men!), because the response to it can be overpowering. Learning what that energy is like, and allowing yourself to surrender and let this energy flow through you can be purely delightful.

Sharing sexual energy with a partner works on many levels to build your bond with one another. In the early development of a relationship, taking the step to become sexually intimate marks an important test of determining your compatibility. The excitement stimulates a series of changes in your feelings about yourself. Whereas women of previous eras may not have considered it to be important if they were sexually compatible with their partners, today's woman is more aware. Women are more likely to take on an assertive role in sexual relationships, instead of passively waiting for their partners to ignite the fires of passion. Even women who do not feel comfortable taking the lead are likely to be more open about their desires to share sex with their partners.

What About Love?

The meaning of love has been pondered, argued, and remains difficult to define. We know it when we feel it—or do we? This feeling is highly personal. Loving energy is an expression of Venus. Compassion is an expression of Neptune. Wild attraction is expressed through Uranus, passion through Mars, the energy ranging from deep bonding to obsession is an expression of Pluto. As we have seen, the energy of your Moon stimulates nurturance and caring, while Saturn energy is also protective, albeit critical. All these qualities, and more, are part of a loving relationship, and your entire being is involved in any relationship.

Over the changing course of your life, your needs from relationships will change and transform. As you get to know yourself more fully, you discover your motivations for developing your relationships, and may also find that you do not need certain things. As for love, it is not, first of all, something that comes to you from beyond yourself. Love resides within you, and is expressed through you. When you are stimulated to feel a particular way, those are *your* feelings! One of the key factors in healthy loving seems to involve the sharing and support which stimulates mutual positive self-esteem.

As an astrologer, I have learned to view life in a manner which involves integrating many factors, and the experience and process of loving is truly a multifaceted expression. When examining the concept of loving, there is always a dynamic involved which requires allowing energy to flow. Loving is never just giving, nor is it simply receiving. Loving involves opening the heart from within, allowing the flame of love to warm and inspire you to feel. Then, the next step is to project that feeling into your life through your creativity, through giving to others, or through simply radiating love. As that energy flows outward, you also must open to receive, because there is always a return of the flow! This is the nature of the relationship between the Fifth and Eleventh Houses in your astrological chart: the giving and receiving of love. Many women do just fine with the giving part, but have trouble when it comes to simply receiving love. There are so many qualifications you can place upon yourself: I'm not good enough, not pretty enough, not successful enough, not enough—period. Or there can be blocks, like "love hurt me once, so I will never allow anyone to get close again." Or, "I failed to reach my expectations in creativity, love, or whatever, so I will never do it again." These attitudes and fears block the flow of love. So, you may be able to send it out (in a limited way), but you have trouble letting the flow return to you. Strangely enough, if you're blocking either end of the energy spectrum—giving or receiving—loving seems incomplete, and is certainly less fulfilling.

By exploring the meaning of the Fifth and Eleventh Houses in your astrological chart, you may uncover the easiest ways to open to this process, which, at its highest level, can be a natural exchange of energy. The planetary rulers of these houses (those planets which correlate with the signs on the cusps of the houses), gives you a strong clue about what you seek from loving relationships. If you have stubborn energies like Saturn or Pluto in either of these houses, it is a strong probability that giving and receiving love may never seem quite "equal." You control the way these energies work. Perhaps you are the one blocking the flow!

Showing appreciation and reminding yourself what you appreciate about your partner is a crucial part of nourishing love. Consciously taking the time to express appreciation for one another is mutually nourishing. However, women tend to express their appreciation and stroke their partner's ego, and may not receive the same treatment in return. If you need this reinforcement (and who doesn't?), you may have to begin by talking to your partner about your concerns. Even if you have to make time for this in the beginning and it feels a bit awkward at first, give it a try. These expressions literally feed a loving relationship.

Sometimes, a sense of lack stimulates an attraction, and can lead to developing a relationship. For example, if you are feeling deficient in some way, you may try to fill this deficiency by attracting someone else who has mastered it. In most cases, this is an unconscious process. The sign on the cusp of the Seventh House in your chart shows what you unconsciously seek from a partner. Many times, this sign and planets within the Seventh House indicate what you have difficulty "owning" within yourself. In reality, this area of your chart indicates the type of partner *you* need to become! Once you've taken possession of those qualities within yourself, your entire approach to partnering will change!

Another factor which lurks at the heart of intimate relationships is the question of personal worth. Outside of the planetary influences already explored, you'll gain more insight by studying the dynamics between the Second and Eighth Houses in your chart. If the Second House represents your personal worth, and the Eighth House represents the worth you perceive from your partner, it is possible that you will attempt to focus upon one side or the other and achieve a very lopsided value system within your relationship. When you are expressing mutual appreciation for one another, the nature of each individuals' personal worth deepens. If you're in a situation which reinforces the other person and leaves you cold, take another look! What are you missing? There *is* the ever-present argument between heart and head— "I know it's not everything I want, but I love him or her so much!" Because there are so many levels of love and loving, there are many "reasons" for becoming involved. Yet if you are using "love" as an excuse for staying in a situation which defeats, undermines, or abuses you or your needs, think again. If you are staying in a relationship for all the "conveniences," but do not feel love, you have another problem on your hands! It all comes down to self-worth, which is at the heart of love. Once again, the ball is in your court!

Trouble-Shooting

CONTRASTING AND COMPARING

One of the fantastic things about life is that you get more chances with every breath! You are continually determining the experiences and circumstances which bring you positive support and good feelings, and also may have a running list of the things you do not like or appreciate. Relationships force you to learn things about yourself: a type of illumination which is sometimes comforting, other times, distressing, but you also remember. Whether conscious memory, subconscious memory, or repressed memory, you remember what has happened before. That's how everyone learns!

Along with that memory is often-unfinished emotional business. We all have heard ourselves say things we heard our mothers say when we were young, stopped, and thought, "Wow! I cannot believe I said that!" This is your subconscious mind at work (your Moon). Outside of the apparent blunder of calling a current lover or partner by the name of an old love, we do the same thing in relationships. One client of mine does not own an iron. In her first marriage, her husband wanted everything ironed. (After all, his mother ironed everything: including the sheets, handkerchiefs, and even his dad's socks!) In the beginning (in the 1950s), she ironed her clothes and her husband's, and with the advent of permanent-press fabric, was happy to stop ironing. When she started working, she began to send out some ironing, like shirts, to the cleaners. Other things, she let go. One weekend, her husband remarked that she had certainly become lazy. She was incensed. "Lazy?! What do you mean? I have a full-time job, do all the cooking, most of the cleaning, and everything else!"

"Well," he said, "you certainly do not keep up with your ironing!"

Now, granted, there were other apparent problems in this relationship which lurk like menacing ghosts within the preceding conversation. The end-result of this relationship saw the woman throwing out the iron and ironing board and vowing never again to iron— at least, not for a man! In one session with me, she commented that she was very interested in a relationship. We were examining the two charts, talking about possibilities, strengths, pitfalls, when she asked, "Can you tell if he'll want me to iron?" We both laughed. Heaven help the man if he suggested it. I advised her to talk to him about this issue before it lead to something else, and to discuss with him her concerns about maintaining a stronger sense of balance or equality within the relationship.

Other, more traumatic, emotional circumstances also leave their mark, and can result in your recoiling in situations in a non-sensical manner. When this happens, you may be dealing with old memories which are triggered by an unhappy, difficult, or unresolved emotional trauma from the past. Women with strong Saturn and Pluto aspects to personal planets frequently hold onto the past more tenaciously. If you have an emphasis in fixed signs (Taurus, Leo, Scorpio, or Aquarius), you may also find it difficult to release the past.

Early conditioning which is based upon stimulating fear, shame, or guilt also makes its mark in relationships and can cause confusion. If a young girl is raised in a home where shame and guilt are continually used to shape her behavior, she is likely to seek out the same circumstances in her adult relationships as a woman. Many people shake their heads, wondering how someone can stay in an abusive relationship. It's all too easy when you have nowhere else to go, and when your self-esteem is so low that you feel you deserve no better.

Even if you are not caught in the extremes, you're likely to find that you respond to your current partner based upon your previous circumstances. Changing those responses has to come from a conscious effort. Releasing the past must also be done in a conscious manner, but one step is required before you can begin. You must give yourself permission to end your attachment to an old relationship.

To move forward in relationships, it is necessary to release the past. If you have issues, they will always be there, but they are *your* issues, and *you* must deal with them. Many women still hang onto old love as though it belongs in some sacred scrapbook. That emotional attachment will color every relationship you have once the current one is done.

If at all possible, when you end a relationship, tell your ex good-by. Really look at them and say, "Good-by." And mean it. Then do your inner work. Release your need to stay attached to that person. In one of my women's prosperity classes, I offered several suggestions for releasing exercises for old relationships. One of the best exercises, which was shared with me by a female friend years ago, deals with personal attachment to an old love.

EXERCISES FOR LETTING GO

Lie down in a comfortable place. If at all possible, lie outside, under the sun or moon, on a blanket or air mattress. Breathe deeply and release as much tension as you can. Imagine that you are wrapped, like a mummy. This wrapping represents your attachment to your lover. Ask for support, guidance, and assistance from your higher self, and if you feel a strong connection to any spiritual guides or beings, such as angels, or have a special connection to any archetypes such as Astarte or Isis, request their assistance. Starting at your feet, feel the bonds releasing. Breathe deeply. Your helpers gently and gradually unravel this wrapping. Stay in touch with your feelings all along the way. At some point, you may remember a touch or a caress. Let it go. When your torso is unwrapped, you may feel a deep sense of loss or hurt. Let it go. If you need to cry, allow the release Once all the wrapping is removed, your helpers carry it to a fire, and it is burned. For a few minutes, allow yourself to relax and feel the freedom. When you do get up, carefully integrate back into your present reality. A shower or swim is often a good accompaniment to follow this exercise.

In another class, I suggested a releasing exercise for old relationships, or a relationship which is ending. Envision yourself and your former lover or partner walking together toward a car (or boat, if that seems more fitting). Stand before the car, and ask that the car be blessed with the protective light of unconditional love. Face your partner and look into their eyes. Tell them good-by. Open the car door, usher them inside and hand them the keys. Then, see them driving away. You walk away and get into your own vehicle, which is protected and shielded, and go your own way.

In the class, one woman asked if she could process all her old relationships at once. I responded that it might work to use a bigger vehicle. "Use a van or a bus," I suggested, "and just have all your old lovers line up, tell them good-by, have them board the van and drive away."

"A van won't hold them all, " she said. "Could I use a train?"

So, if you have to, use a train!

Dealing with Conflict

Conflict is a necessary part of life, and certainly arises in any relationship. Some women (and men, too) have shared that they feel conflict means things are not going well. After all, if you're fighting, you don't love one another, right? Wrong! Healthy, open conflicts can provoke a more positive connection with your partner. Avoiding conflict can poison your relationship. Of course, there is a difference between disagreements, reasonable anger, and knockdown, drag-out fights! Physical and psychological abuse does not qualify as healthy conflict, either.

In some relationships, where strong Mars energy forms the connection between lovers or partners, conflicts arise on a regular basis. In fact, we have all seen the relationships which seem to begin out of some form of conflict, like disagreeing about politics. Attraction can provoke conflict, too. To take the risk of becoming involved with someone in the first place, you experience internal conflict of one type or another, but when conflicts do arise in a relationship, there are ways to deal with them so that the relationship wins.

First, you must allow yourself to know your own limits when it comes to anger. If you reach a certain point and can no longer reason or hold a rational conversation, teach yourself to know that place. Make an agreement with your partner that if either of you asks for a "time out" to cool down, you will honor it. Continuing to escalate a conflict can lead to real problems, if you do not know how to stop. You also must agree that you will return to the scene of the battle and examine together what happened. Leaving conflict unresolved does not work. It will emerge again on its own if you fail to address it.

One of the best exercises I've used with clients to be more attentive to conflicts is quite simple. All you need is two chairs, placed close together. Sit on the chairs, opposite one another, and move them close enough that your knees are touching. Then, begin talking about what had upset you in the first place. Every time you start to feel angry, make sure you are still touching one another. Really dive into the conflict. In the process of all this, neither of you is allowed to blame the other person. You can express your fears, frustrations, and anger, but you must own the feelings. Many times, couples discover that their upsets are the result of a lack of understanding, or that something has become blown out of proportion.

OWNING YOUR RAGE, ANGER AND FRUSTRATION

Women are frequently guilty of both conflict-avoidance and repression of anger. Messages like, "it's not nice to show anger," or "it's not spiritual to get angry," are both useless and counter-productive. Whatever feelings you have, they are there. Telling yourself they do not exist does not make them go away. Unexpressed frustration, anger, or rage becomes emotionally and spiritually toxic. Not only can this damage a healthy relationship, but it can hurt you. The key is in finding a way to express those feelings which is less destructive. When you're experiencing frustration, anger, and rage, you're in touch with the energy of Mars—and Mars is about taking action! You may have no choice about the feelings, but you do have some choices about the way you express them. In extreme cases of anger or rage, some people seek out a way to use the energy so that it does not consume their lives in a destructive manner. For example, crime victims who, in outrage and pain, go about taking steps to change laws or their enforcement in such a way as to create better protection, may use their anger to motivate them into action. Mothers Against Drunk Driving (MADD) was just such an undertaking.

If you're holding back anger or rage, you may find that you become angry in situations which do not call for anger. If you are legitimately angry, you have the right to express that feeling, and, in responsibility to yourself, need to express it in some way.

I've seen hundreds of circumstances where women have experienced painful abuse at some point in their past and were unable to release their rage. That rage can work like a magnet to attract a partner who is also enraged, but who may lash out at you instead. These situations can become highly volatile and destructive unless one or both of the partners chooses to address their feelings honestly and to find healthy ways to express them.

The balance of the *modes* (cardinal, fixed, and mutable) in your chart may clue you in to your most "comfortable approach" to expressing yourself. If you are strongly cardinal (Aries, Cancer, Libra, and Capricorn), you are likely to take charge and get things done (and may be impatient in the process!), and may initiate changes which allow room for growth. With a fixed nature (Taurus, Leo, Scorpio, or Aquarius), you can endure through eternity, taking your problems with you (or may even allow them to bury you in the process). You may even allow your own stubborn attitudes to get in your own way! If your nature is mutable (Gemini, Virgo, Sagittarius, and Pisces), you're comfortable with the idea of consensus and even compromise, and may prefer to work around problems.

Another circumstance which arises all too frequently involves the "typical" male/female exchange. Females allow their males to express the aggression, anger, and power (Sun and Mars energy). Males allow their females to express the tenderness, emotionality, and sensitivity (Moon and Venus energy). We all know that this model does not work, but it pervades even the most consciously aware relationships in some form. Perhaps it is easier for one partner to express certain types of emotion—after all, we each have our strengths and weaknesses. Acknowledging and owning all your feelings is a good start toward becoming whole, and it is a crucial ingredient for a growth-oriented relationship.

POWER STRUGGLES: CONTROL, SEX AND MONEY

Maintaining a reasonable balance of power within a relationship is no small feat. Some relationships involve a strongly one-sided power base, in which one person takes charge, calls all the shots and directs all the action. The other person (who frequently feels like a non-person) takes the orders, yields to commands, and never questions authority. This is the model of an unhealthy power base!

It is no accident that the sign which has the affinity for partnerships is Libra. This sign, in its highest expression, allows for a continual shift in the balance of power. When the weight on one side of an issue brings the scale down, then the other side of the issue has to be addressed. It is rare, in true Libra form, for the scale to be still. The balancing action is continual, since circumstances and energy are continually shifting. Libra, in its negative sense, can appear to maintain a balance just for appearance's sake, yet never quite reaches it. This is the behavior when a person agrees just to keep the peace. You have Libra somewhere in your chart, so you'll probably recognize this behavior in some capacity. If you have difficult aspects to Venus and/or Mars in your chart, you may also be a perpetrator of placating behavior which does nothing but postpone the inevitable confrontation with the truth. To have a working partnership, both parties must give and take.

In a relationship involving two individuals, the ideal is for each to experience a positive affirmation of their autonomy through the relationship. You have probably learned that it does not work to try to "divide" everything into half-portions. You may have some skills or strengths which your partner does not possess, and vice-versa. In the realm of control, striving for the ideal of *shared power* is almost a requirement if a relationship is to survive and thrive.

Negative control frequently arises out of an individual's feelings of lack or loss, and is usually accompanied by underlying fears. Saturn, Pluto, and Mars in their worst expressions operate through negative control: attempts to force another to bend to your will. If you are the perpetrator of negative control, stop for a moment. What are you afraid of losing? What would happen if you allowed another person to do things their way? Can you keep your own personal boundaries in tact? Sometimes, control occurs because you have not set your own boundaries, or do not know how to maintain them!

If you are a victim of negative control, then you have another set of questions to explore. What do you gain by allowing another person to hold the power? Could it possibly be that you do not know how to take responsibility for yourself (or are you unwilling to . . .)? Where does your security reside?

To reclaim your personal power, you must first realize that someone else does not have it! You may have hidden it, or you may have had an experience in which it seemed to be taken from you. But you *can* access that power. It just takes practice, patience, and inner courage. Small steps are the best beginning. Start by looking in the mirror again. Tell yourself that you deserve to have an honest, open relationship, and that you will begin by being honest with yourself.

Power struggles frequently emerge in the bedroom. To open to a sexual encounter with another person, a certain level of vulnerability is exposed. Now that women are talking more openly about their sexual needs and desires, the old concepts about sex are pretty basically useless. For a long time, the only acceptable form of sexual encounter involved a man taking the lead, fulfilling his desires, and a woman going along with it. Not only is this a sad picture, but it is also pretty boring. This model, along with others in the patriarchal society, allowed men to take advantage of women, and kept women in the role of victim. Although it meant that the pendulum had swung a bit too far, Lorena Bobbitt certainly brought a new image into the world of a sexual relationship gone awry! While Pluto was transiting in Scorpio from 1984 through 1995, there was very little left to the collective imagination in regard to sex. So, now that the doors have opened, how will the nature of sexual relationships be altered? You are an active participant in writing that story!

Sexual sharing allows you to reach a level of intimacy with a partner which strengthens your bonds. It is part of the alchemy of love. Sex is not a favor to be granted or withheld as some form of blackmail. It is, among other things, a form of communication. But sex can be part of a power play, and is frequently experienced in that manner by both men and women. If you are enraged, you may use sex as part of your vengeful plans in some manner.

Money issues are another form of power struggle. In astrology, the part of your chart which relates to shared resources also is connected to sex. Surely you've had battles which pointed out these correspondences?! Your sex life suffers because finances are bad. Couples who joyfully share themselves on every level can create greater abundance. If there is blocking on any level, it filters into all elements of a relationship — including financial abundance (or a lack of it). How many times have you seen a young couple, poor as church mice, who love one another so dearly. You think to yourself that young love will change all that, and that somehow will turn things around. It's not a false myth. This is a universal truth: Where love is shared and nurtured, all things grow!

Control of finances within a relationship cannot be a one-way street, or the relationship will suffer. In premarital counseling with clients, financial issues become just as important as discussions about love, family planning, spiritual concerns, physical attraction, and other factors which play a part in a total relationship. In the early stages of a marriage, I always suggest that couples have three bank accounts — one for each individual and one joint account, especially if both partners are employed. (No, I do not work for a bank!) The way these accounts are to be handled should be discussed and planned. Secrets and devious planning do not work. If such things are necessary, there is a problem with trust in the relationship. One person cannot carry the burden of financial responsibility alone, when two people or a family are involved. Even if only one partner is employed, decisions about spending which affect the partnership or family should be shared for the best possible outcome. Hiding important details about finances may be a symptom of a deeper problem. Perhaps it is not a big problem, but you must, at least, acknowledge it if it is there.

JEALOUSY

Closely related to power struggles within intimate relationships is the experience of jealousy. Many times, jealousy arises when the core connection in a relationship has eroded and the vitality of the relationship itself is undermined. Then, anything which threatens the integrity of your bond can seem like a threat. Inevitably, when you're feeling jealousy, you are in a struggle with yourself. At the core is your sense of self-worth.

Jealousy can arise when a relationship is built on a weak foundation, especially if you feel that you never quite measure up to your partner's expectations. Then, if confronted with a situation in which your partner seems to be more interested in someone or something else, you begin to feel insecure. Sometimes, a twinge of jealousy is a good hint that you may need to do some work on your own personal evaluation, and it may not indicate that anything is wrong with your relationship. However, if you continually feel that you must compete or work extra hard to keep your partner's interest, then it is time to take another look at the relationship and its support of your personal worth. If you began the relationship at a personal low point, and found that your partner provided a strong support and positive encouragement, then you may be using your partner as a crutch for your own self-esteem.

The opposite can also be true. I frequently counsel women who complain that they did all the work of encouragement, support, and understanding, helping to shape their partner, only to have him leave. "I feel like I got him ready for his next relationship," is not an uncommon lament. If you have a history of relationships which have this theme, then you are working toward award-winning codependency. Your chart may indicate strong Moon, Venus, or Neptune influences which could make it difficult to keep your boundaries intact. You may also have trouble owning your own Sun and Mars. By that, I mean that you may project these qualities of self-assertiveness, strong will, and personal power onto the man in your life, but may not be comfortable embracing them as a part of yourself. A healthy relationship will normally involve support, and may include periods in which one partner seems to be the stronger while the other gets on their feet. In the ideal situation, the tables can turn, and the relationship still prospers.

Jealousy can also arise between partners within a relationship. It is not uncommon for a man to feel jealous if his wife or lover is more financially successful or otherwise self-assured. You may also feel some form of jealousy, especially if you share the same line of work. One of the best remedies for these feelings is to work on developing positive personal assertiveness — to start using your own Mars energy to accomplish your personal aims.

If jealousy is arising because you feel threatened by something or someone else outside your relationship, concentrate on the areas in which you feel vulnerability. Ask yourself what you have invested in these concerns. Determine what you can do to alleviate the pressure you're placing upon yourself by trying to satisfy these issues. Focus instead upon creating a feeling of greater self-acceptance. Fill yourself with the energy and vitality of love, which is not only personally satisfying, but highly attractive!

The Evolution of Love

An intimate relationship not only involves the lives and energy of the people involved, but it develops a life of its own. We expect changes in our relationships with our children, because they are growing and need different things from us during the periods of their personal development. The process of mothering is, indeed, a process of personal evolution for the woman and for the child or children involved. Moving from absolute support and intensive attachment to the experience of sending a child away from the nest is a long journey. Yet our relationships with lovers and partners also evolve and change over time. However, many couples become concerned because some of the changes seem to diminish the quality or passion within the relationship.

As an astrologer, I usually chart the course of a relationship by studying the astrological indicators present in the charts of the individuals involved and the charts of the relationship itself. The techniques of *composite* and *relationship* charts are quite useful, and I also try to obtain the chart for important events in a relationship. The chart of the first meeting is always significant, as is the chart of a marriage. These are techniques which I will not attempt to discuss here, but which you might want to explore. From these "core" level charts, which show the energy basis of the relationship, I extend toward exploring the cycles as they occur throughout the course of the relationship. It is always fascinating to correlate changes and shifts — like the decision to live together, time of marriage, birth of children, purchase of a home, etc. — with the cycles of a relationship. But the most illuminating factors involve the "internal" changes which occur in a relationship. Loving is not a static process. It involves periods of strong action, impatient waiting, passionate embrace, cool detachment, close comfort, and more. All the changes add color and texture to the relationship.

As you mature on a personal level, it only makes sense that your relationships will also undergo a maturing process. In astrology, everything is related to *cycles*. The concept of a cycle is that, at some point, it will repeat itself. Some cycles take a long time to return, like cycles of Saturn, which require about twenty-nine years. Others, like cycles of the Moon, repeat themselves in twenty-nine days! Yet through each of these repeating cycles, we gain a different perspective. Our first look at a relationship produces an impression, but rarely does it give a broad picture. It takes the experience of time, the repetition of cycles, to see the same thing, but with different eyes.

One of the beautiful things about astrology for me has been the awareness of shifting perspective. I've seen cycles come and go, for myself, and for my clients. In the process, something new is added each time something "old" is repeated. A healthy relationship will grow, change, mature, and transform. Sometimes the endings arise through separation, divorce, or death, but as a woman, you and I have learned that even as we change, what has been woven into the fabric of our souls will always remain. Regardless of how a relationship ends or transforms, the awakening you experienced through the relationship has altered your sense of yourself, and that is what you maintain. Once again, you and I have come full circle. Embrace yourself.

NOTES

1. "Change the World, and Godspeed," *Time Magazine* 145:24 (June 12, 1995), 82.

BIBLIOGRAPHY

Anand, Margo. *The Art of Sexual Ecstasy*. Los Angeles: Jeremy P. Tarcher, 1989.

Bach, George and Wyden, Peter. *The Intimate Enemy*. New York: William Morrow, 1969.

Beattie, Melody. *Codependent No More*. San Francisco: Harper and Row, 1987.

Beattie, Melody. *Beyond Codependency*. San Francisco: Harper and Row, 1989.

Covington, Stephanie and Beckett, Liana. *Leaving the Enchanted Forest*. San Francisco: Harper and Row, 1988.

Garcia, Jo and Maitland, Sara. *Walking on the Water*. London: Virago, 1983.

Lerner, Harriet Goldhor. *The Dance of Anger*. New York: Harper and Row, 1985.

Person, Ethel S. *Dreams of Love and Fateful Encounters*. London: Penguin, 1988.

Ross, Ruth. *Prospering Woman*. Mill Valley, CA: Whatever Publishing, Inc., 1982.

Madalyn Hillis-Dineen

Madalyn Hillis-Dineen began her study of astrology with the Uranian system and has practiced and taught Uranian techniques since 1980. A frequent lecturer at conferences throughout the United States, she coordinated the Uranian/Cosmobiology tracks for the 1992 and 1995 United Astrology Congresses. She has written for various publications including the NCGR Journal and had a monthly column in Horoscope Guide. She is also a certified Astro°Carto°Graphy interpreter.

An active member in the astrological community, Madalyn was awarded the 1995 UAC Regulus Award for Community Service. She is the clerk of the National Council for Geocosmic Research and has served two terms on the Steering Committee for the Association For Astrological Networking. In 1994, Madalyn joined Astrolabe, Inc., a leading astrological software firm, as their Director of Marketing. She is listed in "Who's Who in the East" and "Who's Who of American Women."

For twelve years, Madalyn was a happily "single again" mother of two children, Mark and Katie. In 1996, she married a man in touch with his spiritual side. They all reside in Brewster, Massachussetts, on Cape Cod, where Madalyn maintains an astrological practice in addition to her work at Astrolabe.

Madalyn Hillis-Dineen

On Singleness: Choosing To Be Me

As we approach a new millennium, growing numbers of women are living all or part of their lives in a state of singleness. Whether they've chosen it with blissful abandon or it has been thrust upon them by circumstance, these women face similar social, economic, and psychological challenges. If you believe the statistics, it is likely that most will remain single. In fact, a forty-year-old woman's chances of getting married are said to be about the same as her being kidnapped by a terrorist. At the risk of sounding a bit like Dan Quayle, it isn't as easy to handle the challenges of being single (with or without children) as Murphy Brown makes it look. If you don't believe it, spend time where women congregate and listen to their stories.

We like to think that we are enlightened and that we live in a society that tolerates a variety of lifestyles. After all, this is the 90s—there's no stigma attached to being single anymore. While words and phrases like spinster and old maid may be gone from our vocabulary, many of us still define a woman's worth in terms of her relationship to men. Though societal attitudes toward the institution of marriage may be changing, albeit slowly, our unconscious attitudes about male/female relationships have changed little. If this were not the case, why are there still so many married and unmarried women willing to stay in psychologically, not to mention physically, abusive relationships rather than face the day without a man?

Many women believe they are single simply because they just can't seem to find Mr. Right—you know, like that one married man who *will* leave his wife. How many women have gone from one unavailable or distant man to another, endlessly trapped in a cycle of hope and despair? They seem hooked on roller-coaster relationships that take them to dizzying heights and plummeting depths—sometimes all in a week, day, or hour. There is the never-ending belief that this relationship will be different and then the accompanying shame and anguish when it turns out to be just one more variation on the same theme. You have everything in common but he lives 3,000 miles away. Or, he's just next door but he's eccentric, emotionally distant and only interested in you when you're not interested in him. He's divorced but his ex-wife still owns him—emotionally, as well as financially—and he's done all that couple stuff already anyway. He's your soul mate, your one true love but you can't be together for some tragic reason or other, making your relationship with him especially tantalizing because the illusion of perfection remains intact.

Some women find themselves single again as a result of divorce or widowhood. A good number of them battle, on a daily basis, the financial insecurity and emotional terror of living alone. This is especially true when a woman first re-enters the single state. For some, it may be the first time they have ever lived alone in their lives. Even though she may have suffered through financial woes and periods of loneliness in marriage, the very fact that she is single adds a new complexity to her life.

Remember the movie, "An Unmarried Woman." It traces a newly divorced woman's process of becoming single from her initial anger and resentment right through to her own glorious self-emergence. By getting to know herself and making her own choices, she made contact with an inner strength she never knew she had, but the people around her, including some of her women friends, were not sure how to react. After a divorce or death, many "singles again" experience changes and even endings in long friendships. Why do we do that to each other and to ourselves? Some of us really believe that it is men who are the enemy.

The world of self-doubt, loneliness, and fear, however, is not purely the domain of the "single by default." Even the most enlightened, career-driven, "single by choice" women often find themselves second-guessing their decision, and, if their own economic and emotional worries weren't enough to deal with, they are frequently subjected to well-meaning but bruising comments from family and friends. *"I just want you to settle down and be happy before I die."* (Hidden message: You need a man to take care of you. You're not able to take care of yourself and you couldn't possibly be whole and happy on your own.") *"You have so much to offer. Why hasn't some nice guy married you already?"* (Hidden message: You have a lot going for you but you'll really be valuable when a man confirms it by wanting you.) *"Well, you don't really have time for a relationship anyway. You're so wrapped up in your work."* (Hidden message: Are you frigid, simply selfish, or too emotionally crippled to share your life with someone else?) The presumption that no woman would willingly opt to remain unmarried and that, therefore, there must be something wrong with her makes it nearly impossible, even today, for anyone except the very brave to openly and unabashedly choose to be single. So, the most self-assured, confident and independent single women will inevitably question, if only for a moment, whether their life would indeed be better if they were one half of a couple rather than one whole person alone.

Of course, singleness is not all pain and suffering, especially when a woman makes contact with the possibilities within herself. It may be for this very reason that so many of us are alone these days— to experience the joy of discovering ourselves. Even the most reluctant of single women often realize that the longer they are single, the more they begin to recognize their own inner power, glory, and strength. Once you've come to know and appreciate yourself, the more discriminating you are likely to be about the quality of your relationships. Living unhappily with a man is not an acceptable alternative once a woman is happy with herself. When a woman takes control and responsibility for her own life, it becomes impossible for her to enter into relationships unless they are based upon mutual respect and encourage each individual's personal autonomy.

When you examine the charts of women who are single, the common theme seems to be the need to define oneself. The horoscopes of women who openly and enthusiastically choose to be single will tend to have a preponderance of masculine or active energies. Look for a strongly placed Sun, Mars, Saturn, and/or Pluto. Often, the feminine planets, Moon and Venus, are placed in fire and air signs. Their charts tend to be more impersonal and work- or service-oriented and may have a Virgo/Aquarian kind of flavor. However, you will frequently see elements that point to conflicting needs of space and intimacy in the charts of women who are, shall we say, reluctantly single. There may be more dominance in the feminine signs, but there is usually a strong Saturnian and/or Uranian flavor as well. They may not openly choose singleness, but their behavior and choices in relationships usually tell another story. Often, it is this very failure in relationships that propels them on to develop independence, successful careers, and a higher sense of self-esteem.

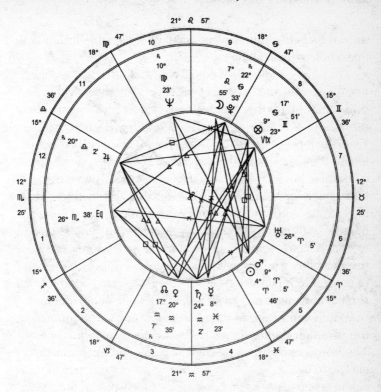

Chart 1. Gloria Steinem[1]

It shouldn't surprise us that the chart of one of the leaders of the contemporary feminist movement, Gloria Steinem, is a wonderful example of a dominance of active, masculine energies at work. She has Scorpio rising and its ruler, Mars, is conjunct the Sun in Aries in the Fifth House. Her Ninth House Moon in Leo makes a trine to that fiery combination. Venus is conjunct Saturn in Aquarius and they straddle the IC from either side. There is little in this chart that points to the need for the type of emotional fulfillment one traditionally gets in marriage. In fact, it rather aptly describes exactly who she is—

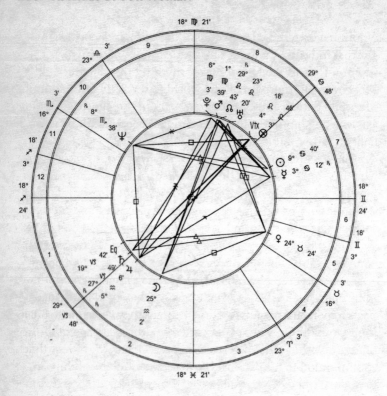

Chart 2. Princess Diana[2]

a publisher, writer, and champion of equal rights for women and men.

In contrast, we can look at the chart of Princess Diana who chose marriage but who, through divorce, will undoubtedly have to develop her independence and autonomy. As a Cancer, Princess Diana certainly would desire emotional intimacy, but the Moon, ruler of the Cancer Sun, is in the detached and anything but emotional sign of Aquarius. Emotional independence is what's needed here but it's usually only learned through painful experiences centered around erratic behavior and emotional extremes. Her Venus is dignified in its own sign of Taurus, indicating a great desire for loyalty and trust. Yet, it squares Uranus which promises anything but dependability. Moreover, out there for all the world to see is the midpoint of Mars and Saturn at the 15-degree mark of the Taurus/Scorpio axis, making her quest to understand and accept her own sexuality a rather public affair indeed.

What seems to be common in the horoscopes of women who are single, whether they believe that they want to be or not, is the need and the opportunity to develop wholeness within themselves. Astrologers will tell you that many women will actualize their Sun and Mars through the men in their lives and men will often experience their Moon and Venus through women. There is an intoxicating sense of wholeness that occurs when we integrate, within ourselves, our masculine and feminine energies. This is especially true for those with difficult aspects to personal planets because it means they've begun to heal their wounds. Once we can create a healthy marriage of those energies within ourselves, we have the chance to reflect that soulful union in a relationship with someone else. Being single doesn't necessarily mean that you will stay that way, but knowing and loving yourself is certainly a prerequisite to having a healthy, meaningful relationship.

Pulling Your Own Strings

Personal autonomy is one of the greatest lessons to be learned from being single. And, it is an essential ingredient for those in search of wholeness and happiness. Taking responsibility for one's own life is necessary for living happily, whether single or married. When you take responsibility for the state of your relationships, emotions, finances, and career—you don't shift dependence or blame, if things go wrong, to anyone else. This means that your spirits, work, or health don't rise or fall based upon the mood swings or telephone habits of the current man in your life. Your happiness becomes your responsibility and a function of your attitudes and perceptions. Your well-being is not dependent upon anyone or anything outside yourself. It is only by first taking responsibility for oneself that true personal freedom is possible.

Women who develop a sense of their own autonomy welcome making decisions for their own lives. They are not so apt to make the stupid choices that undermine their autonomy and self-esteem in the name of love. If this means staying single, then so be it. For a lot of women this takes courage. It is often much easier to be with a man than to be alone. According to Dr. Laura Schlessinger, author of the *Ten Stupid Things Women Do To Mess Up Their Lives*, women often use relationships to avoid the hard work it takes to fulfill their own potential. A woman who lacks a strongly developed sense of self is likely to be stupid when it comes to these ten things: attachment, courtship, devotion, passion, cohabitation, expectations, conception, subjugation, helplessness, and forgiving. On the other hand, a woman who respects herself approaches life as a chooser, not a beggar. When you begin to make clear choices, you tend to live life wholly and without guilt, recrimination or blame.

Astrologically, Saturn holds the key in determining how important the lesson of independence is in the individual's life. Through Saturn's placement by sign, house, and aspect, we have a clue as to how and where we can assume autonomy in our lives. Not coincidentally, it is in these very areas where we are likely to have been most wounded as well. The source of our doubts and fears is always the appropriate battleground to overcome them. Fear paralyzes us and cuts us off from our own self-potential. Once we meet the fear head on, it is possible for us to break through and achieve true personal fulfillment.

Many people simply remain paralyzed in self-destructive behavior patterns, holding on to their fear for dear life. Fear disappears when you replace it with a clear sense of self that starts from trusting in your inner strength.

The Saturn theme is universal in the charts of many single women and its expression takes a variety of forms. Saturn is often found in aspect (usually "hard") to relationship-oriented planets like the Sun, Moon, Venus, and Mars. Saturn may be angular (near the cusps or in houses 1, 4, 7, and 10). Or, you may see a number of personal planets in Capricorn and Aquarius, the signs Saturn rules. A good example of someone who meets all these criteria is Louisa May Alcott, a Sagittarian who had Saturn rising in Virgo squaring Mercury, which was also in Sagittarius. Her father was an educator who was acquainted with the great thinkers of the day like Henry David Thoreau and Ralph Waldo Emerson, but who could not earn enough to keep his family out of poverty. Because of her father's irresponsibility, she was forced to use her writing talent to support herself and her sisters. As you'd expect from someone with an Aquarian Moon, she took a great interest in social issues and was a champion of women's suffrage, education, and prison reform, but she was particularly immersed in the right of women to work to support themselves and fought for their economic equality. This was due, no doubt, to the fact that she also had Venus in Capricorn. Saturn also makes a minor hard aspect (11-1/4 series) to both her Moon and Venus.

The Sun/Saturn individual usually experiences some feelings of either being unloved or unwanted by the father and, for a woman, this influence usually affects her relationship with all the men that follow. In the case of a very strong father figure, the child may never feel good enough or deserving enough of her father's love. Often the individual strives to earn the father's love and respect in vain, for he very likely is the difficult-to-please type and there is almost never enough the child can do to secure

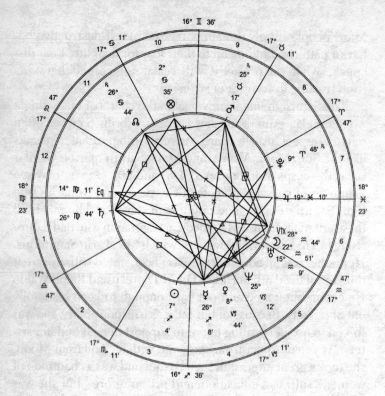

Chart 3. Louisa May Alcott[3]

this much-coveted acceptance. Sun/Saturn can also manifest as a weak, ineffectual, or absent father. In many cases, real economic hardship accompanies the situation as well. One way or another, though, the Sun/Saturn individual eventually must carve out their own identity, recognize that they are on their own, and learn to be independent.

In relationships with men, Sun/Saturn type women will often find themselves going from one unfulfilling and cold relationship to the next, looking for and rarely finding approval or love. Many Sun/Saturn types transfer all their emotional

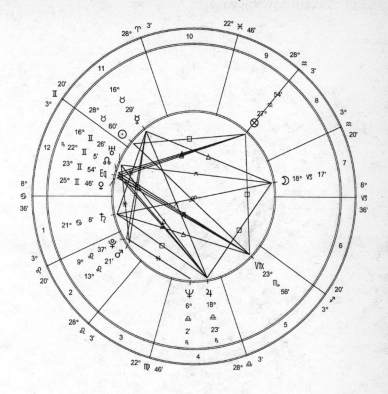

Chart 4. Cher[4]

dependence from Daddy to husbands, only to find those men missing in action when they need them the most. Some women are inexplicably attracted to unreliable men, thereby forcing them to rely on themselves. Many of these women end up accumulating a tremendous amount of disdain and contempt for men. It is through rejection that the Sun/Saturn individual often gets the opportunity to work hard at understanding themselves. Real self-mastery is possible with this combination, as we will see when we examine Oprah Winfrey's chart in detail.

With Moon/Saturn, women will often question their own femininity and their ability to nurture, usually stemming from

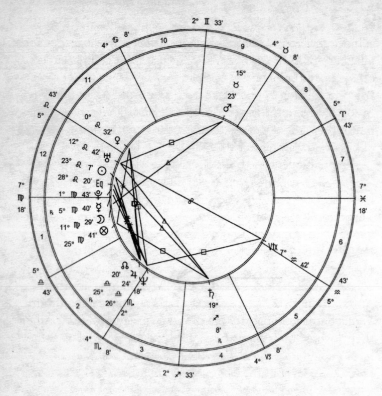

Chart 5. Madonna[5]

a difficult relationship with their own mother. They may feel
that their mothers resented them, constantly reminding them
of the hard work and the many sacrifices that were made on
their behalf. In order to earn the love and nurturing that they
so desire, they often will take on a subservient role, subjugat-
ing their needs to those of others. They tend to be pragmatic
about emotions and may find it difficult to let feelings flow. Circumstances often burden these women so that taking care of
others becomes a duty or obligation, rather than a joy. However, this aspect also affords the individual the opportunity to

achieve real emotional freedom once they learn to accept and take care of their own needs. They are then able to care for others out of free choice, without feeling resentment or guilt. It is interesting to note that both Cher and Madonna have Moon/Saturn hard aspects in their chart. Their music celebrates the right of women to assert their own sexuality instead of passively waiting to be fulfilled.

Femininity is also a question for women with Venus/Saturn aspects. Self-esteem is always a real issue and they may never feel attractive enough, no matter how good looking they are. They seem to zero in on imperfections, rather than capitalizing on strong points. They will usually have painful love experiences and the fear of being hurt again often leads them to be extremely cautious when it comes to relationship, or they may become involved in encounters that lack meaning or substance rather than risk the loss of something more meaningful. Venus/Saturn people will often find it difficult to share either their love or their money because they never feel as if they have enough of either. Venus/Saturn types are plagued with painful insecurities which generally stem from a fear of losing what they have because, deep down, they don't feel they deserve it. However, when the Venus/Saturn individual learns to accept and love themselves, they are capable of giving and accepting love and affection. Moreover, it is through their understanding of loss and suffering that they have the possibility to develop true compassion. Mother Theresa, a Virgo with a Venus/Saturn square, is an excellent example of someone who has dedicated her life to selfless giving. Maya Angelou, the black poet whose work is a triumphant celebration of the struggle to overcome adversity, has both Venus and Mercury in Pisces squaring Saturn in Sagittarius. Mia Farrow, an Aquarian who epitomizes unconventional single motherhood, has Saturn in Cancer involved in a t-square with the Moon in Capricorn and Venus in Aries.

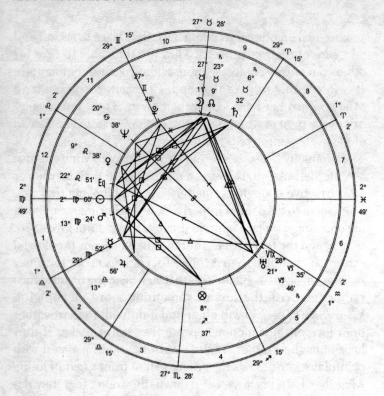

Chart 6. Mother Theresa[6]

Women with Mars/Saturn aspects often experience frustration in their relationships with men. They can find themselves attracted to men who are controlling and sometimes even cruel. Often, they have feelings of shame or guilt regarding their sexuality which usually is due to strict or religious upbringings. These are people who grew up hearing no a lot. Energy flow is an issue and they can be prone to spurts of activity, rather than consistent effort. They tend to sabotage themselves by pushing too hard or not enough. There is an inevitable conflict between the nature of Mars which wants to act and Saturn which

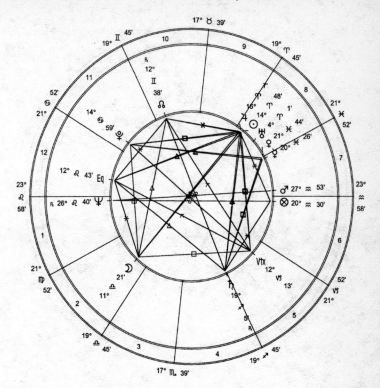

Chart 7. Maya Angelou[7]

would tend to deny, question, or impede action. Many may overcompensate for their inhibitions by having numerous encounters in search of a partner with whom they can experience sexual pleasure. They are also quite capable of, and usually do experience periods of celibacy. However, as with the other Saturn aspects, satisfaction for these individuals is not a function of anything outside of themselves. Rather, it has to do with allowing themselves to act without fear and to believe that they can get what they want. Once they learn to accept their sexuality and to understand how it works, they are quite capable

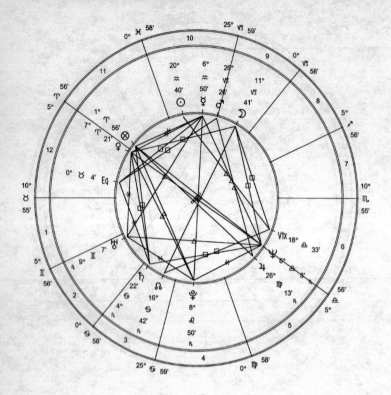

Chart 8. Mia Farrow[8]

of achieving and enjoying physical pleasure. Mars/Saturn individuals have the opportunity to develop a good deal of discipline and to achieve consistency in their behavior and energy patterns. In its highest expression, it enables the individual to act responsibly and with integrity, to do unto others as they would have others do unto them. St. Teresa of Avila, an Aries with Aries rising, used her Mars/Saturn opposition to reform her Carmelite convent from a haven for rich girls who eschewed marriage into a contemplative order of nuns dedicated to changing the world through prayer and meditation.

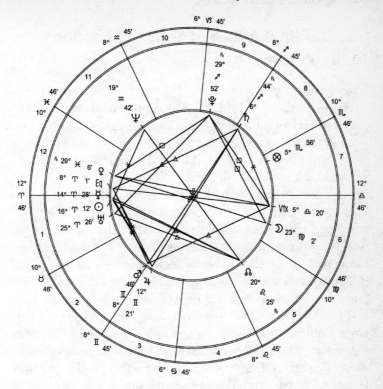

Chart 9. St. Teresa of Avila[9]

The emphasis on Saturn is not meant to imply that it is the determining factor in being single. Often, there are strong Uranus, Neptune, or Pluto themes that accompany Saturn in the charts of single women as well. However, it is essential to understand the function and action of Saturn in our chart before we can properly utilize the other outer planets. Once a firm foundation has been built, we are then free to innovate, dream, and transform.

The Cardinal Axis and Your Connection to the Whole

Uranian astrologers use the cardinal axis or eight-armed cross to represent the world at large. The eight-armed cross is comprised of the four cardinal ingress points (0 degrees of Aries, Cancer, Libra, and Capricorn) and the 15-degree points of the four fixed signs (Taurus, Leo, Scorpio, and Aquarius). In essence, we are dividing the 360 degrees of the zodiac by 8. The cardinal ingresses correspond to the four seasons and mark for us the turning points in the earth's connection with the sun, the giver of light and life. Many astrologers who specialize in predicting world events use the cardinal ingress charts as a kind of quarterly birth chart for the earth. The 15-degree point of the fixed signs is halfway through each season and represents the peak of intensity for that period. Since the connection between the sun and earth is marked on this cross, it represents the world at large. Cultures throughout the ages have celebrated these eight turning points with various holidays or traditions, just as we celebrate Christmas, Easter, and Halloween. This division by eight is not exclusive to our observation of the sun. We also follow the eight phases of the Moon, from new to full and new again and we sing the eight tones of the musical scale.

As the planets move through time and space, their connection with this axis is ever-changing, making each day different and new Planets are certainly connected to the cardinal axis when they are in conjunction or even in a minor hard aspect to one of the eight arms of the cross, but this is not the only way a planet can be connected to this axis. Uranian astrologers also look at the symmetry of the planets around each of the eight arms of the cross. In other words, they look for planets whose midpoints would be posited on the cross as well. Just as this technique is useful to describe world events on a particular day or place, we can also use the position of the planets at birth

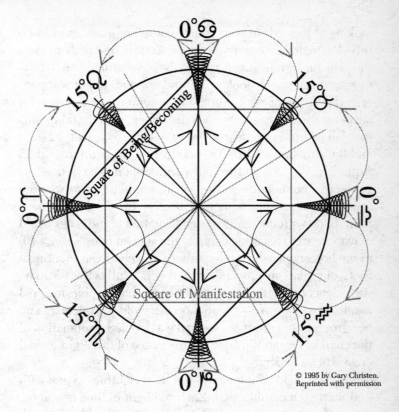

Diagram 1. The Eight-Armed Cross

relative to this eight-armed cross to describe the unique connection of the individual with the world at large. After all, the
planets are constantly moving in relationship to one another and
thereby define the course of human history in the broadest
sense as well as in everyday ways. How you fit into this universal,
ever-changing rhythm is quite elegantly defined in how the
planets were arranged around the cardinal axis at your specific
time and place of birth.

Astrologically, the "whole of humanity" is represented by the
cardinal axis, and your place in this whole can be described by

looking at this axis in your chart. There are many ways to do this. Uranian astrologers often use 360-degree dials to view the planetary arrangement around the eight-armed cross. However, you can simply look at a 360-degree midpoint sort generated from your favorite computer program or order one from an astrological chart-casting service. Then, look for midpoints that fall within a one-degree orb of 0 Aries, 0 Cancer, 0 Libra, and 0 Capricorn, and 15 Taurus, 15 Leo, 15 Scorpio, and 15 Aquarius. We look to the four cardinal points to define our subjective connection to the world, enabling us to sow the seeds for our self-unfoldment. However, the fixed points have more to do with the material manifestation in the outer world of who we are. This is analogous to the angular houses (1,4,7,10) in the horoscope which tell us about ourselves, our emotional roots, our relationships, and our career in a subjective way. The succedent houses (2, 5, 8, 11) describe the measurable, material results of who we are—our money, our children, our taxes and our group interactions. As we make a detailed examination of the chart of Oprah Winfrey, the relevance of this eight-armed cross will be illustrated

Any search for wholeness in the chart rightfully begins with examining the cardinal axis. Each moment in time is unique, just as there are no two people who are exactly alike. Though we may be born alone and die alone, our lives are not lived in isolation. Defining your connection to the whole is an important step in the process of living life happily and successfully on every level—physically, mentally, emotionally, and spiritually. One of life's great dichotomies is that although we are certainly separate individuals, we are also part of a greater whole. Every action you take affects the people around you and, in fact, the whole world. Yet, how insignificant we usually feel that we are. Once you are in touch with where and how you are connected to the universe, with your higher purpose, so to speak, you come to know that nothing you do is insignificant. Understanding your place in the larger scheme of things is the first step toward taking responsibility for your own life.

Oprah Winfrey: A Single "Everywoman"

Known simply as Oprah to her legions of adoring fans, this Aquarian superstar remains single, despite a long, devoted relationship with Stedman Graham. Though they appear to have transcended the "will they/won't they marry" media hype of a few years ago, their marital status was once a very hot topic. You couldn't check out of a supermarket without Oprah's image staring out at you, like some pathetic poster girl for singleness. In a way, it's laughable. Wondering whether Oprah will marry Stedman seems a bit like asking if Golda Meir can type, but the taunting tabloid headlines insinuating it was Oprah's weight that was keeping Stedman from the altar still seem unnecessarily cruel, especially in view of her horoscope.

Even more insidious, though, for the rest of us, and no doubt a real question for Oprah herself, was the underlying message beneath all this speculation: that she would be happier, more okay, if she were married. And, if this is true for the incredibly talented and successful Oprah Winfrey, where on earth does that leave the rest of us? It appears that, for now, she has answered by saying she's okay enough, thank you, and continues on with her life, her work, and her relationship with Stedman. She did us all a great service by not succumbing to that kind of pressure, but that shouldn't surprise us. Her horoscope clearly reflects that the essence of her life is not about her wealth and fame or even the tremendous obstacles she overcame to achieve her stunning success. It's not about personal happiness at all. Ultimately, her life is about being mindful of the power she has to change the lives of millions and the sacred responsibility that goes with it.

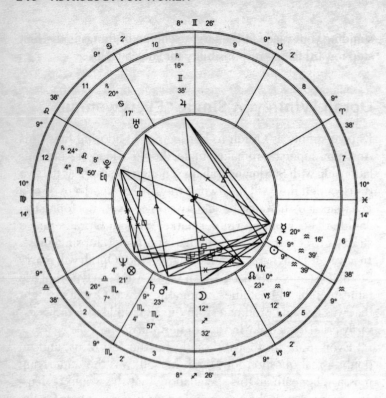

Chart 10. Oprah Winfrey[10]

Oprah Winfrey was born on January 29, 1954 at 7:50 P.M.
CST in Kosciusko, Mississippi[11] at nearly the exact moment of
a superior conjunction of Sun and Venus in Aquarius. Not only
has she achieved phenomenal popularity and success
(Sun/Venus) in television (Aquarius) but, to the millions who
watch her daily, Oprah is "everywoman's" best friend. This intimacy with the masses is so befitting someone with both Sun
and Venus in Aquarius, the so-called least personal sign of the
zodiac. It's not that Aquarian types aren't capable of personal
relationships, it's just that their life purpose often includes

broader, more universal themes. Their own self-fulfillment usually comes from community with others of like mind, and group interaction empowers these individuals to do their personal best. They function well in relationships that begin with friendship and which have a focus outside the relationship, such as a common interest, political cause, or philosophy.

Oprah has Virgo rising, placing her all-important Sun/Venus conjunction in the Sixth House of health, service, and work. Mercury, her ascendant ruler, is also in Aquarius and in the Sixth House, accentuating the Virgo/Aquarian emphasis even more. She is a legendary perfectionist, a tireless worker, and as famous for her weight problems as she is for her career successes. A firm believer in community service, her participation goes further than merely writing checks. She takes an active role in the causes and people she supports, but there is no doubt that a Sixth House placement of an Aquarian Sun and Venus presents a good deal of difficulty, especially when it comes to self-acceptance. The quest for perfection often has its roots in extreme self-criticism, and what two signs are more associated with an ability to critically analyze than Virgo and Aquarius? As demanding as this placement suggests Oprah may be of those around her, it is certain that she holds herself to an even higher standard. This placement of the Sun and Venus also reiterates that she is likely to find personal happiness through work and service to humanity and that these themes provide a common thread in her more intimate relationships.

Oprah's powerhouse of a Sun/Venus conjunction also happens to be in a rather exact square with Saturn in Scorpio, turning that formidable pairing into two of the most difficult astrological aspects a person can have. These are two of the very aspects most often associated with feelings of abandonment, rejection, and low self-esteem. Saturn is in the Third House, further suggesting that her mental attitude and her feelings about herself are reflected in her health and diet patterns. Still,

Saturn in Scorpio blesses one with determination and the capacity to fight insurmountable odds when necessary. For Oprah, it becomes the very struggle to love herself that is the key to unlocking her enormous potential for success.

It is important to explore the relevance in Oprah's life of being born at such a significant point in the Venus cycle, the moment of superior conjunction. Since the superior conjunction occurs when the Sun is between Venus and Earth, the combination takes on a dualistic quality, much in the way an opposition aspect operates. There is enormous potential for either good or evil and the fundamental lesson of this placement is about the choice between the two. The issue of right and wrong is not only pivotal to the person's experience but tends to be played out quite openly. It is no coincidence then that Oprah led a nation in finally talking about the sort of things polite people never talked about—things like incest, child abuse, rape, and discrimination. In the process, she shared her own pain as a survivor, thereby inspiring others to do the same. While her childhood abuse has long been public knowledge, she only revealed in 1995 that she had been involved in a particularly destructive relationship during which she used cocaine. What makes revelations like these so important for all of us is not the fact that she chooses to share these intimate facts with the entire world. The real value is in the example she has set on how to get beyond the kinds of life circumstances that leave most people in despair. Her dedication to the arduous task of self-knowledge, self-acceptance, and self-love empowers millions of others on the same path of healing themselves and taking responsibility for their own happiness.

The charts of children whose parents were unmarried or divorced often have Sun or Venus in combination with Saturn, and Oprah's is no exception. The child of a young unmarried couple, she was plagued throughout her childhood with self-esteem issues stemming from feelings of shame and inadequacy about being poor, illegitimate, and black. Soon after Oprah's birth, her mother moved to Milwaukee to find work and Oprah was left in the care of her paternal grandmother, who has been characterized as a strict disciplinarian. True to her Aquarian nature, the spirited child proved too much for her grandmother and she was sent to live with her mother in Milwaukee. Here, she faired no better and, in 1962, her mother decided that eight-year-old Oprah should be sent to live with her father and stepmother in Tennessee. Life in Tennessee proved to be beneficial for Oprah. Her father and stepmother encouraged her in her academic work and provided a loving (Sun/Venus), yet firm (Saturn), environment. Oprah thrived in these surroundings, excelling both academically and socially. That this first glimpse of her real potential should occur in her eighth year is noteworthy, since it coincides with the eight-year Sun/Venus synodic cycle. In the very year that the Sun and Venus again made a superior conjunction in the very same degree as they had at her birth, Oprah Winfrey had her first taste of real achievement.

However, this positive situation only lasted a year. Oprah went back to Milwaukee to visit her mother during summer vacation and, when it was time for Oprah to return to Tennessee, her mother refused to let her go. As is so typical with challenging Saturn aspects, just as your dreams and hard work are being recognized, something occurs to prevent complete enjoyment and realization. Often, the person will sabotage the situation themselves but, especially early in life, circumstances beyond the individual's control may dictate the unwelcome outcome. We can only imagine the rage, self-hatred, and guilt that Oprah must have felt during this time. Even though her father protested, did she blame him for not doing enough to keep her with him? She surely must have felt rage at her mother for uprooting her again, but what child wouldn't wonder what they had done wrong—if only I were good enough, more lovable, perhaps this wouldn't have happened.

To make matters worse, it was during the ensuing five years in Milwaukee that she experienced sexual abuse at the hands of male relatives and acquaintances. She suffered this humiliation in silence though she "acted out" with typical teenage rebellion. In 1968, she was sent back to live with her father in Tennessee, and by the time of the second return of the Sun/Venus superior conjunction in 1970, she had readjusted to her new environment and was well on her way to laying the foundation for her formidable career. It is important to note here that in 1986, the year of her fourth synodic return of the Sun/Venus superior conjunction, her TV talk show first aired nationally (September 8) and she met Stedman Graham after experiencing years of abuse and instability in relationships. In 1994, the year of her fifth synodic return, Oprah never looked better, having lost weight due to changes in exercise and diet, and she even wrote the introduction for a low calorie cookbook, *In the Kitchen with Rosie: Oprah's Favorite Recipes*, written by her personal chef, Rosie Daley.

Difficult aspects, especially squares, from both Sun and Venus to Saturn are a double whammy for any woman. These aspects would typically represent both difficulties in relating to men (Sun/Saturn) as well as creating doubts about her own femininity (Venus/Saturn). Until a Sun/Saturn individual truly learns independence and autonomy, there is a tendency to be involved in relationships which re-create childhood hurts rather than ones which foster healing and wholeness. Some shun relationships altogether rather than go through the feelings of abandonment and rejection that seem part and parcel of their dealings with men. With Venus/Saturn, the person needs to learn to love themselves and to believe in their own worth. Often, they crave love, though they may appear cool and disinterested as a defense. There is an emptiness inside that can never seem to be filled no matter how much they are loved or how much they accumulate, and the truth is that the void will remain until they learn to love and accept themselves. Once they have bridged that gap, they are capable of real sharing and commitment.

Both these aspects can also contribute to a woman's success in the "male" world of business. The Sun/Saturn person often spends a lifetime working hard. This may begin purely as survival—if I don't take care of myself, no one will. Yet, it is often through work achievements that these individuals begin to like and believe in themselves, so while relationships may fail them, work sustains and rewards them. Venus/Saturn types really get creatively juiced through work and often give a great deal of loyalty and devotion to a particular job, boss, or company, and though women with Venus/Saturn may question their femininity, they often feel comfortable dealing with men on men's terms.

There is no doubt that Oprah Winfrey has experienced both the most positive and negative aspects of her Sun/Venus/Saturn combination, but it is in the positive way that she has been able to work with these energies that make the exploration of her horoscope of genuine value to others who may have strong Saturn themes in their own horoscopes. While Saturn poses challenges, limitations, and obstacles, it nevertheless also presents the chance to add structure to whatever planets it touches. In Oprah's case, she has the opportunity to marry the force of the ego (Sun) with discipline (Saturn) and can approach her life mindful of the importance of personal responsibility and master of her own destiny. Through learning (Saturn) to love and accept (Venus) herself, compassion, understanding, and true commitment becomes possible in her relationships.

A close look at this Sun/Venus/Saturn combination reveals that it makes another very important planetary connection, one which beautifully explains why Oprah was able to make such positive use of these rather difficult aspects. Mercury, the planet of communication, is in antiscia with Saturn.[12] This means that

Mercury reflects her Saturn onto 0 degrees of the Cancer/Capricorn axis, part of the eight-armed cross. Therefore, Mercury and Saturn work together in the world arena. Since the Sun and Venus are inextricably linked with Saturn, their public expression is also realized through Mercury. Further, Mercury most truly reflects the Sun and Venus onto 15 degrees of the Leo/Aquarius axis, which represents manifestation of creativity and group values in the world at large. Therefore, communication (Mercury) is the appropriate vehicle for her to achieve popularity and success (Sun/Venus) in the outer world.

Another formidable aspect in Oprah's chart is a rather tight square between a Third House Mars in Scorpio and a Twelfth House Pluto in Leo. While this combination certainly accounts for the sexual abuse and violence she suffered, these planets also endow one with the ability to fight back. Certainly, this aspect is also descriptive of her role as a producer—she certainly would want to run the show! Mercury is also involved in this combination, making a t-square with Mars and Pluto. We already know that Mercury is connected to the cardinal axis through Sun, Venus, and Saturn and so there is a direct link between the effect of sexual abuse and her ability to turn those destructive experiences into an opportunity to speak for all those without a voice.

The mechanism with which she is able to take control of her life is so clearly described in this Mercury/Mars/Pluto combination. Even during the time that she was experiencing sexual abuse, she escaped through reading and study into the world of ideas, and it is no secret that she is a firm believer in the concept that you can create your life through the power of your mind. What's more, she shares her valuable secrets with anyone who cares to listen. Her television program is a virtual showcase for physical, mental, emotional, and spiritual self-improvement techniques, but it is through her spontaneous reactions to her guests that we have a real window into her thoughts and her soul. While writing this piece I tuned into Oprah one afternoon for inspiration. She didn't disappoint me. The show was about, of all things, wedding day disasters. One distressed California couple showed video of the collapse of their outdoor wedding tent, thanks to a torrential rain and hail storm. The bride revealed that, as a result of this tragedy, she believed her marriage was doomed from the start. "But," Oprah replied, "I thought rain was supposed to be good luck. So, when it turned to hail, why wouldn't you just think that it sort of solidified things?"

Oprah knows that true miracles occur when we choose to change how we think. More than that, she strives to empower others to create miracles in their own lives, fully aware that these changes in perceptions are what will ultimately change our world. Whether or not Oprah Winfrey ever marries Stedman Graham, or anyone else, for that matter, seems irrelevant in light of her life and her horoscope. Her true purpose lies in the ability she has to influence millions of people to join her on a path of self-love and spiritual growth. After all, she's there every afternoon to remind us that if she can do it, so can we!

Honoring the Masculine and Feminine

Since the movement of Pluto through Libra, we seem to be involved in a process that has led more women and men to be alone. The divorce rate skyrocketed during the years between 1972 and 1983, and we are still dealing with the repercussions of this transit on our idea of the roles of men and women in relationship. It's interesting to realize that those who were most affected by this transit were born with the spiritually potent sextile of Neptune in Libra and Pluto in Leo. This is the generation that has the opportunity to achieve true spiritual union by understanding the power of the self.

As Pluto went through Libra, tearing at the very fabric of Neptunian dreams of perfect relationships, the distinctions between men's and women's roles began to blur. Because they had to survive emotionally and economically, many women were forced to toughen up, to be agressive and to compete with men in the workplace. Men also had to deal with the havoc Pluto wrought on their relationships. Many men were forced to do for themselves all the things they grew up believing a woman would do for them. Men, too, became single parents and had to learn how to comfort their children as well as cook the bacon they brought home. What's more, they had to learn to cope with their own emotions. Married or unmarried, they were urged to develop their feminine side and to talk about their feelings, while women went through assertiveness-training and started getting jobs that traditionally belonged to men. Thus, the transit of Pluto through Libra seeded the possibility for a whole generation to achieve spiritual wholeness through understanding and honoring the masculine and the feminine as equally important and powerful. At the same time, the movement of Neptune through Sagittarius trined a generation's Pluto in Leo and self-help groups, methods, and philosophies emerged to help lead the way to self-realization.

Pluto moved into Scorpio and Neptune into Capricorn, making squares to their natal positions in the charts of an entire generation, forcing them to deal with their actions. In some ways, the gulf between men and women, especially the single ones, seemed to broaden. It became increasingly apparent that there was real economic fallout from divorce and it was easy to blame each other for monetary woes. With Neptune in Capricorn, the economy was shaky anyway. The pie-in-the sky, unlimited financial boon of the preceding years became a thing of the past just as AIDS brought the sexual revolution to a jolting halt. Even though sexual and economic realities should have brought men and women together, it seemed to further fuel an already malignant distrust. Man-bashing became a sport wherever single women congregated, while men's violence against women escalated. The very same women who treat men as the enemy wonder why they don't have a relationship, and it seems that men's fear of drowning in a world of feelings causes them to build walls and deny that they care for the very women who are most able to meet their emotional needs.

As Pluto moves through Sagittarius and Uranus, and then Neptune through Aquarius, they will activate that Neptune/Pluto sextile again, bringing the challenge to the "me" generation more clearly into focus. We may continue down the road of isolation, to be sure. After all, we'll be able to indulge in virtual reality sex, a definite plus for an aging generation. It's likely that our social safety nets will undergo a transformation and we'll need to find inventive solutions, like group living, to the problems of health care and retirement, but it is continuing the process of attaining spiritual wholeness that is of real importance.

Women who have mastered independence and self-reliance now are beginning to reconnect with the real power of the feminine that they hold inside—the ability to be nurturing, intuitive, and loving. Perhaps women have made it to the so-called man's world so that they can contribute the very special spiritual gifts that they have to offer. The goddess is emerging and demanding equal time. There is a resurgence of a belief in angels, those glorious entities that unite the masculine and feminine. Remember, though, the archangels were men who were in touch with their spiritual side. The men in our lives have the possibility to be angels, too. A man in touch with his inner self is also empowered by the same spiritual joy of finding wholeness. These are our brothers and sons, as well as our friends and lovers. The future is about enabling each other on the road to self-realization.

As Marianne Williamson states so beautifully in *A Woman's Worth,* "Spiritual growth is like childbirth. You dilate, then you contract. You dilate, then you contract again. As painful as it all feels, it's the necessary rhythm for reaching the ultimate goal of total openness. The pain of childbirth is more bearable as we realize where it's leading. Giving birth to our selves, our new selves, our real selves, whether we are men or women, is a lot like giving birth to a child. It's an idea that is conceived, then incubates. Childbirth is difficult, but holding the child makes the pain worthwhile. And so it is when we finally have a glimpse of our own completion as human beings—regardless of our husband or lack of one, our money or lack of it, our children or lack of any, or whatever else we think we need in order to thrive and be happy. When we have finally touched on a spiritual high that is real and enduring, then we know that the pain of getting there was worth it, and the years ahead will never be as lonely."[13]

NOTES

1. Gloria Steinem. Born Mar. 25, 1934, 10 P.M. EST, at Toledo, OH (41N39, 83W33). Source: Machey-Saunders Data Collection, Astrolabe, Inc., Brewster, MA, 1989.

2. Princess Diana. Born July 1, 1961, 7:45 P.M., at Sandringham, England (52N50, 0E30).

3. Louisa May Alcott. Born Nov. 29, 1832, 5:30 A.M. UT, at Germantown, PA (40N2, 75W10). Source: Blackwell Data Collection, Astrolabe, Inc., Brewster, MA, 1989.

4. Cher. Born May 20, 1946, 7:25 A.M. PST, at El Cerrito, CA (32N48, 119W34). Source: Machey-Saunders Data Collection, Astrolabe, Inc., Brewster, MA, 1989.

5. Madonna. Born Aug. 16, 1958, 7 A.M. EST, at Bay City, MI (43N36, 83W53).

6. Mother Theresa. Born Aug. 27, 1910, 4:57 A.M. CET, at Skopje, Yugoslavia (41N59, 21E26).

7. Maya Angelou. Born Apr. 4, 1928, 2:10 P.M. CST, at St. Louis, MO (38N37, 90W12). Source: Machey-Saunders Data Collection, Astrolabe, Inc., Brewster, MA, 1989.

8. Mia Farrow. Born Feb. 9, 1945, 11:27 A.M. PWT, at Los Angeles, CA (34N4, 118W15). Source: Machey-Saunders Data Collection, Astrolabe, Inc., Brewster, MA, 1989.

9. St. Teresa of Avila. Born Mar. 28, 1515, 5:51 A.M. UT, at Avila, Spain (40N39, 4W42). Source: Blackwell Data Collection, Astrolabe, Inc., Brewster, MA, 1989.

10. Oprah Winfrey. Born Jan. 29, 1954, 7:50 P.M. CST at Kosciusko, MS (33N03, 89W35).

11. Source: herself during a demonstration of the Timisis Life-Clock on a TV show, as cited in Lois Rodden's *Data News* #53, June 1995.

12. The antiscia of a planet is that point equidistant on the opposite side of the Cancer/Capricorn axis from the planet. Therefore, the midpoint between the planet and its antiscia will always be 0 degrees of Cancer/Capricorn. Antiscia are also helpful in finding planets with equal declination. Contra-antiscia is measured off the Aries/Libra axis and will point to planets that are in contra-parallel to each other. Antiscia and contra-antiscia are the basis for the concept of the eight-armed cross as used by Uranian astrologers. Using the eight-armed cross also involves measuring symmetry around 15 degrees of the fixed signs as well as looking for planets in antiscia and contra-antiscia. The concept

of antiscia and contra-antiscia dates back to the time of Ptolemy, making it much older than Uranian astrology which was developed at the turn of this century.

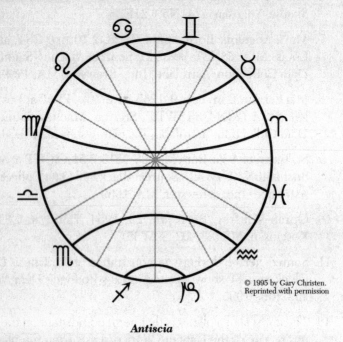

Antiscia

13. Marianne Williamson. *A Woman's Worth* (Ballantine Books. New York. 1993), 138–9.

Ronnie Gale Dreyer

Ronnie Gale Dreyer is an internationally known astrological consultant, teacher, and lecturer. In addition to numerous articles, columns and gift books, she is the author of *Venus: The Evolution of the Goddess and Her Planet*, *Vedic Astrology*, and *Moon Guides to Love and Life* and is currently writing a book about astrology and alternative health.

Ronnie holds a B.A. in English/Theater Arts and studied Jyotish (Vedic [Hindu] Astrology) both privately and at Sanskrit University in Benares, India. She co-founded the first astrological computer service in the Netherlands where she lived for ten years, was the official Dutch representative for Astro-Carto-Graphy, and was an editorial consultant for new age and self-help books at several publishing companies.

Ronnie is the secretary of the Association for Astrological Networking (AFAN) and is on the staff of the New York Astrology Center. In 1994, the Indian Council of Astrological Sciences awarded her the Jyotish Kovid certificate for "helping to promote Vedic Astrology through teaching and writing."

Ronnie Gale Dreyer

The Impact of Self-Esteem

What is Self-Esteem?

ith the recent proliferation of 12-step recovery programs, ranging from Alcoholics Anonymous to Adult Children of Alcoholics to Debtors Anonymous, the term "self-esteem," which Webster's Dictionary defines as "confidence and satisfaction in oneself," runs the risk of becoming not only misused, but inextricably altered in our vocabulary.

In the first place, nobody ever seems to have "high self-esteem," or self-confidence, anymore. Lately, it seems more people than not are suffering from "low self-esteem," a catch-all phrase for every insecurity we may experience, and the fashionable but glib answer to the question of "what ails our society." In fact, low self-esteem or what used to be called an "inferiority complex" (to which nobody dared own up), may range from simply lacking confidence in a particular area, which most of us have experienced at one time or other, to becoming so filled with self-loathing that it paralyzes and prevents us from attaining happiness or success. Because the concept has become so overused, the true significance of what it means to truly feel confident and possess the self-respect and self-love which enables us to reach the pinnacle of success has almost lost its meaning.

Although self-esteem issues obviously affect both sexes equally, it is the intention of this chapter to focus on how a woman's self-image influences not only her self-expression, but her ability to be discriminating in her choice of relationships. While men may also suffer from low self-respect and benefit from the rewards of high self-esteem, women, by virtue of what Dr. Susan Forward terms "cultural support for women's dependency," are more likely to succumb to a dependent role in professional and personal relationships. According to Dr. Forward, women are more easily convinced that they are weaker, i.e., needing someone "stronger," even if that strength is ultimately enacted as abuse, that is, "any behavior that is designed to control and subjugate another human being through the use of fear, humiliation, and verbal or physical assaults. In other words, you don't have to be hit to be abused."[1]

Men, on the other hand, have always been conditioned to be performance-oriented and self-supporting, so that any intimation of esteem problems will often remain hidden beneath the surface of an outwardly successful lifestyle. In fact, men may overcompensate to a great extent because it is more stigmatic for males to openly admit to any insecurity.

Astrological Indicators of Self-Esteem

To determine whether the attainment of self-esteem, i.e., feeling good about yourself, is an easy task or an arduous road attained through conscious efforts at self-improvement, it is necessary to view the entire horoscope in accordance with its planetary cycles. Despite the fact that in-depth horoscope analysis is always in the end recommended before reaching conclusions regarding the individual's assets and liabilities, it is still possible to isolate key factors when trying to understand a particular area of the chart.

Although difficult configurations and planetary combinations, regardless of the planets involved, present conflicts which may throw off self-confidence, I have utilized the Sun, which represents the self, and Venus, which signifies the love and value placed upon that self, as basic indicators of self-esteem. By zeroing in on these two planets, we can instantaneously assess precisely how a woman perceives herself and how that self-image may impact her choice of partners. Conversely, by examining a man's Sun and Venus we can evaluate how his own self-esteem, or lack thereof, eases or prevents his spouse's journey toward wholeness. Viewing the Sun and Venus equally applies to a man's chart, but because this book is directed toward the condition of women, I will be using the feminine gender.

Whereas a positively placed Sun in the horoscope represents the ability to remain autonomous, maintain a sense of purpose and generally take charge of one's life, the individual with its negative counterpart will generally lack confidence, have a weak or undefined sense of self, or simply be incapable of standing on his/her two feet. If Venus is well-positioned in the chart, we possess an inner strength, beauty, and general feeling of worthiness which, as a result, radiates outwardly and attracts people who wish to absorb some of that "feel good" energy. Conversely, by refusing to acknowledge or accept our inner beauty and strength, we feel undeserving of, and consequently reject, life's pleasures and benefits. This can manifest as the denial of Venusian rewards ranging from physical appearance and personal relationships to sexual enjoyment and financial security.

By judging the horoscopic Venus, we immediately recognize that the capacity for self-love clearly dictates how we value ourselves within our personal and professional relationships. If we feel worthy of love, we will seek a partner who will treat us with high regard. If there is a certain degree of self-loathing, then we may deny ourselves pleasure as a way of saying "I don't deserve to feel good," resulting in negation of relationships or gravitating towards someone who is unattainable, difficult, or, at its most extreme, abusive.

Although there are many indicators in the horoscope which contribute to the way we feel about ourselves, afflictions to the remaining planets may not paralyze one's overall relationships as will afflictions to the Sun and, especially, to Venus. While a prominent Mars may provide physical strength and the courage to be assertive and straightforward, a powerless Mars will not necessarily be detrimental to our sense of self-worth, unless accompanied by a weak Sun and/or Venus. Even the most dominant Mars cannot always reverse or alter the effects of a weak Sun or Venus, unless Martian assertiveness and forcefulness has been sufficiently internalized. As we will see in the section on O. J. and Nicole Brown Simpson, the aggressive nature of their strong Martian energies acted as a temporary facade, until their true insecurities, reflected by their weak Venuses, were put to the test.

After analyzing the chart to determine the level of one's self-esteem, it is necessary to view the cycles of our lives as evidenced by the transits and progressions, to determine when we will be blessed with renewed self-confidence or, conversely, when unfavorable circumstances could potentially lower our morale. For the most part, stressful aspects to the Sun and Venus will present times in our life when values and self-esteem are challenged. If, in fact, some of those conflicts have already been worked through at the time the configuration is activated, the period will be somewhat manageable, since we know what to expect and can transform adversity into an opportunity for self-improvement and growth.

Case Studies of Nicole Brown Simpson and Hillary Rodham Clinton

To illustrate how differently two women dealt with the issue of self-esteem throughout the cycles of their lives, I have utilized the charts of Nicole Brown Simpson (see chart, page 267) and Hillary Rodham Clinton (see chart, page 284). Although these women appear to have nothing in common, what links them are their attraction and subsequent marriages to charismatic men with whom they led charmed, public lives and an awareness that motherhood was an important key to their self-fulfillment.

Whereas Nicole Brown Simpson relied on her beauty and sexual magnetism to propel her through life, Hillary Rodham Clinton's assets have always been her intelligence and a passion for her beliefs. While each woman fought to carve her own niche, Nicole Brown Simpson's road toward establishing her own identity was more obscured than that of Hillary Rodham Clinton's, who, due to her prominent Sun, always knew who she was and where she was going.

Because Hillary Rodham Clinton overcame certain insecurities to become an accomplished professional, she attracted a self-assured man who was not threatened by an intelligent, successful spouse. Bill Clinton learned the lessons of his positively aspected Venus, and, as a result, wanted a woman with whom he could forge a working partnership. Nicole Brown, on the other hand, did not have a strong self-identity at the time she met O. J. Simpson (see chart, page 264). As a result of his own afflicted Venus, O. J. viewed Nicole as a beautiful accoutrement who would enhance his own lack of self-esteem off the playing field. Rather than forming a marriage of equals, these two needy people attempted to provide the other what each lacked inside.

Of the two women, Nicole Brown Simpson has the more profoundly afflicted chart, consisting of three separate t-squares with one involving the Sun and another involving Venus. Due to a series of transits and progressions which alternately activated each of her t-squares, her journey toward achieving self-esteem was arduous and, unfortunately, tragic. Hillary Rodham Clinton, on the other hand, was able to use her strong Sun to offset her Venus squares and develop a fierce sense of self-worth, succeeding in life where Nicole Brown Simpson could not. While the Sun and Venus may indeed give indications about the level of self-esteem, it is only through an examination of the entire chart and its planetary cycles that we can fully understand where the root of certain difficulties lie and how they may be overcome.

Although there are countless ways to analyze a horoscope, I will be employing very basic chart interpretation (planets in signs, houses, and in aspect to one another) for character analysis, and transits, secondary progressions and solar arc directions to illustrate the unfolding of events in the lives of these strikingly different yet, in some respects, similar women.

NICOLE BROWN SIMPSON[2]

Who would have believed, other than an astrologer or therapist, that concealed beneath the facade of beautiful, wealthy and glamorous Nicole Brown Simpson was a woman filled with contradictions, complexities, and insecurities which may never have been completely overcome even had she lived. Taking a closer look at one of the most difficult horoscopes I have ever encountered ultimately reveals the real story behind the mask—a grand trine in water and three separate t-squares (Venus-Saturn-Moon, Sun-Jupiter-Pluto, Mercury-Uranus-Neptune).

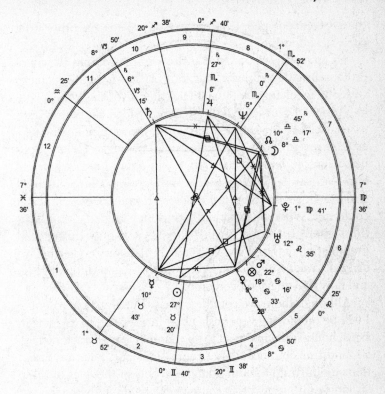

Chart 1. Nicole Brown Simpson[3]

Grand Trine (Venus-Neptune-Ascendant). The grand trine
between Venus (9 Ca 28), ruler of her Taurus sun and Libra
moon, Neptune (5 Sc 0), ruler of her Pisces ascendant, and
the Ascendant itself (7 Pi 36)[4] is, by most standards, the more
beneficial signature. Since Neptune, her ruling planet, trines
both Venus, planet of beauty, and the Ascendant, indicator of
appearance and character, Nicole was blessed with a beautiful
face and figure, and developed a charming, winning personality to match. Given the fact that her Sun sign is Taurus and
Moon sign is Libra, two Venus-ruled signs, it is not surprising

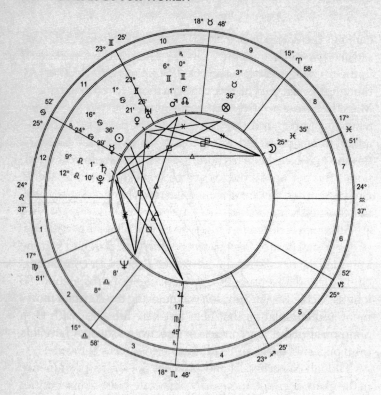

Chart 2. O. J. Simpson[5]

that sensuality, pleasure, and preoccupation with looks and money would be important factors throughout her life. In addition to being exceptionally beautiful due to the connection between Venus and the ascendant, Neptune's influence added an element of mystery, romanticism and idealism. It also made her highly impressionable, prone to deceptive relationships and caused her to gravitate toward O. J. Simpson, a man whose offers of a romantic, heightened, glamorous, but somewhat unrealistic, lifestyle she would misjudge.

In Nicole Brown Simpson's relocation chart for Los Angeles, where she lived for most of her life, Neptune (5 Sc 0 r) exactly conjoins the Ascendant (5 Sc 43), further emphasizing the dissatisfaction with her identity and the desire to immerse herself in the exciting lifestyle which O. J. Simpson afforded her. Although it is not part of this configuration, Neptune's trine to Mars, her most positively aspected planet (sextile to Sun and trine to Jupiter) and the only planet not part of a t-square, added to her projected sexual image which masked insecurities she may have been harboring. From a psychological standpoint, this set up a situation which could have made Nicole Brown Simpson feel it was incumbent upon her to keep her partner constantly interested—an extremely large burden to bear.

Although a dominant Mars gives her a flair for athletics, strong sexual desires (especially coupled with the chart's strong Venusian flavor) and an almost insatiable need for constant excitement and adventure, it is not a planet of introspection. So long as Nicole Brown Simpson was enjoying the constant movement and stimulation that her "fast-lane lifestyle" with O. J. Simpson afforded, any conflicts or insecurities she may have felt, even on a subconscious level, were temporarily set aside.

Though Mars instills and physical power, its prominence in the chart does not necessarily obliterate built-in insecurities which lie beneath the surface. For better or worse, Nicole and O. J. Simpson each possessed a powerful Mars whose excitement, passion, and aggression became the hallmark of their relationship, overwhelming the serenity and self-assuredness which their afflicted Venuses and Nicole's Sun could not supply. It was only later in life that she learned how to manifest positive Martian energy—enterprise, assertiveness, adventure, and enthusiasm— without necessarily relying on her beauty or sexual prowess.

T-Square (Sun-Jupiter-Pluto). Although the trines provided advantageous personality traits and initiated the fortuitous circumstances of her life, including her initial meeting with O. J. Simpson, the extremely rare combination of three t-squares and the series of transits and progressions which activated them led to the destructive and, ultimately, fatal aspect of her life. While her Mercury-Uranus-Neptune configuration indicates that she did not always exercise good judgment, and that she often lacked clarity of vision, I have limited my discussion to the t-squares involving the Sun and Venus.

Consisting of a Third-Ninth House exact opposition between the Sun in Taurus (27 Ta 20) and Jupiter in Scorpio (27 Sc 06r) forming an out-of-sign square with Pluto in Virgo (1 Vi 41) in the Sixth House, this t-square presented direct challenges to her self-confidence (Sun). Due to an inability to define who she was and what her goals were, Nicole Brown Simpson may have been, oftentimes, unable to cope with the responsibility and intensity that accompanied her role as O. J. Simpson's wife. Fueled even further by her frustration and her need to be in control due to the fixity of the Sun Jupiter opposition, this t-square created power struggles, that is, rebelling against the partner's authority and, at the same time, resenting her dependence on him. Because there is so much frustration and repressed anger hidden within Pluto's squares, this configuration often leads to self-destructive patterns and, in Nicole Brown Simpson's case, anger and violence as a way of releasing pent up frustration and/or punishing the self.

The Sun in Taurus opposed to Jupiter in Scorpio (the most exact aspect in her chart) also represents the dissipation of one's energies due to the indulgent and wildly undisciplined nature of Jupiter which expends much too much time in social situations. With a flair for the dramatic and a desire to go beyond the realm of the ordinary, her self-confidence (Sun) was based on lofty yet unrealistic visions which, due to her lack of knowledge, she was unable to enact. As the apex of this t-square, Pluto, when positively aspected, evinces magnetism and power, but when negatively aspected, as it is here, signifies the inability to handle that power. There is a repression of confidence (Sun) and an inability to expand one's horizons (Jupiter) which alternates with the need to be confrontational and, in extreme situations, violent (Pluto).

Due to the constant challenges to her autonomy (Sun) and the potential destruction Pluto squares are capable of unleashing, Nicole, like most people with heavily squared charts, would have been better able to cope with the responsibilities thrust upon her after her thirty-fifth year—the year of her death. Had Nicole Brown Simpson lived, I have no doubt that she would have become an extremely strong-minded, able woman learning to take charge of her life and, perhaps even, a company or organization—patterns that had begun to emerge at the time of her death. Ironically, it is through her death that the promise of her t-square is being fulfilled; her name has become a national symbol for battered women's groups.

Although Mars should theoretically provide a positive outlet for the Sun and Jupiter, which it sextiles and trines, its placement in the fallen sign of emotional Cancer in the Fifth House emphasizes physical enjoyment, adventure, and sexuality, but hardly lessens the indulgence of the opposition. In fact, the volatility of Mars in Cancer in the Fifth House, though positively aspected, does not function as a balancing factor for this particular t-square. It was, however, her role as mother, signified by the Fifth House, which finally gave her the autonomy she was seeking and something she could call her own.

T-Square (Venus-Saturn-Moon). Although Nicole Brown Simpson's chart is filled with intricacies, conflict, and inconsistencies, her lack of self-esteem is most revealed within the Venus-Saturn-Moon cardinal t-square, which goes to the very heart of her tempestuous relationship with O. J. Simpson. It is also through the transits and progressions to this t-square that her journey toward self-discovery begins to unfold.

In this particular configuration, Venus is in Cancer (9 Ca 28) in the Fifth House opposing Saturn in Capricorn (6 Cp 15 r) in the Tenth House and squared by the Moon in Libra (8 Li 17) in the Seventh House. To begin, an afflicted Venus placed in the Moon-ruled sign of Cancer fosters insecurity which makes it imperative for these people to create a protective, familial environment. Like Venus in each of the water signs, this place-ment's instability often breeds co-dependent behavior whereby one person controls the emotional climate by making the other completely dependent on him or her. Because Venus in Can-cer people often find it simpler to be caretakers rather than seek assistance (which would reveal their own neediness), they tend to excuse rather than strengthen the partners' weaknesses.

In the case of Nicole Brown Simpson, this general defini-tion of Venus in Cancer is especially true, since it not only squares the Moon, its ruling sign, but Venus and the Moon are mutually receptive (Venus in Moon-ruled Cancer and Moon in Venus-ruled Libra), making the indulgent nature of this square that much more intense. Since O. J. Simpson's Venus is also in Cancer, he was driven by his insecurity, i.e., bestow-ing lavish gifts to prevent Nicole from leaving and, after their divorce, to persuade her to return. These two individuals, who shared the same insecure Venus, failed to develop their indi-vidual strengths which could have, in the end, held their mar-riage together.

I have found that Saturn's hard contacts with the Sun and Venus are probably a woman's most difficult aspects, since Saturn represses, denies, and ultimately challenges the indi-vidual's basic identity (the Sun) and/or ability to love (Venus). Because Nicole Brown Simpson and Hillary Rodham Clinton have the Venus Saturn opposition and square, respectively, I will elaborate on this particular aspect combination.

On its most basic level, Venus-Saturn contacts may indicate a relationship with someone who is either older, very responsible and/or a father/teacher figure. If that aspect is positive, i.e., sextile or trine, there will be mutual admiration and the ability to grow together even if, at the onset, one person may look up to the other. In keeping with Saturn's penchant for fidelity, loyalty, and longevity, this type of relationship frequently endures, especially if the Saturn figure continues to be a source of strength and commitment throughout the course of the relationship.

If, however, the aspect is a difficult square or opposition as it is here, it is "understood" that the teacher figure in the relationship, i.e., O. J., is not only more experienced, but superior. What often happens is that once the "inferior" student grows, learns, and even surpasses the partner, tension will arise and, unless the nature of the relationship changes to one of equals, the union usually dissolves. In the case of the Simpsons, the marriage became shakier as Nicole grew stronger and more self-assured.

On the other hand, the Venus-Saturn opposition just as often indicates relationships with younger men, especially in the charts of women who years earlier were attracted to older men due to insecurity and an unwillingness to compete with someone of equal stature. Once these women have attained maturity and self-confidence, they are often attracted to younger men, thereby reversing the role they once played. After her divorce in 1992, Nicole Brown Simpson surrounded herself with a younger crowd who were envious of her lifestyle, even though her assets were acquired by virtue of being O. J. Simpson's wife.

While relationships with older or younger people is one of the most traditional interpretations of this aspect, the more psychological and profound enactment of the Venus Saturn square or opposition is the effect it has on one's self-image. Since Venus has already been established as the significator of self-love, the opposition from Saturn, especially when involved in a t-square, becomes a restrictive influence. After enjoying the drama, sexual innuendo and provocation provided by Venus in the Fifth House squaring the Moon in Libra, Saturn comes along to punish and/or discipline. At its most extreme, this may take the form of relationships with someone like Simpson who never failed to remind Nicole of her inferiority, and who eventually abused her physically and emotionally.

One of the best explanations of Venus-Saturn aspects comes from Liz Greene who, in *Saturn: A New Look at an Old Devil*, states that

> "The typical Venus-Saturn woman carries deep feelings of inferiority and unattractiveness—regardless of how physically appealing she may be . . . for these women [men] it is terribly important to be loved, admired, and thought beautiful."[6]

Because there is an innate displeasure with the self, one may overcompensate by becoming vain and almost compulsive about physical appearance, often deluding oneself into believing that the admiration of others will conquer the insecurity within. Dr. Greene even goes so far as to say that Venus-Saturn aspects are often found in the charts of prostitutes who use beauty and sex to compensate for the fact that they do not regard themselves as beautiful. Although Dr. Greene feels that this issue primarily applies to women, I have always felt that men are equally affected by a lack of self-esteem.

As the apex, or focal point, of this configuration, the Moon in Libra in the Seventh House represents Nicole's desire, above all, to be an accommodating wife and devoted mother. Funneled through her identity as the spouse of a famous husband, her "need to be needed" served as an outlet for the tension created by the inadequacy of the Venus Saturn opposition, which places an extremely low value on how she viewed herself. This particular t-square seems to say "I cannot make it on my own. However, if I make my partner feel wonderful about himself I will be needed and, therefore, loved. I will also, in turn, feel better about myself as a woman."

Because the Seventh House Moon constantly needs feedback and reassurance from the partner, its square to an already insecure and mutually receptive Venus emphasizes the indulgence, vanity, and extravagance of the aspect—qualities perpetuated by her relationship with O. J. Simpson who also has Venus in Cancer squared by the Moon in Pisces.

Since the North Node signifies the area of life one struggles with in order to feel spiritually fulfilled, its conjunction with the Moon in the Seventh House made it imperative for Nicole to have a successful marriage. Because the ability to hold her marriage together probably became the key to her feelings of self-worth as a woman, she avoided its failure at any cost and stayed under adverse circumstances. Additionally, Hindu (Vedic) Astrology teaches that the North Node is compulsive and, therefore, any planet with which it comes in contact takes on those characteristics; her "need to be needed" by a partner is almost obsessive. In the end, it was motherhood (Moon) which empowered Nicole Brown Simpson and, as a result, relieved the tension of the t-square. Emphasis on her marriage, however, prevented her from discovering her strengths and, therefore, unwittingly reemphasized the Venus-Saturn opposition.

Nicole Brown Simpson's Journey to Self-Esteem

Now that we have analyzed how her t-squares with the Sun and Venus may have affected her self-image, let's see how transits and progressions activated those t-squares and influenced her choices on her journey towards self-esteem. In order to isolate certain events, I have focused on several turning points in her relationship with O. J. Simpson—their first meeting in May, 1977, their marriage on February 2, 1985, the assault and battery on January 1, 1989, filing for divorce in 1992, and the events of 1994 which led to her murder.[7]

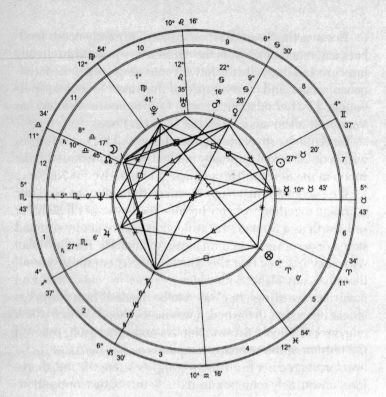

Chart 3. Nicole Brown Simpson[8]

May–June 1977—Meeting O. J. Simpson.
Nicole Brown graduated from high school, moved to Los Angeles and met O. J. Simpson, a celebrity whose background and lifestyle were completely different from hers, within a month after her eighteenth birthday. Because her life had always revolved around high school activities including being elected homecoming queen, it would not have been unusual for her to experience an identity crisis once she was away from home and living on her own.

If we progress her chart to her eighteenth birthday, May 19, 1977 (using both solar arc and secondary progressions), there are several noteworthy conjunctions formed between her progressed and natal planets. Because some are separating aspects, it is probable that her life took a turn in a new direction during the summer of 1976 when Nicole went to Greece to visit her sister Denise, who was on a modeling assignment. Although it is documented that Nicole was homesick and felt out of place, the vacation may have nevertheless initiated a desire for excitement and a yen to socialize with celebrities and jet-setters.

By solar arc direction, progressed Mercury (28 Ta 1) conjoins her natal Sun (27 Ta 20) which not only sets off the control issues and power struggles intrinsic to its t-square with Jupiter and Pluto, but indicates quite clearly that she will change (Mercury) her identity (Sun). More pointed is the fact that progressed Venus (26 Cancer 45) sextiles the natal Sun and trines natal Jupiter. Since these aspects are applying, the indication is that the series of events introduced by Mercury (change) will be completed the following year by Venus (relationships). It is obvious that when O. J. Simpson came into her life in June, 1977, he stimulated not only her social life (Jupiter) but her sense of self (Sun). Since Sun opposing Jupiter is the most exact aspect in her chart, any transits or progressions activating this position will be enormously powerful in effecting change.

But the most exact progressions occurring at the moment of her meeting with O. J. Simpson are the semi-sextile of solar-directed Mars (9 Leo 33) to natal Venus (9 Cancer 28) and the trine of solar-directed Neptune (22 Scorpio 17) to natal Mars (22 Cancer 16). Together, these combinations perfectly describe the sexual, volatile, romantic, and deceptive nature of her relationship with O. J. Simpson. With these types of progressions hitting her chart, it is no wonder that a tremendous transformation was about to occur.

Other indications that this period in her life would present an incredible turning point include transiting Uranus setting off the grand trine of Venus, Neptune, and the ascendant, and her progressed New Moon, which meant that in her secondary progressed chart for May 1977, the Sun and Moon were at the same degree. The progressed New Moon is always a time of change and the beginning of a completely new cycle, culminating in the progressed full moon fifteen years later. Whenever the progressed new moon occurs, one should be alerted to the changes that are occurring internally as well as externally. Had Nicole Brown Simpson known that this was a period when the opportunity for inner transformation presented itself, she might not have devoted herself to O. J. Simpson but followed an altogether different course of action.

February 2, 1985—Marriage of O. J. Simpson and Nicole Brown. While pregnant with their first child Sydney, Nicole Brown married O. J. Simpson on February 2, 1985, when transiting Saturn (27 Scorpio 14) set off her t-square by exactly conjoining natal Jupiter (27 Scorpio 6 r), and opposing her natal Sun (27 Taurus 20). With Saturn bearing down on Jupiter, the planet of abundance and indicator of childbirth in Hindu (Vedic) Astrology, one's luck and optimistic outlook will immediately be limited. Furthermore, Saturn's opposition to the Sun likely revived inadequate feelings about the self and could have made her painstakingly aware of the limitations which confronted her. Unless Saturn is well-positioned in the birth chart, this is certainly not the best transit under which one would choose to be married. Had she consulted an astrologer, the wedding would not have been set for a day when Saturn conjoined her Jupiter and opposed her Sun, once again setting off the power struggles of the Sun-Jupiter-Pluto t-square. What should have been a joyous day marked the beginning of a marriage where physical and emotional abuse, the manifestation of their inequality, escalated causing their union to slide steadily downhill.

Had these two people, and especially Nicole, been farther along in their journey toward self-esteem, Saturn might have been able to weave its wisdom into this difficult planetary configuration. Unfortunately, Nicole had still not experienced her Saturn return—a time which marks the passage between child-like fantasy and emotional reality—or motherhood which, in her particular horoscope, was the key to her autonomy and fulfillment as a woman.

Because O. J. Simpson's Neptune (8 Libra 8) exactly conjoins Nicole's Moon (8 Libra 17) and squares her Saturn (6 Capricorn 15 r) and Venus (9 Cancer 28), transits setting off her Moon and, in turn, the cardinal t-square will also set off his Neptune. If two people are experiencing the same difficult transit, it is impossible for either of them to maintain a sense of objectivity. Because Neptune cannot deal very well with reality, the square which his Neptune makes to her Saturn resulted in a conflict between the illusion and glamour (Neptune) with which he viewed their relationship, and Nicole's desire for security (Saturn), especially with impending motherhood. This is especially evident during her Saturn return when transiting Saturn conjoined her natal Saturn but squared O. J. Simpson's Neptune.

New Year's Day, 1989—O. J. Simpson pleading no contest to assault and battery—Nicole Brown Simpson's Saturn Return. Throughout the years, I have discovered that people with heavily squared charts, such as Nicole Brown Simpson's, do not begin to feel at ease with themselves until after Saturn returns to its natal position between the age of twenty-nine to thirty, and in some cases not until the age of thirty-five, when Saturn makes its subsequent square to itself. It is only after the Saturn return that an individual can develop the type of maturity needed to approach the problems presented by this type of natal placement.

Very often, relationships formed prior to the Saturn return mirror unresolved relationships with parents, a portion of which are worked through with the spouse. Because we finally begin to develop a sense of our own identity, the Saturn return brings a new level of maturity whereby a childlike partnership has the opportunity of transforming into one between two adults. If the transition is not attainable, the union most likely ends, or simply continues in the same vein. On the other hand, any new partnership initiated has the potential of representing maturity and, therefore, fulfillment.

In Nicole Brown Simpson's case, the transiting Saturn-Neptune conjunction exactly conjoined natal Saturn and activated the Venus-Saturn-Moon t-square once again, initiating issues reflecting her role as dependent wife and mother. Once she entered a new period of maturity, the roles which she thought were the defining features of her life could no longer satisfy her. With self-esteem and the need for self-determination on the rise, it was incumbent upon the relationship to reflect those changes—or else split apart.

This is exactly what happened during the now famous incident on New Year's Day, 1989, when O. J. Simpson pleaded no contest to battering his wife. According to Sheila Weller, author of *Raging Heart*, the Simpsons returned from a party where, in addition to consuming alcohol (Neptune), Nicole was probably flirting a bit more than O. J. would have preferred. Had this type of disagreement taken place between two people who trusted each other, there might not have been such a violent reaction. However, since the transit not only activated Nicole's t-square but O. J.'s singleton Moon in Pisces in the Eighth House, his reaction was emotional and uncontrollable. The fact that his Moon is the dispositor of Venus in Cancer further connects his rage to his basic insecurities. At the same time, Nicole's Sun-Jupiter-Pluto t-square was once again activated by transiting Jupiter (26 Taurus 41 r) which conjoined her natal sun, opposed her natal Jupiter and brought out the more negative Jupiterian aspects of fanaticism, aggrandizement, extravagance and, of course, power struggles.

Because the Venus-Moon-Saturn t-square sets up her conflict about being defined by a relationship, its activation demanded that the relationship be restructured or else it would be doomed to fail. In addition, her secondary progressed Moon (11 Scorpio 13) was about to conjoin her progressed descendant at 12 Scorpio 25, and secondary progressed Venus at 10 Leo 59 was in a separating conjunction to secondary progressed Mars at 9 Leo 57.

Between 1989–92, anyone with major cardinal configurations was bound to be deeply affected by transiting Saturn which accompanied Uranus and Neptune through Capricorn. Since O. J. and Nicole each have Venus in the insecure sign of Cancer, there were major upheavals in the marriage. Each was experiencing major transits to Venus, that is, challenges to their basic definition of self-worth, which naturally spilled over into the quality of their partnership.

On this particular day, O. J.'s chart saw transiting Uranus at 1 Capricorn opposing his Venus thus setting up a t-square with natal Neptune. In addition, transiting Neptune was squaring Neptune which also aggravated the square. While not necessarily a violent transit in itself, it challenges whatever makes one feel powerful or, in the alternative, vulnerable within the course of a relationship. Because both he and Nicole experienced major transits during 1989–1992, it was obvious that their marriage could not continue on the same course.

1992–94—Divorce, Attempts at Reconciliation and Murder. Due to the fact that Nicole Brown Simpson's Saturn return coincided with physical abuse, it was predictable that unless their relationship underwent a transformation, the violence would either continue to escalate, or the marriage would have to end. According to Dr. Susan Forward whom Nicole Brown Simpson consulted in March 1992, Simpson recognized a little bit of herself and O. J. in Forward's book *Men Who Hate Women and the Women Who Love Them*.[9] Since Dr. Forward specifically deals with both men and women suffering from low self-esteem, Nicole Brown Simpson may have finally acknowledged that this dynamic defined the marriage and, shortly thereafter, filed for divorce. The incentive to obtain the divorce and declare her independence was brought on by several astrological factors.

One of the most noteworthy astrological indications of 1992 was the progressed Full Moon, a time of fulfillment which, in Nicole Brown Simpson's case, meant a declaration of independence, i.e., filing for divorce and the end of the cycle which began fifteen years earlier during her progressed New Moon of 1977, when she initiated her relationship with O. J. Simpson.

Although she was distinctly aware that feelings of independence were leading her in a new direction, she was unable to make the complete break and was, once again, easily led to believe that she could not survive on her own. Had her self-esteem been more fully developed and internalized, she probably would not have made repeated attempts at reconciliation, even after the divorce was final.

Astrologically speaking, progressed Venus conjoined Uranus by solar arc direction which not only cries out for independence but instills confidence and sustains her attempts to make it alone. Because this conjunction also activated the square between Uranus and Mercury, ruler of the Fourth and Seventh Houses, her newly found independence also indicated that she could not become her own person unless there was a dramatic change, i.e., movement, in her domestic affairs. Because O. J. Simpson's Pluto conjoins Nicole's Uranus, her declaration of independence instantly activated his violent emotions, and it was during this period that the infamous 911 tapes recorded O. J.

breaking down the door to Nicole's house and threatening her with violence.

It is ironic that some of the progressions (progressed Full Moon and progressed Venus conjoining Uranus) of these last few years point to autonomy, emancipation, and fulfillment, indicating that Venus was finally getting the reassurance it had always sought. Ironically, a month before her death in June 1994, Nicole finally overcame her insecurities and declared that there would be no more reconciliations.

It is unfortunate that Nicole did not meet O. J. at a time in her life when she had already developed a sense of liberation and feeling of self-respect. But then again, if she had, someone like O. J. could not have enticed her with the promise of things that she may have been able to attain on her own.

HILLARY RODHAM CLINTON

After seeing the disastrous results wrought by the relationship between two people who both suffer from a poor self-image, Hillary Rodham Clinton stands out as a paragon of accomplishment, strength, and sensitivity for women who may be struggling to achieve balance in their personal and professional lives. From an astrological standpoint, Hillary Rodham Clinton does not have the same complex configurations which beset Nicole Brown Simpson and is, therefore, not subject to a barrage of difficult transits and progressions at almost every point in her life.

While her triumphs have been recorded by the press and in popular biographies, information about her personal life is more difficult to ascertain, unlike Nicole Brown Simpson whose intimate secrets have been splashed all over the media. As a result, this section may be somewhat shorter but, hopefully, not less insightful, in addressing the difficulties which Hillary Rodham Clinton may have encountered in her private and, at times,

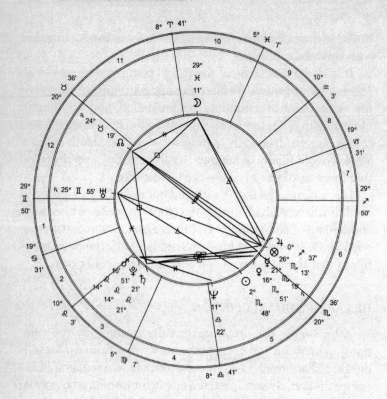

***Chart 4. Hillary Rodham Clinton*[10]**

professional life. Although it is difficult to isolate factors in order to judge the level of self-confidence, I will concentrate, for the most part, on how her dynamic Sun yet afflicted Venus contributed to Hillary Rodham Clinton's professional success and personal predicaments, to the extent that we know them, or may wish to conjecture. (Throughout this chapter, I will be using Mars and Pluto as the co-rulers of Scorpio.)

Hillary Rodham Clinton's Sun (2 Sc 48) is placed in Mars/Pluto-ruled Scorpio in its natural Fifth House, and forms trines with Uranus (25 Ge 55r), the ascendant (29 Ge 50) and the midheaven (5 Pi 7). Due to Scorpio's physical and

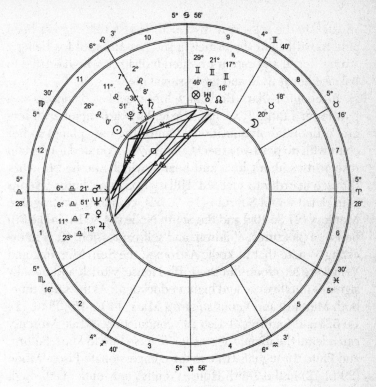

Chart. 5. Bill Clinton[11]

psychological intensity, the strength of her well-positioned Sun in aspect with Uranus, the ascendant and midheaven provides her with the tenacity, self-confidence and ambition she needed to follow through and accomplish her goals. With no difficult aspects attached to the Sun, Hillary Rodham Clinton always had a strong sense of purpose which sustained her through the ups and downs which may have beset her personal life from time to time. The trine to Uranus allowed her to break through the fixed conservatism which Scorpio sometimes imparts, and revel in her need to be different, provocative and even a bit revolutionary. It is only due to the fortitude of her well-aspected Sun situated in the self-expressive Fifth House that she has been able to withstand the criticism she has endured for being a strong, vocal, and career-oriented individual who has tried to balance her private and professional life.

Although Hillary Rodham Clinton achieved success as a partner in a Little Rock law firm and a board member of several influential organizations, Venus, the only planet in her chart with no positive aspects, may have accounted for certain insecurities about love and beauty which she had to work through in order to succeed. Hillary Rodham Clinton's Venus is in detrimental Scorpio (16 Sc 52), conjoining retrograde Mercury (21 Sc 19r) and the South Node (24 Sc 19) in the 5th house of pleasures, children, and self-expression. (It is interesting to note that in Vedic Astrology, the Sun, Mercury, and Venus are also found in the Fifth House, wthich additionally signifies intelligence and higher education.) At the same time, both Mercury and Venus square a Mars (14 Le 16), Pluto (14 Le 52) and Saturn (21 Leo 21) conjunction. While Mercury can release the mental aggression of its square to Mars, Saturn, and Pluto through its trine to the compassionate Pisces Moon (29 PI 12) in the Tenth House, Venus's only outlet is through Mercury. Since Venus is easily filtered through Mercury, Hillary Rodham Clinton's intelligence and mental aggression made her attractive to and envied by others. These qualities, in fact, beguiled Bill Clinton, who called Hillary the smartest girl in Yale Law School.

It is easy to see why, during the 1992 Presidential campaign, Hillary Rodham Clinton may have been accused of pulling the strings in her marriage. Not only is Venus disposited by Mars, a fiery planet not known for its understatement or tactfulness, but it is placed in a fiery house which further accentuates its "detrimental" qualities. Because the term "detrimental" relates to the position of Venus in the Martian-ruled signs of Aries and Scorpio, Hillary Rodham Clinton is not likely to view relationships in terms of the typical male-female role models and, even though Scorpio is an emotional water sign, diplomacy, cooperation, and soft-spokenness are not necessarily the qualities which her Venus allows.

With Venus in Scorpio in the Fifth House, Hillary Rodham Clinton would prefer to express herself as individualistically and intensely as possible, but instead might find herself either holding back or being furtive for fear that her forcefulness will be viewed as aggression and would thus be unacceptable. Further weighed down by squares of Mercury and Venus to the three malefic planets, Mars, Saturn, and Pluto, she is fiercely argumentative and a fighting, obstinate idealist—qualities not particularly fitting for the way society would expect a woman to behave. It is only because she has proven herself to be a brilliant attorney and champion of humanitarian causes that Hillary Rodham Clinton has been able to rise above the squares' aggression and insecurities.

Like Nicole Brown Simpson, who shares the negative Saturn aspect to Venus, there is bound to be a certain degree of insecurity regarding her self-image, and perhaps difficulty in expressing her needs within a relationship. Although we do not have details of her marriage to Bill Clinton or know intimate details about her personal life, we do know that conforming to society's image of beauty was never first and foremost on her mind. More concerned with communicating (Mercury) her ideals (Uranus) than looking beautiful by society's standards, early photographs of Hilary Rodham Clinton show an almost deliberate attempt to hide her shapely figure by dressing dowdily and masking her eyes with huge, owl-rimmed glasses.

On the one hand, this is quite indicative of an independent Uranus on the ascendant who intentionally needs to make a statement and assert one's uniqueness by rebelling against society's attitudes toward women. Had a more positively aspected Venus been available to her, the lessons of diplomacy and cooperation, which her husband knows so well, might have offset an almost compulsive need to make a personal statement. While the use of excessive beauty aids, clothing, and jewelry are ways to camouflage insecurities, intentionally downplaying one's sensuality or the importance of traditional beauty merely because it is dictated by society, is another side of the same coin. If we look at the evolution of Hillary Rodham Clinton over the years, it is evident that she has been taking more pride in her physical appearance without being obsessed with it—possibly because the rebellious girl is gone and the mature woman has taken her place.

What is, in fact, most important about the combination of Sun and Venus in Scorpio in the Fifth House is the importance of children as a means of fulfilling self-worth. Although she has only had one child (though she has said on numerous occasions that she wanted more), her involvement with the Children's Defense Fund has been one of the most meaningful aspects of her career.

Hillary Rodham Clinton's Journey to Self-Discovery

As with Nicole Brown Simpson, I have chosen several periods in Hillary Rodham Clinton's life when traditional transits and progressions may have brought the issue of her self-esteem into focus, keeping in mind that the details of her personal life are not publicized, nor are they as dramatic as the events surrounding the death of Nicole Brown Simpson.

April 1962. We do not know much about her youth except that her parents, especially her mother, always encouraged her ambitions. According to David Maraniss, author of *First in his Class: A Biography of Bill Clinton,* this period was a key time in her life, when her ideas suddenly took shape and she began to formulate her libertarian belief system.

Whenever the Sun and Venus, indicators of the self and the values we place upon that self, conjoin each other by progression, it signifies a period when one's deepest desires are realized. (Bill Clinton, for example, was elected president of the United States—the culmination of a childhood dream—when his progressed Sun conjoined his natal Venus.) Since Venus is the midpoint between her Sun and Jupiter, we can assume that Hillary Rodham Clinton experienced something very profound in 1962 when her progressed Sun conjoined natal Venus by Solar arc direction which, in turn, meant that her progressed Venus conjoined natal Jupiter. Although she was only fifteen years old, Hillary Rodham Clinton's involvement with a Methodist church group and its activist minister fueled her desire to work for social causes which would, in fact, become her life's work. Had this event not occurred during the progression of the Sun and natal Venus, her introduction to social idealism may have turned out to be an isolated event; however, experiences which take place during this powerful progression indicate an important achievement, thus renewing a sense of self-worth. Because Venus is in her Fifth House, it is by no means coincidental that her activism revolved around the Children's Defense Fund and other issues relating to the rights of minors in our society. (Because Nicole Brown Simpson's progressed Sun would have conjoined her natal Venus at the age of forty-three, one could only speculate what that may have signified.)

Wellesley College—1965. Because this time of her life was marked by the New Moon Progression, her identity (Sun) would be permanently altered and the balance of her life redirected. Although attending college is an important transition in anyone's life, its effect on Hillary Rodham Clinton was more penetrating than the usual student experience. Whereas many teenagers enroll in colleges near their hometown only to return upon graduation, Wellesley, an established East Coast institution, represented not only an environmental change (she was from the Midwest) but a political conversion, during which time she switched her allegiance from Republican to the more popular liberal causes which came to define her public persona. Excelling in whatever she did, Hillary Rodham was named valedictorian of the graduating class of 1969 and, as is customary, prepared a speech for the commencement exercises which was to follow that of the guest speaker, Republican senator from Massachusetts, Edward Brooke. Enraged by what she perceived to be Brooke's reactionary stance against the student demonstrations, Hillary Rodham ripped up her notes and spontaneously gave a rousing speech defending freedom of speech and the right to protest, for which she received a standing ovation.[12]

Yale Law School and Meeting Bill Clinton—1969–1971.
Hillary Rodham entered Yale Law School in 1969, met Bill Clinton in 1970, and began living with him in 1971. Astrologically speaking, solar arc Neptune conjoined her Sun bringing romance, idealism, and, perhaps, a bit of deception into her life. More significantly, Venus moved by secondary progression into a trine with the Mars-Pluto conjunction thus fulfilling its potential contained in the natal square. At the same time Bill Clinton entered Yale Law School and met Hillary Rodham in 1970, his progressed Venus trined his midheaven, thus combining love and career.

Any period wherein natal squares progress to trines often affords the opportunity to resolve conflicts inherent in the original aspect. Because Bill Clinton has been quoted as saying that he wanted to marry the smartest woman at Yale, he was able to appreciate, rather than fear, the power and potential volatility inherent in this intense square aspect which forces confrontations regarding relationship, jealousies, and power struggles. Meeting Bill Clinton at a time when this square is first activated and marrying him when it is again activated is a signal that this issue will indeed be confronted during the course of their life together. Although we know from their own admission that the Clintons' marriage had its ups and downs, and perhaps even its indiscretions, there are not enough actual facts on which to make a judgment. We can guess, however, that Hillary Rodham Clinton's strong sense of self helped her overcome marital adversity.

August 1974–October 1975—Moving to Arkansas and Marriage to Bill Clinton. After turning down numerous offers from prestigious Northeastern law firms, Hillary decided to "follow her heart" to Arkansas and become a law professor at the University of Arkansas Law School. Choosing between love and career is always a difficult choice, but especially troubling for those with hard Venus-Saturn aspects, who are usually confronted with these options at some point their lives. Since there is always the instinctive feeling, despite their accomplishments, that they are unlovable and will remain unloved, these people often feel they must seize the opportunity for marriage before it is too late. At other times, they put their profession first and deny themselves the pleasures of love.

In Hillary Rodham Clinton's case, she may have instinctively seen great career potential in her relationship with Bill Clinton stemming from the fact that they met when secondary progressed Venus trined natal Mars-Pluto, thereby fulfilling the tension and promise of the square. Additional factors include her Venus in Fifth House Scorpio and general fixed sign emphasis, which provides the tenacity and patience in new living situations, and the water/fire sign emphasis which, above all, makes her an emotional person who listens to and follows her heart. After all, the Moon in emotional, romantic Pisces indicates that while she may reason things through, if she is in love, she probably cannot concentrate on much else. Furthermore, having no earth planets makes her extremely desirous of stability which Bill Clinton provided since he felt strongly that Arkansas would be the foundation for his political career.

Because her Sun is positively aspected and Venus is well channelled through Mercury, she generated enough self-esteem to be a stimulating partner for her politically savvy husband. While Nicole's Brown Simpson's beauty (Venus-Neptune-ascendant) was an asset in the glamorous Hollywood circles in which O. J. Simpson traveled, Hillary Rodham Clinton's intelligence benefitted her husband's political career. They appeared to the electorate as a modern couple whose marriage was based on mutual respect not on traditional male-female power struggles. She may have also realized that support of her husband's career provided an arena where she could exercise her own political beliefs.

If we look at the transits and progressions for the period between August, 1974, when Hillary Rodham Clinton moved to Arkansas, and October 1975, when they were married, there were transits which indicated a great sense of self-liberation. As opposed to the date of the Simpsons' marriage when Saturn activated Nicole's already difficult Venus-Moon-Saturn t-square, the Venus progressions in Hillary Rodham Clinton's chart at the time of their marriage are quite amazing and, most astrologers would agree, perfect for a long-lasting union. In 1975, Venus moved by secondary progression to trine natal Saturn, completing the journey the planet began when it trined the Mars Pluto conjunction while she was at Yale. Because Venus is now trining Saturn, her marriage has the potential to ease the tension between work (Saturn) and love (Venus) first set up by the natal square. It also means that her union with Bill Clinton will be a partnership of love and work even though remnants of the natal square still bring up issues of jealousy, hostility, and power struggles. Additionally, the Sun had progressed to Jupiter, her descendant ruler, and Uranus had transited the Sun, making it seem that the marriage encouraged her to express herself. In fact, the threads appearing to hold the marriage together lie in the fact that each is not seeking to find an identity within the other—merely the other's support.

Birth of Daughter Chelsea—February 27, 1980. Rather than focus on the course of her successful career as partner in the Rose law firm and activist for social issues, I have concentrated on the events of her personal life and how they further elevated her image as a woman. On February 27, 1980, when daughter Chelsea was born, Hillary Rodham Clinton's secondary progressed Mercury conjoined her natal Venus in the Fifth House. Because two of her Fifth House planets were activated at this time, it is fairly certain that her experience as a parent, like her work with the Children's Defense Fund, evoked a renewed sense of confidence in herself and was a means by which her aggressive square from Mars, Saturn, and Pluto could be tempered. Additionally, she experienced her exact full Moon progression in February 1980, which reveals that motherhood has indeed given her great fulfillment and self-realization.

In keeping with the significance of the new Moon and full Moon progressions, the birth of Chelsea could be seen as the end of one cycle of ambition and the beginning of a new cycle where her caring, maternal qualities would come into focus, as well as her public activism and role as the Governor's wife. Since the Pisces Moon in the Tenth House is the most elevated planet in the chart, motherhood (Moon) coupled with her compassion and public interest in social causes (Tenth House) offset the Third–Fifth House squares. Although she earned great respect as an attorney yet was criticized for being a career woman, it is quite evident from her horoscope that Hillary Rodham Clinton's self-worth was indeed elevated through her parenting experience. It is not my intention to show that women must choose motherhood in order to raise their self-esteem. In Hillary Rodham Clinton's case, this was one of many factors that added to her strong sense of purpose.

First Lady—Rejection of Health Care Bill and Retreat from Public—1993–1995. Rather than discuss Hillary Rodham Clinton as a political asset and partner to husband, I would like to address the events of 1993–95, for once again she has been confronted with very revealing transits and progressions.

After her appointment as chairperson of the committee to reform health care in 1993, public opinion switched from judging Mrs. Clinton harshly, to embracing her as first lady. She noticeably changed her image by dressing fashionably and was polite and soft-spoken during interviews—traditional Venusian qualities still widely accepted as appropriate for women and which, earlier in her life, she rebelled against.

At the time of this writing in June 1995, Hillary Rodham Clinton has all but vanished from public view due, in part, to the complete dismembering of the health care bill which she helped engineer, as well as other public accusations and possible scandals. Having undertaken the most idealistic and worthy task of trying to provide health insurance for all Americans, she utilized both her assets and her liabilities, leaving herself vulnerable to criticism once again, as in the 1992 Presidential campaign. Although public scrutiny and defeat may have shaken her self-confidence, it is difficult to reach any definitive conclusions about how the first lady feels, because we are not privy to this information. We can only conjecture that her overly sensitive Moon in Pisces in the Tenth House caused her to perceive public defeat as a personal attack.

To get a better handle on what may be going in with the First Lady, let's take a closer look at the noteworthy transits and progressions of the period. One of the major transits she experienced in Autumn 1994, when the health care packet all but died, was transiting retrograde Venus conjoining her Scorpio Sun and Venus. Normally, 1–2 day transits of Venus to natal planets and angles go completely unnoticed. However, the transits of retrograde Venus are significant when contacting a

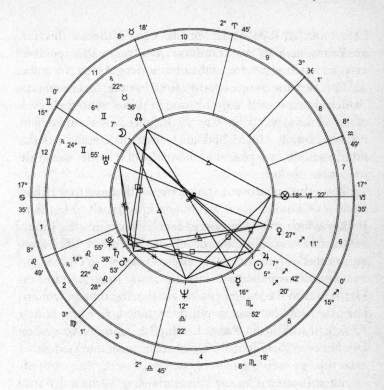

Chart 6. Hillary Rodham Clinton[13]

natal planet due to the fact that a usual 1–2 day transit can last as long as 2–3 months.

In Hillary Rodham Clinton's chart, transiting Venus first contacted her natal Sun on September 11, 1994. After going retrograde, Venus stationed exactly on her Sun on November 19, 1994, before finally going direct on November 23, 1994. At the same time, transiting Venus contacted her natal Venus between October 3–5, 1994, retrograded over natal Venus between October 21–23, and transited it for the final time on

December 24, 1994. At the same time she withstood this transit, Venus made its own transition from cooperative, peaceful evening star to aggressive, embattled morning star on November 4, 1994. Because the changeover from evening to morning star (which always occurs midway through Venus' retrograde cycle of 41–42 days) was defined by the Babylonians as a time of increased hostility, Hillary Rodham Clinton, in keeping with that interpretation, was placed in the midst of a battle, which she unfortunately lost.

The other significant transit presently besetting Hillary Rodham Clinton's life is a Jupiter-Pluto transit to her natal Jupiter which rules her descendant. After transiting Jupiter contacted her natal Jupiter briefly in December, 1994, igniting another Jupiter return, or twelve-year cycle, Pluto began its almost two-year transit over her natal Jupiter. Transiting Pluto contacted her natal Jupiter for the first time in January-February, 1995, stationed and retrograded over it in March, 1995, and will finally transit her Jupiter again in November-December 1995. In July, 1996, Pluto once again retrogrades over natal Jupiter, only to go direct one final time in August, 1996.

Since Jupiter rules her descendant, it is this last transit which is extremely significant, since July–August, 1996 will be around the date of the Democratic Convention at which time Bill Clinton may or may not be his party's candidate for President. Due to the fact that Pluto forces one to make dramatic changes, this transit may simply indicate, as it has for the last few months, that the Clintons will be forced to confront certain unpleasant situations that lie beneath the surface. Due to the political pressure cooker that the President finds himself in, as well as the potential strains this transit probably has on the marriage itself, we can assume that while Hillary Rodham Clinton's strong sense of self allows her to bear up reasonably well under public examination, she has nevertheless retreated from the public eye. While there is no way of knowing what is taking place between the Clintons on a personal level, I must speculate that not only is this period taking a toll on their marriage, but also on the First Lady herself, since so much of her self-esteem stems from her ability to act on behalf of her beliefs. For the first time in her life, she has more or less failed.

Since the Seventh House also rules legal battles and public contact, we know that she has been cited in connection with several possible legal skirmishes involving the aftermath of Vince Foster's suicide and real estate dealings in Arkansas. These events have only raised more doubts about her credibility.

In addition to the above-mentioned transits, Hillary Rodham Clinton experienced her exact secondary New Moon Progression at 19 Sagittarius in her natal Sixth House, in April, 1994. We already know from her previous new and full Moon progressions and those of Nicole Brown Simpson, that 1994–95 is the beginning of a major transition and the introduction of another cycle of change. Because the progression falls in her natal Sixth House, we can only presume that there will be a continuation of interest in universal health care issues, but a change in the approach.

My personal interpretation is that rather than be part of governmental policy making, she should continue to stress health care issues on a more personal level, using her eye for detail and her ability to work methodically. This could mean taking a much greater interest in her own physical and emotional well-being, as well as reaching out to people throughout the country—something which helped endear her to the American public in 1993. Since she has already, as of this writing, begun to take an active role in breast cancer awareness, we can only assume that she is utilizing the best qualities her chart offers in accordance with its planetary cycles.

NOTES

1. Dr. Susan Forward and Joan Torres. *Men Who Hate Women and the Women Who Love Them* (The Aquarian Press, London), 43.

2. This chapter was written in 1995 during the course of O. J. Simpson's criminal trial and, as a result, I have tried not to let my personal feelings influence the content. Everything that is stated about the lives of the Simpsons and the Clintons is based on either published material or direct observations. Where I have made assumptions or come to my own conclusions, I have so stated.

3. Nicole Brown Simpson. Born May 19, 1959, 1:00 A.M. CET, at Rollwald, Germany (49N59, 8E51).

4. Although some astrologers do not classify this as a grand trine because the third point is an angle and not a planet, it has been my experience that if a major configuration involves the ascendant-descendant axis as its third point, the personality/partnership will be affected, while the involvement of the ic./midheaven as its third point will affect the parental/career axis.

5. O. J. Simpson. Born July 9, 1947, 8:08 A.M. PST, at San Francisco, CA (37N47, 122W25).

6. Dr. Liz Green. *Saturn: A New Look at an Old Devil* (Weiser Pub., York Beach, ME), 171.

7. All the events in her life are taken from Sheila Weller's book *Raging Heart* (Pocket Books, New York, 1885) as well as through newspaper articles, which are in the public domain.

8. Nicole. Solar Arc Directed Chart. May 19, 1977, 12:00 P.M. PST, at Los Angeles, CA (34N04, 118W15).

9. It is pure coincidence that Nicole Brown Simpson visited Dr. Susan Forward whose book I came across in 1987.

10. Hillary Rodham Clinton. Born Oct. 26, 1947, 8:00 P.M. CST, at Chicago, IL (41N52, 87W39). Source: as told to astrologer Celeste Longacre by Hillary Rodham Clinton.

11. Bill Clinton. Born Aug. 19, 1946, 8:51 A.M. CST, at Hope, AR (33N40, 93W36).

12. This story was relayed by astrologer Priscilla Costello, a classmate of Hillary Rodham Clinton.

13. Hillary. Full Moon Progressed Chart. Feb. 27, 1980, 11:24 P.M. CST. Little Rock, AR (34N45, 92W17

BIBLIOGRAPHY

Dreyer, Ronnie Gale. *Venus: The Evolution of the Goddess and Her Planet.* London: The Aquarian Press, a division of Harper/Collins Publishers, 1994.

Forward, Dr. Susan and Joan Torres. *Men Who Hate Women and the Women Who Love Them.* New York: Bantam Doubleday Dell, 1987.

Greene, Dr. Liz. *Saturn: A New Look at an Old Devil.* York Beach, ME: Weiser Publications, 1976.

Levin, Robert E. *Bill Clinton: The Inside Story.* New York: S.P.I. Books, 1992.

Maraniss, David. *First in His Class: A Biography of Bill Clinton.* New York,:Simon & Schuster, 1995.

Weller, Sheila. *Raging Heart.* New York: Pocket Books, a division of Simon & Schuster, 1995.

Kim Rogers-Gallagher

Kim Rogers-Gallagher is a past President of the Washington State Astrological Association, having been lured to the Seattle area by one too many NORWACS, (NorthWest Astrological Conference). She currently lives in Ridgway, Colorado, (population 463), where she has recently become the proud owner of her very own mountain range, the San Juan Rockies. She is a former member of the AFAN (Association for Astrological Networking) Steering Committee, a board member of ISAR, (The International Society for Astrological Research), and is the Editor *of KOSMOS*, the publication of ISAR. Kim lectures nationally, and particularly enjoys political and mundane astrology. She works with Chiron, Electional Astrology, and composite charts, and specializes in teaching the beginner just how much fun learning astrology can be. Along those same lines, her first book is entitled *Astrology for the Light Side of the Brain*, (ACS Publications). Kim was recognized as a "Most Promising Newcomers" at UAC '92, was a speaker at UAC '95, and is scheduled to speak at UAC '98, NORWAC '97, and ARC '97. She donates a percentage of her income to environmental and animal welfare groups, and shares her nest with far too many pets and a computer who doesn't let her go out much at all.

Kim Rogers-Gallagher

Who Should I Be
When I Grow Up—
And How Do I
Get There?

All Aboard the Evolution Express

*S*ome folks say Earth is a school—a place to learn, take tests and earn our degrees. So, the theory goes, each of us are born at a moment we've selected—when all conditions are right for our next evolutionary lesson to begin. In other words, even before we arrive, we're planning our trip, and we don't jump off the Evolution Express until all the Right Stuff is in all the right places.

What stuff? Well, Cosmic Stuff. Our Universe is chock-full of all kinds of wonderful energies—your astrology chart is your own personal "map," drawn up from the exact time and location of your birth. From that information, a circular, clock-shaped diagram emerges, which shows where every planet, star, asteroid, and comet was located at the moment you made your debut. In a nutshell, it's your blueprint—your cosmic back-pack. It's an owner's manual that shows what you packed into your "tool-kit" for this lifetime—and how best to use it. Everybody's got one, and no two are ever the same-which, in itself, is amazing—but there's more. Since the chart is a map, everybody's got one of everything. Everybody's got a Venus, a Moon, and a Pluto. Everybody's got a bit of Virgo in there, and some Sagittarius, too.

I like to think of each chart as being constructed of four astrological food groups: planets, signs, houses, and aspects. The ten planets (the other eight planets, and the Sun and Moon, that is), represent urges or needs we each have, simply by virtue of our decision to take up residence inside a physical body. The twelve signs show styles of behavior, the way we act out those urges or needs. The twelve houses tell us which area of life will be the set of life circumstances where our planets, dressed in their sign costumes, will come to life, and aspects are "conversations" or "dialogues" that happen when planets are in angular relationship to one another—in other words, a set number of degrees apart. Those four groups are the basic building blocks that all astrology is based upon.

Finding Your Way with Astrology

The point of this lesson is to give you some background, to prep you for what I'd really like to talk about: your life's purpose, because this is where astrology comes in. Much as it can be used for any number of things, the real point of individual astrology, and it's very highest use, is to point out our individual life goals, to help us understand why we're here, what we're supposed to be studying—this time—and what our own particular magical quest might be. Having our maps—and knowing how to use them—is a great way to get off to a good start.

Think of it this way: when you're about to drive cross-country, you have several options. You can put some gas in the tank and wing it, asking directions as you go, trusting that eventually you'll find your destination—through trial and effort. If you'd like to be a little more prepared but still want some degree of spontaneity, on the other hand, you can get a pile of maps and tourist guides and lay out the trip yourself. You can also go to an agency like AAA, to find the fastest or most scenic way to get you where you want to go, and get the latest information on possible delays or detours due to road construction or other inevitables along the way. It's up to you. Regardless of the type of preparation you choose, if you point yoursef in a particular direction, you'll probably get there.

Once you know astrology is out there, and once you know what it can do, you have the same options available to you for your life's journey. You might decide to wing it, to just go on instinct, trusting that the Universe will provide roadsigns and guideposts as you need them. You might opt to get a copy of your chart and learn to do astrology on your own—or you might consult someone who's an expert in the field, and get their help to lay out your trip, one step at a time.

Personally, I recommend number two or three for your long-range planning, and number one at all times. Yes, the Universe will always get you where you're going, and yes, you'll always need to look out for the "directions" it will send along that won't be found on any map—things you wouldn't know any other way than by actually being there. If you've got a time limit in mind, or a particular mode of travel, or if there are certain stops you'd rather not miss, it's a good idea to plan. That's where your own particular chart comes in-it's absolutely invaluable.

Regardless of your sex, astrology is the finest tool there is for exploring that purpose, for finding out why you are the way you are. It's especially helpful, however, for those of us who happened to pick female bodies to live inside this time around, since being a woman in today's world is a lot more challenging than it used to be.

Back not so long ago, when traditional gender roles were followed, a woman's primary, (and usually only) concerns were to marry, bear children, and take care of her family and her home. Somewhere along the way, however, we discovered ourselves—and although our families are no less important to us than they ever were, we're now also considering our own needs, for the first time in many a female generation.

In the process of fulfilling those personal needs, many of us have begun to seek careers of our own—which really means we've had to discover the accomplishment-oriented, assertive sides of ourselves, astrologically represented by those planets and points that were traditionally known as "masculine." The independence and new confidence we've gained from realizing our personal goals and developing the qualities necessary to achieve them has arrived with a cost, however: many of us—and single Moms in particular—are now saddled with the role of SuperMom or SuperPartner, working two full-time jobs—first, at the career of our choice, and then, by tending to our families and our homes, after five.

All of that juggling is exhausting, to say the least. It's also not an easy task. Those traditional societal roles teach men and women to "do" their charts very differently. Traditionally speaking, in fact, each sex is taught in both subtle and not-so-subtle ways to develop some energies and ignore others. Even now, much as we try to deny it, and as "New-Age" as we like to believe our thinking is, as women we're encouraged by society to perfect those astrological energies traditionally thought of as feminine—that is, our Moons and our Venuses—and to "hire out" the part when it comes to their "opposites"—our Suns and our Mars, both typically thought of as the masculine parts of ourselves.

In order to get a better understanding of those qualities that we are and aren't encouraged to develop in ourselves as women, and how that conditioning affects us when it comes time to make a career choice, let's take a look at both the Masculine and Feminine sides of ourselves through the planets that represent those urges or needs. We'll examine these planets in pairs, since that's how they seem to function in our charts.

Before we get started, here's my disclaimer. When dealing with astrology, it's important to remember that we're talking in a symbolic language. The masculine and feminine archetypal energies I've mentioned are inside each of us, no matter which sex we happen to be. Although those words don't mean what they used to—in other words, they can't be translated literally into "male" and "female" any more—qualities that seem to pertain more to one gender than the other seem to be encapsulated inside each of the planets, and inside each of us. In most of the descriptions of the planets that follow, then, I'll refer to a planet as "he" or "she," and portray them much as if they were cartoon characters. Also, you may find some of the following descriptions to be rather light-hearted in tone. Don't be scared. Just because I sound like I don't take this stuff seriously doesn't mean I don't take this stuff seriously. I do, but humor conjures the archetypes like no other way, and that's how we learn.

First, the Moon . . .

The best way to experience the Moon is to go out on a clear night when she's close to full, and just stare up at her. Truth be told, when the Moon is full, it's hard not to stare. She invites us to look—hypnotizes us, in fact. Watching her is a totally emotional experience. She brings back memories, and makes us sigh. As women, we're naturally in tune with the concept of "cycles" and "seasons" due to the Moon. She's the absolute essence of feminity, matter of fact, perfectly exemplified through the fact that our menstrual cycles work in accord with her phases. She's kept humanity mesmerized for centuries, inspired countless love songs, and provided just the right mood for more than one tender question. Regardless of her "softness," however, her effect on human behavior is quite real, and quite feelable.

It's obvious, then, that the Moon is basically an emotional energy, the place in your astrology chart where the Inner You lives, that person on the inside who, rather than acting, as the Sun does, reacts to what happens around you. As a result, she's also the side of you who builds a nest in the real world to stay safe inside, the side of you who creates a home base from which to nurture both you and others. All those qualities are ordinarily considered feminine functions—and it's no wonder. In the body, the Moon rules the breasts, the ovaries, and the womb, all necessary for creating, nurturing, and housing new life. Life starts inside our bodies. That's the tremendous gift women receive from our Moons.

The Moon is also connected with our Mom, since she was the primary vehicle that nurtured us before we made our planetary debut. Our mother is the person whose subtle, unstated influence created our own attitudes about nurturing and taking care of. This goes for everyone, of course, both male and female—it's hard not to "feel" what someone is feeling when you live inside their body for nine months. As women, however, we can't help but be even more profoundly affected by our mothers. She was not only the nurturer—she was also the parent of the same sex, the ultimate role model.

Profound as she is, however, the Moon isn't the only energy in a woman's chart, and certainly not the only one to consider when looking for ways to ultimately nurture ourselves. She has a partner, a yang that matches her yin, who's in charge of our sense of self. These solar outgoing qualities come under the jurisdiction of the Sun, since it describes vocation. Now, many of us see our vocation as filling the role of mother, but even if performing the Moon's need to nest, nurture, and provide safety is quite fulfilling for many of us for a very long time, even if raising our children is our first priority, it does not last forever. Kids grow up and leave the nests we've created, no longer in need of our nurturing. So it's best to remember to turn our faces to the Sun, to also tend to our selves—whether we're devoted to the Moon's duties for a great portion of our lives or not.

Now, I'm not saying that the Moon's feelings should be ignored when it comes to choosing a life path. Not at all. Although most of the time, our Moons are silent, lest you begin to imagine her as unimportant, think of how the mood (a word which sprung from "moon," by the way) you're in can either make or break your day. The way we feel—our emotional happiness—affects our interchanges with others, our productivity, and therefore how much we accomplish over the course of a day. The Moon is an undercurrent, a wave of responses we ride. It's the emotional backdrop against whose color shades our lives play out, either clashing or contrasting. When choosing a life path, then, it's absolutely imperative to make sure it's a path the Moon can live with.

And Her Partner, the Sun . . .

Basically, one of the most important things any human being can do for him or herself is to get to know their Sun—and to "feed" it. That is, learn everything you can about the Sun in your chart, and make sure you give yourself experiences that wil make you proud to be you. Study the sign the Sun was in when you were born, and put it in life situations reflected by the house it occupies in your chart. This will show you how: the sign—and where: the house—you can most brilliantly be you. Everyone's Sun wants the same things: to shine, to accomplish something important, and to be recognized for it. In fact, I like to teach the Sun to my beginner students by using the example of the television commercial that seems to have been specially designed with that need to be important in mind. You know the one—it's the Army commercial, the ad that taps into your need to shine by telling you to "Be all that you can Be"—Keep on reaching, Keep on growin'—Find your future..." The music is energizing, to say the least. It's stimulating, exhiliarating, and effective, too—an aerobic class for your pride, guaranteed to get you up and out of your chair and marching around the room, primed to go—to do—to accomplish!

Man or woman, you can't help but feel your Sun rev when you hear that music, and listen to the words. It's a perfect description of the Sun—of what it feels like to live life as if it were an ongoing quest, to keep on reaching for your maximum potential. That's what life is all about—reaching and growing, constantly finding our futures—and that's what the Sun in our charts is all about: it's the side of us we came here to specialize in, the inner child that's always hungry for tomorrow. As a result, the Sun is the best indication of career choice in the chart—but often it's also the one spot that's not investigated to any great length.

Think of it this way: in every corporation, there are many departments, each with its own director. All of them are equally important, and all of them have very specific jobs to perform so that the entire corporation can be successful. Well, in an astrology chart, the planets symbolically function as directors or heads of departments inside one large corporation: you. You have a Mercury who runs the communication department, a Jupiter who runs the department of risk-taking ventures, a Pluto who decides when things have gone far enough and it's time to just let go, and a Saturn who makes your rules. Each of them need to do their job well to contribute to the success of you, the corporation.

As with all management groups, however, they each must also answer to an executive director, to a big cheese who gives the final "yes" or "no" to all decisions. The Sun is that executive director, the chief in the chart with the final word on every matter. The Sun itself is the center of our Universe, the warmth and light around which all the planets dance. Your Sun, then, is your center, the astrological body who, more than any other planet in your chart, describes your mission, your *raison d'etre*, your quest. Most importantly, the Sun represents what you enjoy most, and the type of lifestyle that suits you best. With all that going for it, and taking into consideration that once we do choose a career, it takes up at least a third of our lives, doesn't it make sense to follow the Sun's bliss when deciding what we really ought to be when we grow up?

Well, sure it does. Of course, for women, that's easier said than done. When it comes to making a choice about a career—about following our bliss, that is—we're faced with a couple of immediate obstacles. First of all, as we've already seen, most of us weren't encouraged to actively pursue a career. That was what our husbands were here to do for us—while we tended the home fires, perfecting our Moon skills. Consequently, many of us chose men who reflected energies we had, but didn't express-and that goes for our Suns in particular.

Male or female, bringing the Sun and Moon together—putting them on the same "team" by merging their abilities and purposes—is a primary step toward self-actualization. We both need to be keyed in to what we really want to "be." and what makes us feel safe and secure, emotionally. The Sun is the person on the outside that goes out into life to seek experiences that will further it along the path toward The Quest. The Moon is the person on the inside who reacts to what comes to her via the Sun's actions—and she can hold the Sun back from its next step if she's not feeling protected. The two are the first matched pair that need to be balanced if we're to truly discover our life's work. They unite to create a perfect balance of action and emotion—and that's what it's all about.

There's a second pair of energies that also form a team of sorts, two more planets that represent a "masculine" and a "feminine" side of ourselves. These energies are represented by Venus and Mars, and we'll visit with them first. Since Venus is the feminine planet in the pair, she's the energy that women are traditionally taught to develop, and since Mars is the masculine energy, he's the one we're taught to stifle. Let's take a closer look at each planet separately, and then talk about how bringing the two together can help us to figure out how to further our career goals in the world.

Venus

First, meet the Lady Venus. She's the Queen of contentment, satisfaction, and pleasure—the goddess of love and beauty. Her unofficial title is head of the department of nice things. She's the side of us that attracts, rather than pursues, that knows how to magnetize and draw what we love to us by smiling sweetly rather than by chasing it down. Venus expresses herself in two ways, each of which is represented by one of the two signs she rules, Libra and Taurus.

The Libran side of Venus represents the urge or need inside each of us to relate to an other—to love and be loved. This side of Venus makes her the head of the relationship department, since you've got to be with someone to use that nice, polite side you've been polishing up. She's the technology that drives you out on a Saturday night to try to find your "other half." She's the urge to couple that makes you search for a partner until you find one, sometimes at any cost. You'll recognize Venus easily at the very beginning of a relationship, when you're on your best well-mannered behavior, when absolutely everything the beloved does is just fine in your mind, no matter what it is. Walk across your back? Sure, fine. Sit through a doubleheader? You betcha. Venus, matter of fact, can even be a bit deceiving at the beginning of a relationship, mainly because she completely disguises her counterpart, the assertive Mr. Mars— whom we'll talk about next.

This face of Venus brings out the diplomat and the peace-maker in us, and calls forward our abilities to cooperate, har-monize, and compromise—all for the other. This Libran side of Venus, then, is also in charge of reminding you of your man-ners. She emerges when you need to engage in charming smalltalk, light chit-chat, and social niceties. The weather, mat-ter of fact, is a very Venusian—and Libran—topic. Venus loves social situations where folks don't come together for any other point than to enjoy each other's company. Her earthly repre-sentative is copper, a metal that mixes easily with all other metals, that wears pastels well when it's heated. Copper is a per-fect "alloy"—which sounds an awful lot like "ally," . . . and the lady is into partnerships, after all. . . .

Then there's the Taurus side of Venus, the part of her that specializes in nice things and nice surroundings, rather than nice people. The Taurus side of Venus loves nothing but the best. All your favorite things, in fact. This side of Venus describes what you love, and how you love it. Cats, maybe. Chocolate. A piece of art. A great big pillow. Whatever. Venus is in charge of get-ting those favorite things to you. Since money is what we use to "attract" what we love, she also holds the purse-strings. Money buys more than just things, remember—it also buys experiences, and experiences are why we take up residence in-side these bodies.

Regardless of whether it's the Taurus or the Libra side of Venus, anytime you find yourself smiling just because you feel soooo good, that's Venus. Now, feeling that good makes it impossible not to display behavior that is pleasing to the other, which brings us full circle. In a nutshell, acting nice is a Venus trait.

It's also a trait that's traditionally associated with women. Being sociable, pleasant, and charming—archetypally acting out the part of goddess of love and beauty—was a role we were encouraged to play. Some of the training was overt—"charm schools" and "finishing schools" taught us how to be entertaining, smiling hostesses extraordinaire. Back as recently as the 60s, high school home economics classes gave women lessons on how to cook, clean, and sew—-to be the perfect caretaker and companion. We were also taught to ignore our own needs and be the perfect spouse in far more subtle ways. Women's magazines gave tips on how to catch a man"—everything from cooking his favorite foods to adopting an artificial interest in the Indy 500. All this training we received on how to be nice was yet another obstacle to overcome once we opted to go out into the world and choose a vocation, however, since being nice isn't what you'd call an "edge" in today's competitive world—and especially in today's business world. The times we're living in now require something more along the lines of self-assertion and personal confidence and that's where Mars comes in.

Mars

Yes, it's time to meet our next contestant—Mr. Mars. Get ready, too, because this guy ain't no Venus, he's the head of the department of "mess with me and you die," the dude with the attitude, the guy who makes very, very sure that nobody—but nobody—steps on your blue suede shoes and lives to tell the tale. This is the side of you who just won't take it any more, who takes arms against a sea of troubles when threatened, who fights back when you feel like you're under attack. Your Mars is the warrior inside you, your own personal one-planet swat team. In a word, Mars is your sword, the brave, fearless, and courageous side of you who decides whether to retaliate with the bomb or the pearl-handled pistol when someone offends you—and yes, you bet we girls have one, too. He's the planet we use when it's time to stop doing the Venus—the "we," that is—and time to start doing the "me," and he's most especially skilled at doing the "me" when that "me" involves anger.

Now, most of the images we use to describe how we feel when we're angry involve the image of fire. Makes sense, too—Mars is the red planet, and that's the easiest way to recognize him. Think of how we describe anger. "All fired up." "Seeing Red," for example. "Hot under the collar." Although Mars does bear a strong resemblance to the element it's built of, and although Mars is a truly spontaneous energy, he's not just a loose cannon on the deck. He's got a purpose. He's the strength of your will that gives you super-human power, the push that will get you across a finish line, regardless of whether or not you're actually capable of it physically, just because you want to finish. When your Mars is conjured, you're ready to do anything to avenge yourself—regardless of whether or not you're physically strong enough to handle the offender. Mars doesn't consider the size of the obstacle, or the odds of the outcome. Your Mars just wants you to win. He's in charge of the muscles in the physical body, the side of you who loves competition, equal adversaries, and worthy opponents.

Mars is also in charge of adrenalin, which is manufactured by the body in times of extreme stress—so if you need an extra push of energy to take care of yourself, you'll have it. Ever get so mad that you shake? That's Mars, too. When someone challenges you in some way, whether it's because they yell at you, or just do something that makes you feel as if a line has been drawn in the sand, your Mars reacts as if you're about to be attacked, and turns on the adrenalin machine. You become energized, super-charged with fight-back energy. Now, that can be a problem, because anger isn't always appropriate, but once

Mars been summoned, you can't dismiss him quietly. You've got to use his energy, because it doesn't just go away.

In fact, once you've conjured Mars, unless you give yourself a very strenuous physical task to accomplish—unless you give your Mars a project, that is—he'll find his own way out. His usual style is to find victims to give a little poke to, in lieu of giving one big wound to the individual who called him out. It may take him a day or even a week of poking at innocent bystanders to get rid of all of that energy, too, but it doesn't matter to him at all. Mars will out—no matter what it takes—one way or another.

Of course, Mars isn't just around to "do" anger for you. Mars also describes how you "do" all your actions—the way you initiate any action. So whenever you "do" anything, whenever you decide to act on a decision, whenever you push, pull, yank, swim, or glide, whenever you change your environment to suit your tastes, instead of the other way around, your Mars is what you reach for.

Now Mars does have jurisdiction over the muscles in the physical body, so Mars has traditionally also been an energy men have found easier to express, since they're encouraged to pursue sports, competitive games, and contests. So when Mars got the urge to to "strongarm" a bit, to stir things up a bit, they had—and still have—the perfect outlet for his considerable energy. If their physical activities weren't enough, they were—and are—also encouraged to express the type of me-first energy Mars handles through their jobs. When a man found his Mars getting a little on the cranky side, he worked harder, worked out harder, or headed off for a little touch football. Worked out good.

Mars is another planet we women aren't encouraged to "do." Get angry? A girl? In public? Hardly. It's not "pretty" to get angry. Most of us were taught to go to our rooms if we were going to act "like that." Anger, you see, is not pleasing to the other, and that's what we are conditioned to do—according to society, at least.

Yes, if Venus is how we attract what we want to us, Mars is the way we go off in pursuit of what we want. Sometimes getting what we want means we've got to be pushy, to assert ourselves and not stop until we get what we want. "Pushy," however, is not something women have been traditionally taught to be. In fact, "pushy" is a word that's often used to describe a negative quality in a woman. So going off in pursuit of what we want, even in a career sense, has also not been taught to us. It's a quality we've had to learn on our own, and a recent one, at that. Finding the balance between Venus and Mars, then, between protecting our rights and bending to the wishes of an other, is one of the strongest assets anyone can learn, regardless of sex.

The Balance Point

We've seen how, as women, we're traditionally taught to "do" certain parts of our charts, and not others, how our upbringing and family training classically involved being taught to do our feminine sides, but not our masculine sides. We've seen how, even as modern as we think we've become, we're still taught more about the care and nurturing of our homes and our "others" than we are about how to express our individuality and find the right career direction. We've gone over the planets involved in the drawing of the gender lines, looked at the roles each of them play in our search for a life purpose, and seen how best to turn their positive sides into assets.

Before we go on, then, take a look at the Moon, the Sun, Venus, and Mars in your chart, and try to assess whether or not you're using them on as high a level as possible. Examine how the societal conditioning you received affected you, and your expression of those energies. Once we realize these four planets are in there, once we learn to balance and express both the masculine and the feminine sides of ourselves, we're operating as a whole entity, with no societally imposed blocks. That's no easy quest, but awareness, as always, is the first step.

All that said, it's time to look at the chart in a less gender-specific way. Regardless of sex, there are planets and points in everyone's chart that show the future, others that talk about the past, and still others that show what and where our personal stumbling blocks might be. We'll look first at indications of the future and the past in the pairs of planets and points that contain them.

Indicators of the Past and the Present— What We Brought Along, and What We're Looking For

When it comes to the future and the past, most astrologers agree that certain planets and points are indicators of where you've come from—what you've brought along with you this time—and where you're off to—what you're here to learn. These spots function like "road signs" of a sort, in that they show life experiences with which we're already familiar, experiences with which we're totally unfamiliar, qualities we don't yet know well enough to be absolutely sure about expressing, and characteristics we more or less automatically display. Past places show us where our memories are strong, where we operate on what we already know. Future places show where our areas of inexperience lie, where we're still holding on to the coffee table to walk.

THE SUN AND THE MOON

We've already talked a bit about these two. The Moon, of course, is a lady whose condition in our chart, although subtle, has a tremendous effect on our lives. The Moon is our undercurrent, our emotional script, the comfort zone we seek to recreate over and over again, both through the relationships in which we find safety, and the homes into which we burrow snugly. The Moon represents familiar territory and familiar feelings—like going home for the class reunion. Our life's work should contain elements of her, so that we can feel comfortable, secure, and content in the knowledge that what we're becoming is what we already are—on the inside.

The Sun, of course, is her archetypal opposite, the hero off in search of a quest, who has no idea where that road will lead, but follows along regardless because it must. The Sun in our charts shows the qualities we're out to develop in ourselves this lifetime, the subject of specialization we're here in cosmic college to pursue. The Sun is the part of us that faces the future because it understands that we're all here for a reason. It's an odd quest, too. The Sun is the side of us we're constantly searching for, the aspect of our personalities that we'll never attain completely—because if we did, it would have no reason to continue. Again, our life's work is tied in to the Sun, more than any other point. What we're spending our days doing absolutely must put us in the position of learning the Sun's lessons over and over again, geting the necessary feedback from others to enable us to see ourselves in our creations.

THE NORTH AND SOUTH NODE

Here's an interesting pair—the Nodes of the Moon. Now, the Nodes of the Moon don't really "exist." They're mathematically calculated points that mark the intersection of the Sun's apparent orbit around the earth with the Moon's orbit. The two spots where they cross are significant in that they show where you will combine the energies of these two "lights." Since the Sun is our quest for the future, and the Moon is the memory of the past, this axis contains both fate and destiny, both what we are, completely, and what we need to be. The South Node points to the past, and the North Node to the future.

Regardless of whether or not they actually exist, however, the Nodes are considered to be primary in Hindu or Vedic astrology, the singlemost important indicators of a soul's purpose. James Braha, in "How to Be A Great Astrologer," calls them "a marvelous guidance system that advise[s] which realms of activity to pursue, (the North Node), and the reason for such interests, (the South Node)."

In a nutshell, here's what the nodes seem to point to, in a career sense: if the South Node is, as Seattle astrologer Antero Alli calls it, a place where we are "an adept," those qualities are familiar and easy for us to perform. If they're easy for us, we can reach for them with ease—the same way we reach comfortably for the radio or the windshield wipers in a car we've driven for a very long time. Although some astrologers consider pursuing any South Node activities as being ultimately unhealthy, or possibly dragging us back into the past, experience seems to prove the opposite, especially in the case of the South Node. What's familiar is an asset—so those qualities we know well enough to consider familiar are true assets to us along our life path. They're pieces of our personalities so deeply ingrained in us that we can comfortably rely on their presence at all times.

On the other hand, the qualities represented in the North Node's placement are unfamiliar, or alien to us in some way. They show us our true challenges, new skills we need to learn and develop. The position of the North Node is like a college assignment of sorts. The sign of the North Node describes the qualities we're here to refine, and the house description of the Node tells us in which area of life circumstances we can expect to find that lesson waiting for us. For example, if the North Node is in the Sixth House, it's through challenges we're presented with on a daily basis, as we perform our duties at work, that we receive the training necessary for evolution. Since doing any activities associated with the North Node well is difficult, at least initially, it's also here that we'll receive not just quick pats on the back for success, but feelings of ultimate satisfaction and pride in the new skills we've learned. The North Node points upward, toward what we ought to be, away from what we are.

The nodes are, however, a matched set, a pair of opposites who balance each other, neither of which can exist without the other. The idea behind sucessfully integrating the Nodes into our life's quest is to take the absolute highest expression of the house and sign of the South Node and bring it into balance with the highest expression of the North Node. In other words, use what we already are as stepping stones to help us reach for what we should be.

MORE ABOUT SIGNS IN GENERAL

Whether you're investigating the signs because you're wondering what your Sun and Moon really mean, or you're interested in finding out where the signs of the Nodes are pointing you, it's helpful to keep in mind exactly what a sign is, so here's a refresher. Planets or points are the things we do. Signs are styles of behavior, flavors or filters, or costumes that planets or points wear that describe how we'll act out that type of behavior. The sign a planet or point like the North or South Node is wearing is a description of the way we do the things we do, and there's a whole range of possibilities inherent in the expression of each sign.

Libra, for example, is a sign traditionally associated with the concept of balance, and that's quite true—but it's learning to achieve that balance that is Libra's quest. As a result, Libra planets are often put in the position of learning to restore balance. Now, there are many ways to restore balance to situations that are unsound. There's the quick fix situation, where a Libra planet finds itself taking the easy way out, keeping things calm for the moment by saying whatever the other wants to hear. In that sense, the balance of the moment is rather precariously placed on whether the other is around when the opposing side shows up for a bit of the same medicine. The long term solution, and the side of Libra that requires a bit more work, is to see and tell the truth to both sides, to clearly state the facts, and point out the good in both.

Now, to bring in a bit more of a woman's point of view, I'd like to also mention at this point that half of the signs are masculine and half are feminine, so, again, there are certain sign behaviors that, as women, we're taught to modify, early on. The Fire and Air signs are masculine, for example, and the Water and Earth signs are feminine. You'll find points or planets in your chart wearing signs of both genders, but it's worth another look back to see if there is something about the range of expression inherent in a sign that you were forced to withhold, due to the way you were raised. If that's the case, keep in mind that refining your expression of a particular sign is another way of refining the energy of the planet or sign it's adorning, and another step toward perfecting the energies we need to become who we need to become.

More on Future Points, Via the Tenth House, or Midheaven—Where Your Agent Lives

We've seen how signs differ from planets—those were astrological food groups number one and two. In order to keep on looking for our Life's Purpose, there's one more food group we need to examine: the houses. Now, houses aren't energy sources, like planets, and they're not styles of behavior, like signs. They represent areas of life experience, sets of circumstances we deal with that require different sides of us to handle. For example, the side of our personality we display at work is quite different from the side we take out when we're with our Moms, and that side of us is quite different from the side of us our friends and significant others get to see.

Well, there's a house in the astrology chart that pertains specifically to career, a spot where we can look to find a description of the type of life path that would suit us best—and that's the spot that's straight up, right at what I like to think of as the "roof" of the chart—the Midheaven, or Tenth House. Now, it's up here in this most exposed of houses that we stash the side of us who decides how we're going to act around the subject of authority, both when we're with an authority figure, and when we are the authority figure. Of course, it's through specializing in a single subject that we become recognized as an authority on it, and that's where career comes from. As a result, the type of behavior we'll exhibit, based on the sign on the "door," or cusp of that house, is also a terrific indication of the subject we should be pursuing. If we have the freedom-oriented sign Sagittarius on the cusp of the Tenth, for example, it means we want to be recognized as the type of authority figure who is a philosopher. In order to become a philosopher, then, in order to build a career around those topics, we'll need to set about accumulating a medley of differing life experiences—

because it's experience that makes us wise by showing us what's really important, via the big picture.

Here's another way of looking at it: I like to think that the sign on the cusp of the Tenth House shows the personality of our agent, the side of us that lives up in the penthouse of the chart, that's constantly taking phone calls, setting up personal appearances, and monitoring making decisions on what we ought to do next, to further our career goals. Adopting this type of behavior, then, is also a way to become our own "agent."

And Last but Not Least, Saturn . . .

Any discussion of career would be painfully incomplete without discussing Saturn, of course, since this is the planet who is in charge of the career department. Saturn owns the Midheaven, after all—it's Saturn's office.

Saturn represents the qualities we'll need to develop if we want to succeed at anything—but especially a career. This is the planet with the rings, remember, the planet that holds us back until the time is right, the planet that sets up rules, and structures, and regulations, the planet that may even limit us a little too much, if we're not careful. Saturn is the critical parent inside each of us, the planet in our charts that shows the way we discipline ourselves, the way we just say no to anything that distracts us from our ultimate purpose—our life's work. Saturn's spot in our charts shows what we came here to take charge of. The house Saturn lives inside shows which life circumstances we can look to for experiences that will further us along our paths, and the sign Saturn wears shows the style of discipline and training that will work for us. In a nutshell, Saturn shows where we'll be able to sit still long enough to learn something, and to learn it well enough to master it.

The Real Goal

As women, we need to be aware of the new responsibilities life in these times has placed on our shoulders—and the new opportunities for personal growth, as well. We are able now, like never before, to be whole, functioning individuals, to fulfill ourselves rather than looking to an other to play the part. Since we tend to be more receptive to the intuitive arts, it's important that we choose the best of what's out there to direct us along the way towards achieving our most important goal, self-actualization—and astrology is certainly in that category.

In all, the thing to keep in mind is that the astrology chart represents us—each of us—in our entirety. Everything about us is in there—every talent, every fear, every joy. The key to using astrology successfully, then, is first to understand the whole chart, and then to find activities that involve using as much of it as possible. You'll know when you've found one of those activities, too—whether it's oil-painting, line-dancing, astrology, or stock-market analysis. You'll know because when you find your thing, there'll be a spark of recognition. You'll walk right up to it, grab it, and say, "Ah, yes . . . this belongs to me." Choosing a life path means committing to a career. Building a career means spending an awful lot of time learning to be an expert at something. If you're about to spend all those precious hours out of your life "doing" something, then, make sure it's something you love. Don't worry—you'll know it when you find it.

Roxana Muise

Roxana Muise is a second generation astrologer and metaphysician. She graduated from St. Catherine's Academy in Lomita, California (where she studied the mantic and symbolic arts, such as palmistry and numerology, along with her ministerial studies) and in 1974 was ordained in the Abundant Life Church, a metaphysical-spiritualist church. She began astrological studies in 1968, and graduated from the Scorpio School of Astrology. She obtained her bachelor of science degree with honors in Health Science in 1981 from California State University at Dominguez Hills.

Muise co-founded the South Western Astrology Conference (SWAC), and guided it from 1974 through 1985. She has served as president and membership director, and is now director of archives of the International Society for Astrological research (ISAR), and was a founding member of the board of directors of the United Astrology Congress (UAC). She is a co-founder of the Kepler College of Astrological Arts and Sciences in Seattle, Washington. She is author of *A-YEAR-AT-A-GLANCE, the 45 Degree Graphic Ephemeris* and *The Fourth Sign,* and is listed in the *World Who's Who of Women.* Roxana lectures in several countries and maintains a private practice in Bellevue, WA, where she lives with her husband of forty years.

324

Roxana Muise

The Sacred Sisterhood

O h, Godmother, you taught me so much about life and about the sacred relationships between women! Through your friendship and gentle guidance I learned about my uniqueness, my special talents, gifts, and potentials. In my study of astrology, I learned that as I express through the sign where my Sun resides, I am a unique individual, and also a member of a group of beings who share the Libra Sun sign. That unique duality that my Sun embodies reveals that I am much more than is apparent. Many astrologers say that Libras need to relate with others. I have discovered that all Sun signs share that quality of duality that bids them to manifest more than one of the characteristics of their Sun signs. Ah, but that's only the Sun! The involvement of the other, no less important components of my horoscope symbolize my unique complexity. Those combinations enable me to develop like no other.

You taught me that those components represent many archetypal seeds within me—that I am rather like one of the mythical Kurlon Neskos ceramic dolls of the 3rd dynasty Master of Takwin Hill.[1] This artifact was a symbolic reminder of their philosophy of beingness: it consisted of a large apparent doll that opened to house many smaller dolls—each linked to one another in particular ways. The Kurlon believed that each person is a community of individuals, each with its own style, desires, and world view. As one is examined, the links to others are accessed, and they in turn trigger the seeds of new combinations of potential growth and development.

I saw how those inner parts of me have correspondences and connections with the inner parts of other human beings. Our human nature urges us to develop relationships with other individuals to assist each other in the evolution of our major life processes.

Myths and Human Nature

Human nature is defined by relationships. Relation comes from the Latin, re-latum, meaning: *to tell the story of . . .*

You and I have spoken many times of relationships in ancient times described in stories that we know as myths. The characters in these myths described special powers and abilities. Many had the names of gods and goddesses, and the myths they lived were beautiful, exciting, and terrifying stories of all of the possibilities contained in the minds of the people. According to Carl Jung, these possibilities live in the collective unconscious, and the gods and goddesses are archetypes. Jung believed that each of these archetypes represent a functional prototype or an instinctual behavior pattern present within all people. He compared each archetype to a crystal that resonates to a specific frequency. Frequencies shared between people allow them to play out the myths in their lives together, each person playing the role of one or more of the archetypes. Often famous people, or characters in a movie or the news live out a myth for all of us to observe. We experience those special frequencies in a vicarious way, and learn the lessons without interrupting our own primary myths. Myths are like games that our psyches play— where time and space and reality and dreams are all in the same arena, and not seen as separate.

If the people are aware of an archetypal role they are playing, they can consciously use the relationship to add to their soul's store of knowledge and experience. Many are unaware of the roles that they are embodying, and get caught up in the story as if that is all there is to their lives.

Dear Mentress, you guided me to the writings of James Carse, who writes,

> There are . . . two kinds of games. One could be called finite, the other infinite. A finite game is played for the purpose of winning, an infinite game for the purpose of continuing the play.[2]

A finite game follows a script, which moves toward a specified, inevitable conclusion. In a finite game, there is always a winner and a loser, and the souls are encumbered with the residue of issues left unresolved.

In an infinite game the players are spontaneous and aware, and ". . . relate as free persons. . . ,"[3] and may consciously use all their inner potential and creative abilities to build a positive, loving outcome. Myths are meant to be infinite games; they survive generation after generation and are repeated by many people because they are the living, dynamic patterns of the human condition. If we live our myths consciously, recognizing the archetypal frequencies, we can create new awareness and add new meanings to all levels of our lives.

Myths need not be followed word for word, or deed for deed. The value lies in the resonance of the archetypes involved. All myths involve the principles of process and tension.

The details of each life story are created in appropriate measure to the individual and the culture; and the archetypes may even be used in an entirely different story, but the story must have a beginning, or motivation; a quest, or process leading to a goal, or pay-off; and an ending. The gender of the archetype is not of primary importance. The behavior patterns are easily available to players of either sex, and played out by either with just as much meaning. The true value of living a myth lies in identifying with their concepts, and consciously working toward a healthy and balanced solution to the archetypal challenge.

Early Beginnings of Myths

As early humans observed nature, they created myths to explain the behavior of a world over which they had no control. They saw the similarity in the power of fire, and lightning, and the Sun. They watched the rain, and saw how it nourished the earth and made plants grow. They felt the wind, and wondered about the changes of the seasons. They tried to align themselves with the order of nature's cycles, surrendering to the mysteries of the nature gods and goddesses in return for survival and security.

At first, women joined men in hunting for food, but women soon found that conditions connected with their unique ability of child-bearing made them exceedingly vulnerable, and the first intra-gender relationships began. Inner connections with the sacred and repeatable cycles of the Moon gave them a natural support for their special bonds, and an awareness arose that they had needs that differed from those of their men.

Women soon began to uncover and develop some of their additional gifts—gifts that benefited and supported the whole tribe. They invoked new goddesses to help them develop these talents in supportive clan and family groups, and the notion of the Sacred Sisterhood began to take form.

The first deity that women could relate to completely was the Moon. The triune nature of her cycle was the simplest to follow: In her early phase she was associated with the virginal maiden, love and sexuality, and women's mysteries. (Later in Roman myths, she appeared as the goddess Mens, guardian of menstruation, which means the right moment)

As the Moon approached her full phase, she counted the measure of the months, the birth process, and the bonding of mother and child —the nurturance from the breast that made the difference between life and death. One characteristic of motherhood became the fierce, bold protector of babies from ancient men, who, also observing nature, first saw the small helpless animals as food.

After the full phase, as the orb waned in size, the Moon took on the powerful archetype of the crone, who was the keeper of knowledge, healing, ceremony and night magic, wealth, and the death cycle. One woman of the tribe learned faster or lived longer than the others, She evolved into the wise woman of the tribe, who not only knew the will of the goddesses and gods, but reached inside herself and became the goddess, whenever a needful occasion arose. Her necessity of action became the myth of mysticism, and she became the natural link between the divinities and the people of the tribe. When her physical presence left the earth plane, her province was passed on to another Sister, who had been groomed to take her place. The old wise woman then took her place on the unseen levels of nature, and continued to be a strong force in the lives of the people. She had squared the circle: First integrating the physical with the spiritual whole, then surrounding the cross of matter with the circle of spirit. Her life-spirit and all the Sisters who followed her would serve the tribe for all time.

All of these faces of the goddess, and more, were developed over the ages. The bonds between women of all ages, and all times of history, and all levels of existence became the bonds of the Sacred Sisterhood.

Godmother, I recently noticed a story about women in one of today's primitive cultures, whose lives play out the viable myths of their ancestors, honoring the archetypes that strongly operate within them.

The women of the Huaorani tribe, deep in the Ecuadorian jungle believe that plants have souls. They believe it is the responsibility and the honor of the women to cultivate and harvest them in the sacred lands where food is grown. The men are trusted to protect the tribe and hunt for food animals, but they are not allowed in these sacred places. The women of the tribe are all like sisters to each other. They work together and administer all nurturing aspects of the communal life of the tribe, including preparing the food, healing those who fall ill, and caring for and educating the children until they reach puberty. The boys then join the men of the tribe, where they travel the rite of passage out of the domain of the women. But, the girls are initiated into the sacred ways of women and the Sisterhood of the tribe, and learn to conduct the sacred rituals. Secret stories passed down from their ancestors are given to them verbally, in trust for succeeding generations.[4]

Men and Women, Their Differences

I saw that the differences between the sexes are valuable and important in how they envision and live their processes. I suggested to you that the different and sometimes alien ways of being and becoming of men and women implied that they are two completely different species. You were quick to caution me that the Great Spirit of all Life created those differences with wisdom and compassion; and that we may learn much from each group in every journey that we make on Gaea, our Mother, the Earth.

Our scientists define a "species" as a group of individuals classified under in a common name; a single distinct kind of animal . . . having certain distinguishing characteristics. This is simply a category of biological classification. A sub-classification of species is gender, and our science, as well as some of our religions determine that the primary purpose of human relationships between the sexes is to continue the species.

In most of the gender distinction studies, differences in psychological processes and emotional behavior were initially addressed, but now scientists are finding actual physical gender differences in brain size, neuron and cell density, and are identifying different locations in the brains of men and women for reasoning skills, verbal response, linguistics, speech, melody recognition, and general phonetic comprehension.[5] After correlating their findings, they find that neither gender is generally superior, but that processes and responses differ markedly between men and women in almost every area of life. Perhaps we really are two different but complimentary species.

At birth, all humans begin in a more or less androgynous state. The emphases are on nourishment, bodily comfort, and sleep. As time passes, they want more: Babies are relentless seekers of input and interaction, and are accomplished mimics. They are curious about everything, but very unaware about themselves.

As a child grows, interacting with family groups and playing with others of its age, the dance of relationship begins to educe the basic nature of each child. Each one learns what she or he does best naturally: Lead, connect, or follow; direct, negotiate, or support; yin, yang, or change. As a child approaches puberty, polarization of the individual's basic patterns of physical gender takes place. Cultural expectations and demands, and the powerful persuasions of body chemistry require the child to set forth on its path. Appropriate to the conditions of the lifepath, its psyche chooses mythic archetypes to assist in the process of the child's growth.

Sometimes an individual finds a path that differs from society's expectations. That can present a difficult myth to live, as Hermaphroditus, son of Hermes and Aphrodite, discovered. The water nymph Salmacis fell completely in love with the beautiful youth as he bathed in her spring. When he rebuffed her interests, she asked the gods to unite them in one body so that she could be with him always. The gods granted her prayer, and they were joined in a body that was neither exclusively male nor female, but both at once. He prayed that all the bathers in the spring become bisexual as well; and the gods complied with his prayer, as well.

My learned teacher, I know that many concepts and many levels of meaning may be found in a myth of this type, oftentimes generating more questions than answers.

Mythological Beginnings

Myths containing the same archetypes come from all cultures, but most of our western myths come to us through the stories of the Greeks and the Romans, which reflect the perspectives and attitudes of the predominantly male philosophers, who had command of the places of learning and the leadership of countries. Women held to the oral traditions of story telling, whereas men took to the writing of their ideas. Perhaps this is why women philosophers' works have not been found among the writings of the ancient world.

The male figures in Greek and Roman myths were primarily loners and heroes, who demonstrate a need for a hierarchy or a vertically structured society. In my study of the western myths, I found an enormous number of groups of sisters. In addition to the Heliades, the daughters of the Sun, there were many and various groups of Nymphs, who had charge of various areas of nature: Hyades, who predicted weather, and read the stars and planets; Ionades, who were in charge of health and healing through mineral springs; Nereides for salt water (oceans); Naiades for springs and brooks, rivers and lakes; Oreades, of the mountains and grottoes; Dryades, for the trees. The Hesperides were guardians of the golden apples from Hera's wedding; the Furies were avenging goddesses, relentless pursuers of criminals; and the Graces were filled with beauty, charisma, and the social graces. Then there were the Horae, who were in charge of the hours and the seasons, weather, justice and peace, care and tenderness. They were called upon as helpers of children.

More well known, perhaps, are the Titanides, daughters of Gaea and Uranus, one of whom, Mnemosyne (in charge of memory), spent nine nights with Zeus and gave birth to the nine Muses. Each daughter assumed responsibility for remembering a part of the arts, sciences, creativity and intelligence. Not all the groups of sisters are beneficent. There are the Gorgons, unpleasant, ugly, evil water goddesses, whose images turned men to stone; and the Sirens, half women, half birds, who sang so sweetly, that men who heard them were lured to their deaths. There were innumerable groups of sisters that specialized in many different areas and filled the needs for various archetypes.

Women in these myths banded together toward a common goal, and were bound to each other through similar or complementary characteristics, showing a preference for a horizontally structured society; this is a strong component of the Sacred Sisterhood. Neither structure is superior, but both the horizontal and the vertical are needed to complete the cross of matter.

Concept of the Sacred Sisterhood

Sacred comes from the Latin *sacer*, the same root seen in *sanus*, sane, and in the Greek *saos*, safe; consecrated to or belonging to a deity; venerable, made holy; entitled to the highest respect, reverence. Sisterhood is defined as a group of women having some interest, belief, etc. in common.

There will always be mixed-gender relationships; but exploring, discovering, and developing the wholeness within us is, at times, less confusing when we relate with another who is physiologically, linguistically, and emotionally similar. We feel more freedom and safety to share with them the archetypal processes at great depth and with exceptional clarity.

As my mentress and confidant throughout this lifetime, you have guided me through many relationships. Some were particular lessons that I learned about woman interrelating with man; and those experiences were powerful, exciting, and fulfilling, but since my present journey is in a female body, I want to tell you now how much I appreciate your insight and wisdom as I experienced some of the special bonds I formed with women. I recall some of these experiences through the eyes and hearts and charts of my clients, and the stories of noted women who touch some familiar chord within me. Some, I relive through my own spirit, my own mind, and my own senses. As I remember each one, it is as if time has shifted, and I am seeing each moment for the first time.

You counseled me about the many different ways of women, and prepared me to avail the most from each encounter, each degree of initiation, each point of no return in the path to wholeness in my role as woman. Each woman who brought light to any part of my life gave me a gift of intimate understanding. I consider some of these gifts good and wholesome, and some less than desirable, but they are all valuable, and all of them taught me about love. Even in the realms of love we have many examples of the multi-faceted natures of the archetypes.

Kinds of Love

I learned that there are basically three types of love. The first is a dual love. The primal love of creation gave order and process to our world, then became the love of a sensual or sexual nature. Both are symbolized in mythology by Eros, god of love, or Cupid, as he was later called. His particular ability was to manipulate or sway the passions of both mortals and deities, and cloud their minds to reason. This love supports the myths that we live by, ensuring the creation of an abundance of players for the infinite game of Life.

The second is spiritual love—holy, selfless, and sometimes sacrificial. One such representative in Roman mythology is Agathedaemon, (meaning good genii). She was one of many invisible guardian angel-type nymphs who protected mortals, loving them without favor or judgment. The Greek word for love of God or spiritual love is agape, meaning goodness. This kind of love was held in high esteem by the gods. There are many myths that symbolize the altruistic love of self-sacrifice, such as that of the wise and kindly centaur who was physician and mentor to many young gods and heroes. Chiron, son of Chronos and Philyra, offered to give up his immortality, and die. In exchange for this, Prometheus was released from his eternal torture, and Chiron was awarded a starry place in the heavens for his sacrifice.

Philia symbolizes the third type of love. She had many temples dedicated to her as goddess of friendship. This kind of love is loyal and stable and gentle, and most often is a part of the frequency of the relationships between Sisters. It deals with the fitness of things, easy, familiar relationships, where mutual goals may be accomplished by individuals of like minds.

Many myths contain all three types of love, and are difficult to differentiate, but love is always a part of the motivation of any myth, and is the glue that holds our world together.

Energies of Relating

The two forces, bonding energy and binding energy, form the vital basis for relationships. Binding force is determined by measuring the differences in tension and the direction of the momentum of the energies of two or more entities. When the dynamic tension is just right, the potential for growth is optimum—too much tension and the relationship is blown apart.

Bonding force is determined by the sharing of complementary or similar energies between two or more entities. When many similar energy components are shared, strong bonds of union are formed.

Both types of force are necessary for a successful relationship of any kind. Dynamic aspects between appropriate components of charts are essential to enable the shared passions and goals to grow and develop, and for action and change to take place. For example: conjunctions promote intensity and motivation; squares demand confronting a problem or building a base; semi- and sesqui-squares bring the potential of accomplishment and success. Godmother, you said that it was important to remember that all of the archetypes (gods and goddesses) have dual natures. Just like a magnet, they have positive and negative potentials. Built within a magnet is the principle of opposition, an astrological aspect of relationship, which contributes to filling needs, creates motivation through competition, and offers the gift of perspective.

Aspects of Sameness

Our human relationships need other aspects as well, such as sameness, comfort, unity, and ease of relating, to support and assist in learning and growing, and the building of strength and protection. These qualities can be supported by the so-called soft aspects, such as sextiles and trines. We find parity and similarity within our own gender, which allows us to assist each other to understand our shared characteristics and resolve problems from a shared point of view.

Looking at the individual horoscopes of Sisters for similar characteristics, we find that aspects of fellowship and camaraderie can be found in the following chart conditions: planets in the same sign can show our common characteristics; planets in the same element offer us the potential basis of shared understandings, feelings, awareness, compassion; planets in the same houses or quadrants can indicate similar arenas of life that are being activated; planets distributed in the same hemispheres can indicate similar responses and approaches to life; and planets in parallel (the same degree of declination) can symbolize the creation and strengthening of bonds between generations.

Various planetary aspects that sisters may have in common include: the same planets in squares or major configurations, indicating that the same principles are being developed; repeated families of aspects such as quintile/bi-quintile group, which helps the development and mastery of skills and talents, and the uncanny ability of psychic interaction. Connections between planetary rulers of the houses of relationship (7 colleagues, 3/9 student/teacher, 4/10 mother/daughter, 11 special groups) give us hints about the archetypes being lived.

The use of synastry to find specific connections is another method of identifying the basis of a feeling of community and potential for growth with another sister. Connections between charts that bring feelings of association can include mutual receptions between charts, mutual aspects, and planets that trigger important points in each other's chart. The most important part of the puzzle lies in the identification of the archetypes.

Gods and Goddesses as Planetary Archetypes

Strong goddesses and gods, such as Aphrodite, Demeter or Zeus have several different faces or facets to their personalities, or multiple names given to them by different locations or cultures. The names of these divinities are interchangeable with planetary meanings, forming archetypal bridges between our horoscopes and our myths. Reading the myths is enjoyable and educational, but just knowing the concepts associated with the divinities and their links with the planets is enlightening and revealing when I observe the behavior of myself and others in relationships.

The Moon

The Moon is the most important planet to the Sisterhood. Among the more popular Moon goddesses are: Lucina (birth); Diana (virginal, huntress, procreation, springs, woods, growth); Hekate (the crone, knowledge, night magic, goodness, ceremony, wealth, education, death); Artemis (night, independence, intelligent action, variable energies of the female psyche); Mens (mother and guardian of menstruation); Selene and Luna (night, time, regulation of the months and seasons); Helena (night and healing). The Miorae (the three Fates; Daughters of the night): Klotho or Clotho (she draws the thread from the spindle, spinning the thread of life); Lachesis or Decima (she weaves it into the cloth of life and measures its length, and adds the element of chance); Atropos or Morta (she carries the shears, and cuts the thread of life, bringing death). Together, they are dealers in karma, prophecy, and the natural order and allotted time of the life of mortals.

The Sun

The Sun is androgynous, at once nurturing and protective, powerful and unitive—an indivisible duality. Among the Sun goddesses are: Albina (love and sexuality, the white goddess); Cupra (goodness, day, life/death cycle); Helia (Sun and day); and Phaenna (Sun and day, brilliance and light, the shining one). In many Greek and Roman myths, gods are primarily associated with the Sun, such as Helios, Apollo, and Sol. When the Sun is too brilliant, too strong for women to face directly, the children of the Sun, the Heliades rule the Sun's effects on Earth: the dawn, the day, and twilight. They are associated with compassion. When one of the Heliades, Phaethon, drowned, Aegle (grief) and several of her sisters wept unceasingly until the other gods took pity on them and turned them into tall golden poplar trees, lining the river—their tears became small pieces of amber.

Mercury

Hermes (androgynous, cunning, mischievous, musical, inventive—the Trickster, messenger of the gods, intermediary between the gods and humanity).

Iris (goddess of the rainbow, messenger who delivered divine commands from the gods, guide and advisor to humans, bringer of rain to the crops of the farmers—the rainbow was the signal for them to pay her honor).

Venus

Aphrodite, motherless daughter of Ouranos—she arose from the sea foam where Chronos (after castrating Ouranos) threw his father's testicles—she stands for sexual love, physical beauty, she is considered the mother of the Roman people, protector of gardens and vineyards. Pluto called her Urania (love of all nature), and Aphrodite Panemos (sexual love among humans); Philia (love and sexuality, friendship).

Mars

Ares, lover of Venus/Aphrodite, god of tumultuous storms, particularly in the realm of human affairs—hence, the god of war, pride, fierceness, maleness.

Jupiter

Zeus, chief god of the Olympiades, called: the Thunderer, for his lightning bolts, responsible for the keeping of oaths, purveyor of wisdom (the Solomon of Greek divinities), dispenser of justice, merciful guardian, ruler and preserver of the world, father of the gods and men.

Saturn

Chronos, Kronos, son of Ouranos (who he deposed), father of Zeus, the ripener, the maturer, god of the harvest, keeper of time and cycles.

The three outer planets: Uranus, Neptune, and Pluto, are normally located deep in the collective unconscious, but you, my wise friend and mentress, suggested that when we deepen our awareness of our own life processes, the three great archetypes find a way to express within our lives, generally at great expense for failure, but with commensurate rewards for success.

Uranus

Ouranos, Uranos (the fertility of the original creation of the gods, father of the Titanedes, prophet, first god of the sky, erratic, he deals with changes—but on the order of quick, inevitable, irreversible changes—evolvement, rather than adjustment, such as unavoidable life path changes.)

Neptune

Poseidon, son of Chronos, brother of Zeus, sovereign ruler of the sea and the functions of all water, patron of mariners and sea creatures, associates with the unformed chaos of the mind—the fertile, untapped potential creativity that opens to you in daydreams, or that washes over your consciousness just as you fall asleep.

Pluto

Hades, son of Chronos, brother of Zeus, god of the underworld and of death, symbol of richness from beneath the earth—the elements in mines which must be transformed to be useful; transform, from Latin (*trans*), meaning to cross over on the other side of, to make a complete change; and from the Latin (*form*), meaning shape, image, figure. Those who visit the underworld are completely changed.

Asteroids

More components for refining and defining relationships are the asteroids. Named by their discoverers, many of the asteroids carry the names of mythological archetypes. The meanings of asteroid names began to seep into human consciousness in the early 1800s, when the first four, named after major goddesses, Ceres, Juno, Pallas, and Vesta were discovered. The asteroid belt is full of amazing tales of mythological meaning.

Meaning comes into consciousness linked with tangible symbols in our world. The result is appropriate meaning for those small rocks and their journeys through space. Asteroid names are powerful; they insinuate their mythologies into the fabric of our experience and their orbits interpose their little bodies into our charts, enhancing and supporting meaning deep within our lives. The four largest asteroids carry the Greek or Roman names of some of the most active archetypes in western culture:

Pallas-Athena

Protector during war, goodness, order, practical arts, a virgin goddess. Athena accidentally killed Pallas, her childhood friend and honored her by joining their names. Minerva, the Wisdom-Warrior, reason, thinking, invention, patriotism, intelligent activity.

Juno, Hera

Jupiter's wife and sister, guardian of women and all their cycles and functions, weather, commerce and travel, justice, protector of the form and sanctity of marriage and children.

Vesta, Hestia

Virgin goddess of the hearth, eternal fire of purity, the central nature of the community, consecration of the home as a sacred sanctuary, affairs of the tribe or the family.

Ceres, Demeter

Earth mother, timing and earth cycles, agriculture, harvest, barley, and other grains, purveyor of the cycle of life above the ground—the growing season (mother of Persephone, who is also known as Proserpina, Cora, Kore: alternately, a goddess of healing and purity, and queen of the underworld).

Ceres/Demeter cannot be named without mentioning her daughter. The two had a very close relationship, and their myth is rich in meaning on many levels. The young Kore, (meaning maiden) as she was originally known, was gathering flowers in a meadow. She was observed by Pluto, who was completely captivated by her. He kidnapped her and took her to his kingdom in the underworld where she became Persephone, his queen. Ceres was devastated by her loss, and appealed to Zeus to have her returned. A compromise was made, whereby the daughter would live with Pluto as his wife for one-third of the year, and return for two-thirds of the year to live with her mother above ground in the sunshine, thus describing the cycles of death and rebirth in nature.

I find many asteroids named after goddesses that enliven the myths I live in relevant places in my chart and the charts of my sisters. Often an asteroid with the given name of a sister will be in an important point in my chart. When these points are contacted by transits, symbolic meanings flower into manifestation in my life. If they support the natal promise, they add additional substance and meaning to my myths. There are more than 5,000 named asteroids available to us now, as our technology moves to support our search for understanding.

The Sisterhood in Today's Culture

My wise and blessed teacher, you made me aware of the creation of the cycles that are even now ever-present in our world—the process of being and becoming a woman, and how revered and special is each step in this path. The energy of the Sacred Sisterhood is present and available in our world to support the process every step of the way.

Women of today's culture employ the concept, and relive the mythical archetypes in their lives in many ways. Some of their passages are difficult, through relationships built upon dramatic mutual experiences, such as grief, victimization, terminal illnesses, or shared addictions; or unacceptable behavior, like eating disorders and substance abuse. There are many myths that tell of suffering, shame, victimization, injustice, and self-denial, and many sisters live the lessons of those myths. With the help and strength of another sister who has experienced a similar situation, they may develop the awareness needed to draw themselves into a more constructive completion of their process.

Some women choose to share and support behavior, beliefs, or conditions that are associated with the sacredness of the family. Many specialize in the traditional guilds of homemaking, such as fiber arts, quilting, gardening, food preparation, decorating, the care of children, and other, more unusual talents. Others manifest the literal sacred sisterhood of spiritual or religious holy orders by dedicating their lives to a church or a shamanic tradition, much as ancient women gave their lives and energies to the temple of a favored goddess. Still other women find value in a professional or academic life, while some study and promote body fitness and excellence through sports. Many women join together in support groups of two or more to investigate their spiritual and emotional natures, or to regain the self-esteem that they have lost—or have never yet experienced.

The search for self-esteem is the most prevalent of all the problems that brings sisters together. Sometimes the living of a myth is interrupted; but the psyche will find a way to bring it to completion at another time, especially if it is a prelude to another archetypal involvement.

My Mother, My Friend*

My mother has always been a good friend to me. That was especially important to me as i entered my teens. She was as supportive as a big sister when i entertained friends from school. When the time came for me to leave home, get married and start a family, she was the same understanding friend, always being there for me and offering helpful advice. She was ecstatic

---

*Note to the reader: In this section the lower case i is used to indicate lack of self-hood and low self-esteem.

when i followed her into the same profession, and welcomed me into her group of friends and colleagues, and for a while everything went smoothly. But, as much as i studied, as much as i worked, i still felt inadequate. Then one day came a realization: i wanted to be known as my self, not primarily her daughter, her extension, her shadow.

The pressure was building and building; and i felt there was nothing left but to break free or to die. But how? i felt smothered, captive, stifled. i wrote her a letter; because i didn't want to forget all that i was feeling, and i also wanted to say all i had to say with just the right words. i poured those feelings out on paper from my heart, but i delivered the letter in person, and had her read it while i was there. It was one of the most difficult things i had ever done. In the letter, i told her that i felt that i was only an extension of her, that i felt like i was living a life that she wished me to live. i told her that i was proud to be her daughter, and i knew that she was proud of me, but that now i had to be my own woman. i reassured her that i loved her, and wanted to continue be her friend and colleague, but that it was time for us to cut the umbilical cord. (Time for us to complete the birthing process that we had both slept through.) This last disclosure was not something that i had reasoned out, but a blind intuition, with the addition of some clever words. i had previously heard of the process of rebirthing, but had dismissed it as a technique for very troubled people, or metaphysical dilettantes, but metaphorically this was what we were doing.

She was stunned; she had no idea how i felt, but she saw that it was important to me, and we both dug deeply into our hearts and memories, and found the point of hurt.

Oh, the pain that we both experienced! We cried together, and hugged for so long, and talked at great length—as the energy moved through us. We had finally finished the rite of birth.

My mother and her family were believers in Christian Science when she was pregnant with me, her first child; and they had little or no experience with the medical community. Her water broke on the morning before my birth, and her labor began in the afternoon with mild stomach cramps. Not knowing what to expect, she and her maiden aunt took the bus to the hospital. The doctor was away, and had to be called. He instructed the nurses to give her a general anesthetic until he could arrive. The birth took place with both of us fast asleep. It took the medical team twenty minutes to awaken me and get me to breathe on my own; and my mother, who was also asleep, never saw me until the next morning, when they told her that i almost didn't survive the birth.

> I had been kidnapped and taken into a dark place, as was Persephone. Before Persephone was kidnapped, she was known as Kore. My middle name is Corin. My mother had helped me to live out my myth.

It took us time to fully heal. We continued to work together, and i endeavored to see myself as a separate entity, which was at first very frightening to me. i was unaccustomed to see her as a whole woman without that invisible, but real connection to me. i called her by her given name for a while, until i could call her mother with new and true feelings of the love of a daughter to her mother. My mother, who is a wise and compassionate woman, understood the process that we were experiencing. After she realized what was happening, she was most supportive and loving to both me and to herself. i had always felt close to my mother, but now i had some perspective, and could see some of the many other facets of this loving woman. Recognizing the goddess in another is like mirroring the goddess in myself, and i began to see some of those same attributes in my own life.

Since then, we have developed two separate and distinct relationships. A healthy relationship of mother and daughter (which was impossible for us as long as we were still psychically joined as one), and a relationship within the sacred sisterhood. We worked closely together in the same profession as colleagues with the freedom and awareness to develop more of the special natures of our relationship.

Our charts have combined aspects that produce configurations not present in our individual charts. Her Pluto and South Node complete a grand water trine with my Mercury and my Saturn. My Saturn in this trine opposes her Moon and Mars, which in turn connects to my Venus in her Fifth House, the house of the first child. This indicates a challenge or a difficulty in self-definition or separation as my Neptune conjuncts her Mars. This five-planet opposition completes a grand cross with mutual squares from her Jupiter in my Tenth of parents and careers and my Mars in her Seventh of peer relationships; and oppositions which provide energy for prospective and active co-operation, are essential for reaching goals. My ascendant is closely conjunct her Fifth House cusp and her ascendant is conjunct my Tenth House (career). Both our Mercurys are in Scorpio—mine is disposited by the ruler of the Fourth and hers by the ruler of the Seventh (using Mars as the co-ruler of Scorpio). This gives us a combination of mutual myths—that of mother/daughter (Demeter/Persephone) and self/peer (many myths of the Sacred Sisterhood are connected with this latter axis).

Another grand trine (in earth) is formed by her Venus-North Node, and Moon-Mars, and my Uranus. These interlocking grand trines are composed of planets at early degrees, and our combined charts form the grand sextile, or six-pointed Star of David. This aspect combination underscores the free-flowing communication that made our relationship so rich and meaningful throughout my formative years. The mystical implications of this wonderful mutual configuration imply our many past-life ties, our close spiritual bond, and our mutual interest in metaphysical subjects.

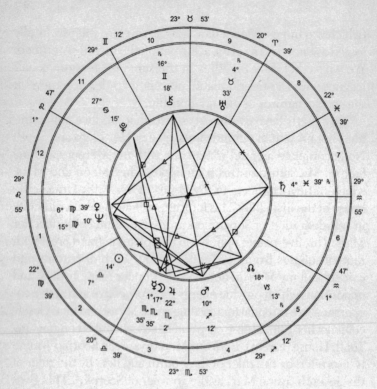

Asteroids: Corinne

Athene	12 Can 31	Juno	0 Tau 13 Rx
Aphrodite	27 Ari 56 Rx	Mentor	8 Vir 56
Cora	12 Leo 07	Philia	18 Vir 50
Demeter	12 Leo 07	Urania	23 Can 18
Diana	29 Libra 19		

Chart 1. Corinne

There are many asteroid connections between our charts, such as our name asteroids in important places in the other's charts. There are also connections between our Suns, Moons, Mars, Venus, and Persephones, Ceres, Demeters, and Coras.

We both have elevated Uranus, squared by sign, and both have fixed angles, squared by sign, and have had many lively, in-

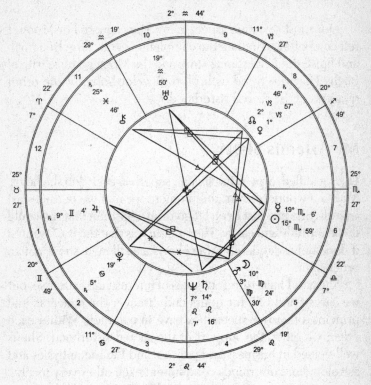

Asteroids: Mother/Friend

| Ceres | 15 Sco 15 | Demeter | 17 Sco 38 |
| Cora | 19 Leo 19 | Persephone | 12 Sagittarius 44 |

Chart 2. Mother-Friend

depth discussions about our different perspectives on astrology and philosophy. We are from different generations, but the bonds shown by parallels of declination between Moon/Venus, Mars/Ascendant, Uranus/Mercury, Saturn/ Chiron, Mercury/Jupiter, Neptune and Pluto/Midheaven, Jupiter/Moon, and North Node/Mars show a very close sisterly relationship.

Our most dynamic aspect is my Mars square her Moon. I felt compelled to initiate the completion of our forgotten myth and finish the Persephone story and the Moon goddess' rite of birth. That rite freed us both to develop some of the other qualities of the sacred sisterhood.

My Artemis Sister

Overqualified, expert, intelligent, superb in every job she holds, Mae is a wonder. From the moment we met we became fast friends. She had just been let go from a position that she could do beautifully and easily. The trouble was that the boss wanted it done only adequately. Mae enjoys a challenge; she is not an order-filler.

She and I have different areas of interest and expertise, but we can sit and talk for hours and discover the concepts and principles that our specialties have in common. Within each other, we enjoy the support of the sacred sisterhood. She is well-versed in business and politics, and I in metaphysics and astrology, and our minds compliment each other very nicely.

As the years turn, we move to different parts of the country, but we stay in contact and our friendship deepens.

Mae's Saturn in Sagittarius conjunct her asteroid Diana (11 Sagittarius 10 Rx) trine her Mars-Uranus, which in turn squares her Neptune-Midheaven indicate her ability to focus on a goal, and concentrate on it to the exclusion of distractions and competition. Her capability and proficiency and her ability to create positions for herself grows, but her vulnerability gets her into situations where people take advantage of her. She has a gracious habit of giving people the benefit of the doubt, and is constantly surprised when people let her down.

She is independent and a problem-solver par excellence; she has gained a reputation for re-organizing a department or a company to make it more efficient and viable, but employers with self-esteem problems are very threatened by her, and co-workers either respect her or fear her. She is very loyal, and expects loyalty in return. Her strength of character attracts both strong and weak men, and her compassionate nature wants to create relationships that are constructive as well as loving and growth oriented.

Mae and I have a wonderful proclivity for experiencing the same conceptual problems in different costumes, and our discussions bring out all the possible options because we look beneath the apparent, beyond the details. Our multiple planetary interactions support a synergistic game of "identify and solve," which we find mutually exciting and nurturing.

Even though we come from different generations, our parallels of declinations show the basis of our inter-generational bonding: Her Jupiter and my Venus; her Lunar Nodes and my Jupiter/Chiron; her Mercury/Venus/Pluto and my South Node/Pluto; her Ascendant and my Mars; her Uranus and my Midheaven.

Since our closest square is Uranus to Uranus, we each sense when life changes are immanent in the life of the other, and we are there for each other to offer alternate options in those times of stress and change. The choice to assist and support a Sister is a positive way to fulfill this aspect.

As well as many close conjunctions, our charts are inter-linked with several configurations: Mae's Sun is the anchor for a grand water trine connecting to my Saturn and Mercury (which is conjunct her out of sign Neptune). That Mercury and Neptune oppose my Uranus along her 4/10 axis and create a T-cross with her Uranus and Mars. Another grand trine is formed by her Jupiter, and my Vertex and my Midheaven, which opposes my Jupiter along my 4/10 axis. A square from her Vertex makes another connected T-cross. Mae's Saturn and Mercury piggyback my T-cross composed of Mars opposing

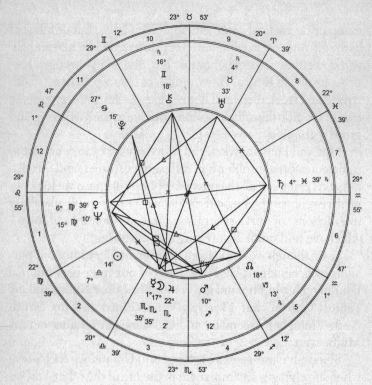

Asteroids: Corinne

Athene	12 Can 31	Juno	0 Tau 13 Rx
Aphrodite	27 Ari 56 Rx	Mentor	8 Vir 56
Cora	12 Leo 07	Philia	18 Vir 50
Demeter	12 Leo 07	Urania	23 Can 18
Diana	29 Libra 19		

Chart 1. Corinne

Chiron, squaring Neptune. A third T-cross is formed across her 1/7 axis that includes my Nodal axis, and her Venus square her Moon. This gives us mutual cardinal, fixed, and mutable T-crosses joined to mutual grand water and earth trines. Since our angles are so involved in these configurations, most of our

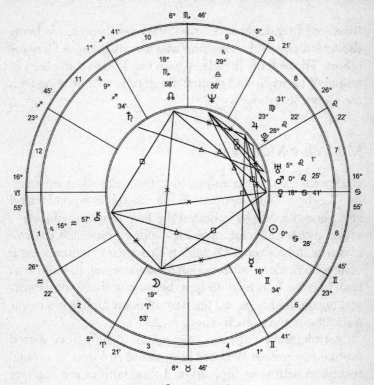

Asteroids: Artemis Mae

Aphrodite	16 Gemini 15	Juno	2 Tau 59
Artemis	20 Gemini 01	Minerva	19 Vir 16
Diana	11 Sagittarius 10 Rx	Philia	18 Sagittarius 40 Rx

Chart 3. Artemis-Mae

projects deal with home and career, and relationships and self-image. Sometimes we merge the qualities of impatience and caution. After we speak together, I feel a little bolder and more confident, and she a little calmer and more self-assured.

Asteroids Diana, Aphrodite, Juno, Artemis, Philia, and Minerva (plus our own name asteroids) from both of our charts make powerful contacts in her chart and in mine. Mae is a treasured friend and sister. As she moves through life living the Artemis myth in a conscious way, life will improve for many others. Through my friendship with her, I learn about the potential of harmony and mutual development of working with the sacred sisterhood.

My Wise Mentress

Godmother, our relationships have been close and meaningful. You have been mentress to me, as well as a good friend and playmate. We have shared the love of many subjects—music, movies, fiber arts, astrology, and yes, especially the love of words and concepts. Our charts share many similarities and connections, along with enough dynamic action to require us both to grow. I say relationships, because we have consciously and unconsciously played the parts of many archetypes in our associations and in each other's myths.

Astrologically, our many connections include three shared mutual receptions: We both have Venus in Virgo, in mutual reception with your Mercury in Libra; both of our Jupiters (mine in Scorpio and yours in Aries—using Mars as co-ruler of Scorpio) in mutual reception with both our Mars' in Sagittarius; and both of our Plutos in cancer in mutual reception with my Moon in Scorpio. Mutual receptions between charts indicate the potential for ease of relationship. It's as though each person can be comfortable with the other person's mental processes. Sometimes we will call each other about the same thing, often finishing each other's sentences. Even though our Plutos are both in Cancer, we come from different generations but we have several parallels that show the links between our different cultural periods. Our Venuses are both at 3 degrees north; my Jupiter and your Uranus are both at 17 south; your Pluto and Neptune and my Midheaven are all at 18 north; and our Vertices are within a degree at 21 south. You taught me the importance of the Vertex and how its contacts trigger realizations of truth. We have truly been able to do this for each other.

One of the most dynamic contacts that we have between us is your Moon square my Saturn. It is our closest dynamic aspect, and suggests a parent/child relationship. However, that has not been the case for us at all. With the many other supporting aspects, such as our individual close Saturn squares— yours to Jupiter, and mine to Mars; the fact that Saturn rules both our houses of peer relationship (using Saturn as co-ruler of Aquarius); and the midpoint of position of the asteroid Mentor from both of our charts at 21 Scorpio 13, conjunct my Jupiter and trine your Chiron, the mentress/student relationship registers as our main myth. Mentor in your chart at 3 Aquarius 30 is trine my Sun, and Mentor in my chart at 8 Virgo 56 is sextile your Sun. Together, we played roles in the myths of Urania, the Muse of astronomy, and Athene-Hygiea, who was dedicated to healing the body and the mind.

Some of the similarities that make for comfort and ease of relating are: Both of us have 3 planets retrograde, one of which is Chiron, one of the most elevated bodies in both our charts; we have both played the part of teacher and wounded healer. We both have seven planets in the lower horizon, including both our Suns, Moons, Mercurys, Mars, and Neptunes. We are both very private women who approach life from a conceptual base.

We are both healers and counselors—you with Chiron opposing Venus, and I with Chiron opposing Mars. Working together, we have been able to assist others in healing their puzzling relationship problems. We both have Moon Quintile Venus, which you taught me is a magical aspect that allows the blending of the voices of the goddesses of the Moon with those of Venus and her sister archetypes, Aphrodite, Astarte, and Philia. The magic facility of the quintile is to synergize the

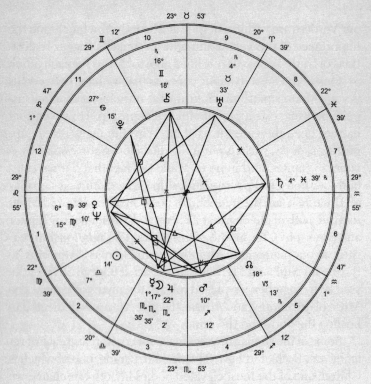

Asteroids: Corinne

Athene	12 Can 31	Juno	0 Tau 13 Rx
Aphrodite	27 Ari 56 Rx	Mentor	8 Vir 56
Cora	12 Leo 07	Philia	18 Vir 50
Demeter	12 Leo 07	Urania	23 Can 18
Diana	29 Libra 19		

Chart 1. Corinne

different energies, and create new possibilities and ideas of how to integrate those energies in our lives.

The Saturn bi-quintile between our charts gives us the alchemical ability to see together beyond the obvious, beyond the apparent processes in life, draw out the deeper meanings and

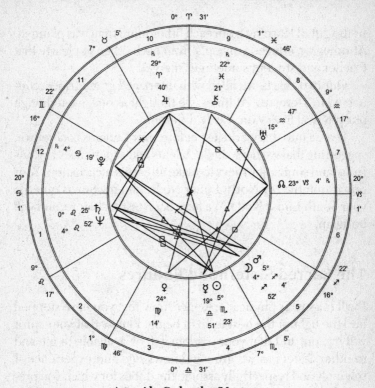

Asteroids: Godmother/Mentress

Aphrodite	13 Vir 23	Urania	29 Aquarius 49
Mentor	3 Aquarius 30	Vesta	10 Sagittarius 35
Philia	29 Sco 57		

Chart 4. Godmother/Mentress

concepts, and offer more stable and practical options and paths to investigate. Often, we used this ability when working on charts of clients. Both of us have Neptune in the First House, yours trine your Moon, mine sextile my Moon. These are also magical aspects that allow the invisibility that is sometimes necessary for a good listener, and that develop into empathic abilities. This magic Saturn aspect between our charts also gave us the gift of learning from each other more than was planned. At times we educed concepts from each other so clearly that teacher and student sometimes merged.

Our two charts are filled with interlaced grand trines, connected to T-crosses. At times, we thought as one, even though our physical lives were vastly different.

I came into this world just before your Lunar Nodal return, suggesting that we have similar talents and experiences to draw from, and similar journeys to make after this incarnation. Your Sun is quintile my North Lunar Node, and my Sun is quintile your South Lunar Node. We have been Sisters before, and will be again.

The Sacred Sisterhood Endures

I will miss your physical presence, now that you have stepped into the light of the next level of being. I know that your spirit will live on, and that your wisdom will be available to me and to other Sisters as we grow in knowledge and experience. I solemnly and respectfully assume the duties for which you prepared me—to continue to learn and grow, and to pass on that which I have learned to other sisters. I joyfully celebrate your graduation, and know that you and I, along with the entire sacred sisterhood will continue to be aspects and voices of the one Goddess, the Sacred Feminine within.

NOTES

1. Jean Luc Picard. "The Chase," *Star Trek, The Next Generation*, stardate 46731.5.

2. From *Finite and Infinite Games: A Vision of Life as Play and Possibility,* by James P. Carse. Copyright 1986 by James P. Carse. Reprinted with permission of The Free Press, a division of Simon & Schuster.

3. Ibid., 15.

4. "Warriors of the Amazon," Television Special *NOVA*, Public Television Presentation, May 1995.

5. *Brain Mind, A Bulletin of Breakthroughs* (Interface Press, Los Angeles, CA), September 1994, December 1994, February 1995.

BIBLIOGRAPHY AND SUGGESTED READING

Aveni, Anthony. *Conversing With the Planets*. New York: Random House, Inc., 1992.

Ann, MA., Martha and Imel, Dorothy Myers. *Goddesses in World Mythology*. New York: Oxford University Press, 1993.

Bell, Robert E. *Women of Classical Mythology*. New York: Oxford University Press, 1991.

Bolen, Ph.D., Jean Shinoda. *Goddesses in Everywoman*. New York: Harper & Row, Publishers, Inc., 1984

Carse, James P. *Finite and Infinite Games*. New York, NY: The Free Press, a division of Simon & Schuster, 1986.

Farrar, Janet & Stewart. *The Witches' Goddess*. Custer, WA: Phoenix Publishing, Inc., 1987.

Funk & Wagnalls. *Standard Dictionary of Folklore, Mythology, and Legend.* San Francisco: Harper & Row, Publishers, 1984.

Grimal, Pierre. *The Concise Dictionary of Classical Mythology.* Cambridge MA: Basil Blackwell Ltd., 1990.

Guttman, Ariel & Johnson, Kenneth. *Mythic Astrology: Archetypal Powers in the Horoscope.* St. Paul, MN: Llewellyn Publications, 1993.

Hope, Murry. *The Psychology of Ritual.* Dorset, England: Element Books, 1988.

_____. *Olympus: Self-Discovery and the Greek Archetypes.* London: Harper Collins Publishers, 1991.

Jung, Carl G. *Memories, Dreams, Reflections.* London: Routledge & Kegan Paul, 1963.

Kirenya, Karl. *Goddesses of the Sun and Moon.* Dallas, TX: Spring Publications, Inc., 1979.

Murray, Alexander S. *Who's Who in Mythology.* New York: Crescent Books, 1988.

Schwartz, Ph.D., Jacob. *Asteroid Name Encyclopedia.* St. Paul, MN: Llewellyn Publications, 1995.

Shorter, Bani. *An Image Darkly Forming.* London: Routledge & Kegan Paul, 1987.

Tannen, Ph.D., Deborah. *You Just Don't Understand.* New York: William Morrow & Company, 1990.

Thorsten, Geraldine. *GOD Herself: The Feminie Roots of Astrology.* New York: Doubleday & Company, Inc., 1980.

Webster's Deluxe Unabridged Dictionary, 2 ed. New York: Simon & Schuster, 1979.

Stay in Touch. . .

Llewellyn publishes hundreds of books on your favorite subjects. On the following pages you will find listed some books now available on related subjects. Your local bookstore stocks most of these and will stock new Llewellyn titles as they become available. We urge your patronage.

Order by Phone

Call toll-free within the U.S. and Canada, **1–800–THE MOON**. In Minnesota call **(612) 291–1970**. We accept Visa, MasterCard, and American Express.

Order by Mail

Send the full price of your order (MN residents add 7% sales tax) in U.S. funds to:

> **Llewellyn Worldwide**
> **P.O. Box 64383, Dept. K860–5**
> **St. Paul, MN 55164–0383, U.S.A.**

Postage and Handling

- $4.00 for orders $15.00 and under
- $5.00 for orders over $15.00
- No charge for orders over $100.00

We ship UPS in the continental United States. We cannot ship to P.O. boxes. Orders shipped to Alaska, Hawaii, Canada, Mexico, and Puerto Rico will be sent first-class mail.

International orders: Airmail—add freight equal to price of each book to the total price of order, plus $5.00 for each non-book item (audiotapes, etc.). Surface mail—add $1.00 per item. Allow 4–6 weeks delivery on all orders. Postage and handling rates subject to change.

Group Discounts

We offer a 20% quantity discount to group leaders or agents. You must order a minimum of 5 copies of the same book to get our special quantity price.

Free Catalog

Get a free copy of our color catalog, *New Worlds of Mind and Spirit*. Subscribe for just $10.00 in the United States and Canada ($20.00 overseas, first-class mail). Many bookstores carry *New Worlds*—ask for it.

ASTEROID NAME ENCYCLOPEDIA

Jacob Schwartz
Foreword by
Demetra George

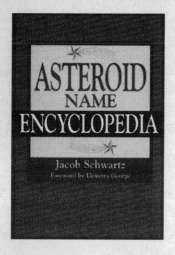

Astrology used to have nothing to do with names. Now it does! Here is the only reference work to include all the 4,000+ asteroids named in almost two centuries. Asteroids are important because they carry the vibrational energy of their names. And, because asteroid names relate to most persons, places, and objects on the Earth—Monica (#833), Chicago (#334), and Toyota (#3533)—they also relate to the events in the lives of these persons, places and objects.

Astrologically, asteroids represent the gate to the individual. Personally named asteroids can define an identity that is more intimate than any other cosmic symbol. While traditional horoscopes are helpful vehicles for self-understanding, placing asteroids in the chart explicitly for people and places by name adds a totally new and exciting dimension.

Is there an asteroid with your name on it? How do the asteroids named for important people in your life reflect actual experiences? Have persons with certain names usually been good for you, or bad for you? The asteroids and their names can explain why!

1-56718-609-2, 448 pp., 7 x 10, softcover   **$19.95**

THE ASTROLOGICAL THESAURUS, BOOK ONE: HOUSE KEYWORDS

Michael Munkasey

Keywords are crucial for astrological work. They correctly translate astrological symbols into clear, everyday language—which is a never-ending pursuit of astrologers. For example, the Third House can be translated into the keywords "visitors," "early education," or "novelist."

The Astrological Thesaurus, Book One: House Keywords is the first easy-to-use reference book and textbook on the houses, their psychologically rich meanings, and their keywords. This book also includes information on astrological quadrants and hemispheres, how to choose a house system, and the mathematical formulations for many described house systems.

Astrologer Michael Munkasey compiled almost 14,000 keywords from more than 600 sources over a 23-year period. He has organized them into 17 commonplace categories (things, occupations, and psychological qualities), and cross-referenced them three ways for ease of use: alphabetically, by house, and by category. Horary users, in particular, will find this book extremely useful.

0-87542-579-8, 434 pp., 7 x 10, illus., softcover $19.95

MYTHIC ASTROLOGY: ARCHETYPAL POWERS IN THE HOROSCOPE

Ariel Guttman & Kenneth Johnson

Here is an entirely new dimension of self-discovery based on understanding the mythic archetypes represented in the astrological birth chart. Myth has always been closely linked with astrology; all our planets are named for the Graeco-Roman deities and derive their interpretative meanings from them. To richly experience the myths that lie at the heart of astrology is to gain a deeper and more spiritual perspective on the art of astrology and on life itself.

Mythic Astrology is unique because it allows the reader to explore the connection between astrology and the spirituality of myth in depth, without the necessity of a background in astrology, anthropology, or the classics. This book is an important contribution to the continuing study of mythology as a form of New Age spirituality and is also a reference work of enduring value. Students of mythology, the Goddess, art, history, Jungian psychological symbolism and literature—as well as lovers of astrology—will all enjoy the text and numerous illustrations.

0-87542-248-9, 382 pp., 7 x 10, 100 illus., softcover $17.95

SECRETS OF A NATURAL MENOPAUSE: A POSITIVE, DRUG-FREE APPROACH

Edna Copeland Ryneveld

Negotiate your menopause without losing your health, your sanity, or your integrity! *Secrets of a Natural Menopause* provides you with simple, natural treatments—using herbs, vitamins and minerals, foods, homeopathy, yoga, and meditation—that are safer (and cheaper) than estrogen replacement therapy.

Simply turn to the chapter describing the treatment you're interested in and look up any symptom from arthritis, depression, and hair loss to osteoporosis and varicose veins—you'll find time-honored as well as modern methods of preventing or alleviating menopausal symptoms that *work,* all described in plain, friendly language you won't need a medical dictionary to understand.

For years, allopathic medicine has treated menopause as a disease brought on by a deficiency of hormones instead of a perfectly natural transition. *Secrets of a Natural Menopause* will help you discover what's best for *your* body and empower you to take control of your own health and well-being.

1-56718-596-7, 224 pp., 6 x 9, illus.   **$12.95**

SENSUOUS LIVING: EXPAND YOUR SENSORY AWARENESS

Nancy Conger

Take a wonderful journey into the most intense source of delight and pleasure humans can experience: the senses! Enjoying your sense of sight, sound, smell, taste, and touch is your birthright. Learn to treasure it with this guide to sensuous living.

Most of us revel in our senses unabashedly as children, but societal norms gradually train us to be too busy or disconnected from ourselves to savor them fully. By intentionally practicing sensuous ways of living, you can regain the art of finding beauty and holiness in simple things. This book provides activities to help you engage fully in life through your senses. Relish the touch of sun-dried sheets on your skin. Tantalize your palate with unusual foods and taste your favorites with a new awareness. Attune to tiny auditory pleasures that surround you, from the click of computer keys to raindrops hitting a window. Appreciate light, shadow, and color with an artist's eye.

Revel in the sensory symphony that surrounds you and live more fully. Practice the fun techniques in this book and heighten every moment of your life more—you're entitled!

1-56718-160-0, 224 pp., 6 x 9, illus., softcover $12.95

SUPERWOMAN'S RITE OF PASSAGE: FROM MIDLIFE TO WHOLE LIFE

Kathleen F. Lundquist, Ph.D.

Midlife transition is uniquely challenging to the "Superwoman" because her success has come too often at the expense of her feminine psyche. For women who have nurtured the more masculine aspects of their psyches for academic achievement, career recognition, and financial independence, life after forty can look grim. *Superwoman's Rite of Passage* is a workbook for high-achieving women who are entering midlife and want to emerge from this transition whole and renewed.

Superwoman's Rite of Passage transforms the challenge of midlife into an enriching personal adventure. Guide yourself through the five stages of a process called "Re-Membering," from which you birth your "Authentic Adultwoman." This process is enhanced by reflective exercises and rituals calling upon nature guides and archetypal goddesses who reaffirm the truth that "You are not alone," "Support is all around you," and "You are not going crazy." *Superwoman's Rite of Passage* is a blueprint for women searching for a sense of wholeness that's been squelched by patriarchal conditioning. Reconnect with your feminine psyche and achieve wholeness.

1-56718-447-2, 240 pp., 6 x 9, softcover   **$14.95**

THE LLEWELLYN ANNUALS

Llewellyn's MOON SIGN BOOK: Approximately 450 pages of valuable information on gardening, fishing, weather, stock market forecasts, personal horoscopes, good planting dates, and general instructions for finding the best date to do just about anything! Articles by prominent forecasters and writers in the fields of gardening, astrology, economics, and cycles. This special almanac, different from any other, has been published annually since 1906. It's fun, informative, and has been a great help to millions in their daily planning. 5¼ x 8 format. **State year $6.95**

Llewellyn's SUN SIGN BOOK: Your personal horoscope for the entire year! All 12 signs are included in one handy book. Also included are forecasts, special feature articles, and an action guide for each sign. Monthly horoscopes are written by Gloria Star, author of *Optimum Child*, for your personal sun sign, and there are articles on a variety of subjects written by well-known astrologers from around the country. Much more than just a horoscope guide! Entertaining and fun the year around. 5¼ x 8 format. **State year $6.95**

Llewellyn's DAILY PLANETARY GUIDE: Includes all of the major daily aspects plus their exact times in Eastern and Pacific time zones, lunar phases, signs and voids plus their times, planetary motion, a monthly ephemeris, sunrise and sunset tables, special articles on the planets, signs, aspects,planetary hours, rulerships, and much more. Large 5¼ x 8 format for more writing space, spiral bound to lie flat, address and phone listings, time-zone conversion chart and blank horoscope chart. **State year $9.95**

Llewellyn's ASTROLOGICAL POCKET PLANNER: Daily Ephemeris & Aspectarian: Designed to slide easily into a purse or briefcase, this all-new annual is jam-packed with those dates and planetary information astrologers need when forecasting future events. Comes with a regular calendar section, a smaller section for projecting dates into the year ahead, a 3-year ephemeris, a listing of planetary aspects, a planetary associations chart, a time-zone chart and retrograde table. **State year $7.95**

Llewellyn's ASTROLOGICAL CALENDAR: Large wall calendar of 48 pages. Beautiful full-color cover and full-color paintings inside. Includes special feature articles by famous astrologers, and complete introductory information on astrology. It also contains a lunar gardening guide, celestial phenomena, a blank horoscope chart, and monthly date pages which include aspects, Moon phases, signs and voids, planetary motion, an ephemeris, personal forecasts, lucky dates, planting and fishing dates, and more. 10 x 13 size. Set in Eastern time, with conversion table for other time zones worldwide. **State year $12.00**

1998 WITCHES' CALENDAR: Celebrate the Craft every day with this entrancing new wall calendar. Charming, original artwork by Tony Meadows accompanies a new seasonal topic each month, including each of the eight Pagan holidays, house blessings, sanctuary gardens, and more. The calendar pages are jam-packed with fun and useful information including invocations, short recipes, herbal lore, and basic astrological data. **State year $12.00**

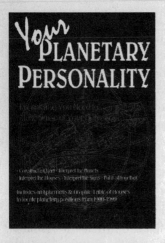

YOUR PLANETARY PERSONALITY: EVERYTHING YOU NEED TO MAKE SENSE OF YOUR HOROSCOPE

Dennis Oakland

This book deepens the study of astrological interpretation for professional and beginning astrologers alike. Dennis Oakland's interpretations of the planets in the houses and signs are the result of years of study of psychology, sciences, symbolism, Eastern philosophy, plus the study of birth charts from a psychotherapy group. Unlike the interpretations in other books, these emphasize the life processes involved and facilitate a greater understanding of the chart. Includes 100-year ephemeris.

Even if you now know *nothing* about astrology, Dennis Oakland's clear instructions will teach you how to construct a complete and accurate birth chart for anyone born between 1900 to 1999. After you have built your chart, he will lead you through the steps of reading it, giving you in-depth interpretations of each of your planets. When done, you will have the satisfaction that comes from increased self-awareness *and* from being your *own* astrologer!

This book is also an excellent exploration for psychologists and psychiatrists who use astrology in their practices.

0-87542-594-1, 580 pp., 7 x 10, softcover $24.95

COME HOME TO YOUR BODY: A WORKBOOK FOR WOMEN

Pamela J. Free

For a woman moving into her 40s and beyond, physical discomfort or pain is the first sign that the grace period on her body has run out. While you can't trade in your body for a new model, you *can* take small, simple steps each day to slow down your biological clock and move through life with new-found freedom, energy and radiance.

Your body is far deeper and wiser than your intellectual mind. *Come Home to Your Body* is filled with practical techniques that will free your body's own wisdom. Learn to move from the belly and heart to prevent stiffness, pain and limitation—without dragging yourself anywhere *near* a gym! You may even have a chronic condition such as arthritis, but that doesn't need to prevent you from experiencing the peace and comfort created from the mystical union of your mind, body, and spirit.

1-56718-290-9, 192 pp., 7 x 10, illus.   **$15.95**

THE NEW A TO Z HOROSCOPE MAKER AND DELINEATOR

Llewellyn George

A textbook…encyclopedia…self-study course…and extensive astrological dictionary all in one! More American astrologers have learned their craft from *The New A to Z Horoscope Maker and Delineator* than any other astrology book.

First published in 1910, it is in every sense a complete course in astrology, giving beginners ALL the basic techniques and concepts they need to get off on the right foot. Plus it offers the more advanced astrologer an excellent dictionary and reference work for calculating and analyzing transits, progression, rectifications, and creating locality charts. This new edition has been revised to meet the needs of the modern audience.

0-87542-264-0, 592 pp., 6 x 9, softcover $14.95